T0212493

Lecture Notes in Computer Science 9968

Commenced Publication in 1973
Founding and Former Series Editors:
Gerhard Goos, Juris Hartmanis, and Jan van Leeuwen

Editorial Board

More information about this series at http://www.springer.com/series/7412

Sotirios A. Tsaftaris · Ali Gooya
Alejandro F. Frangi · Jerry L. Prince (Eds.)

Simulation and Synthesis in Medical Imaging

First International Workshop, SASHIMI 2016
Held in Conjunction with MICCAI 2016
Athens, Greece, October 21, 2016
Proceedings

 Springer

Editors
Sotirios A. Tsaftaris
University of Edinburgh
Edinburgh
UK

Ali Gooya
University of Sheffield
Sheffield
UK

Alejandro F. Frangi
University of Sheffield
Sheffield
UK

Jerry L. Prince
The Johns Hopkins University
Baltimore, MD
USA

ISSN 0302-9743   ISSN 1611-3349   (electronic)
Lecture Notes in Computer Science
ISBN 978-3-319-46629-3   ISBN 978-3-319-46630-9   (eBook)
DOI 10.1007/978-3-319-46630-9

Library of Congress Control Number: 2016952515

LNCS Sublibrary: SL6 – Image Processing, Computer Vision, Pattern Recognition, and Graphics

Printed on acid-free paper

This Springer imprint is published by Springer Nature
The registered company is Springer International Publishing AG
The registered company address is: Gewerbestrasse 11, 6330 Cham, Switzerland

Preface

The MICCAI community needs data with known ground truth to develop, evaluate, and validate image analysis and reconstruction algorithms. Since synthetic data are ideally suited for this purpose, over the years, a full range of models underpinning image simulation and synthesis have been developed: (a) simplified mathematical models to test segmentation and registration algorithms; (b) detailed mechanistic models (top–down), which incorporate priors on the geometry and physics of image acquisition and formation processes; and (c) complex spatiotemporal computational models of anatomical variability, organ physiology, or disease progression. Recently, cross-fertilization between image computing and machine learning gave rise to data-driven, phenomenological models (bottom–up) that stem from learning directly data associations across modalities, resolutions, etc. With this, not only the application scope has been expanded but also the underlying model assumptions have been refined to increasing levels of realism.

The goal of the Simulation and Synthesis in Medical Imaging (SASHIMI) Workshop aims to put all those interested in these problems in the same room, for the purpose of invigorating research and stimulating new ideas on how to best proceed and bring these two worlds together. The objectives were to: (a) hear from invited speakers in the areas of transfer learning and mechanistic models and cross-fertilize across fields; (b) bring together experts of synthesis (via phenomenological machine learning) and simulation (via explicit mechanistic models) to raise the state of the art; and (c) identify challenges and opportunities for further research. We also wanted to identify how we can best evaluate synthetic data and if we could collect benchmark data that can help the development of future algorithms.

The first workshop on "Simulation and Synthesis in Medical Imaging — SASHIMI 2016"[1] was held in conjunction with the 19th International Conference on Medical Image Computing and Computer-Assisted Intervention — MICCAI 2016 as a satellite event in Athens, Greece, on October 21, 2016. Submissions were solicited via a call for papers that was circulated by the MICCAI organizers, through known mailing lists (e.g., ImageWorld, MIUA) but also by directly e-mailing several colleagues and experts in the area. Each submission underwent a double-blind review by at least two members of the Program Committee consisting of researchers who actively contribute in the area. At the conclusion of the review process, 17 papers were accepted. Overall, the contributions span the following broad categories in alignment with the initial call for papers: fundamental methods for image-based biophysical modeling and image synthesis, biophysical and data-driven models of disease progression or organ development, biophysical and data-driven models of organ motion and deformation, biophysical and data-driven models of image formation and acquisition, segmentation/registration across or within modalities to aid the learning of model parameters, cross-modality (PET/MR, PET/CT, CT/MR, etc.) image synthesis, simulation and synthesis from large-scale

---

[1] http://www.cistib.org/sashimi/.

image databases, automated techniques for quality assessment of simulations and synthetic images, and several applications of image synthesis and simulation in medical imaging such as image registration and segmentation, image denoising and information fusion, image reconstruction from sparse data or sparse views, and real-time simulation of biophysical properties. The accepted papers were divided into two general topics of "Simulation and Its Applications in Computational Medical Imaging" and "Synthesis and Its Applications in Computational Medical Imaging" and presented during two oral and one poster sessions, overall covering eight and nine papers, respectively.

Finally, we would like to thank everyone who contributed to this first workshop: Serkan Cimen and Ilkay Oksuz, members of the Organizing Committee for their assistance; the authors for their contributions, the members of the Program Committee for their review work, promotion of the workshop, and general support; the invited speaker for sharing his expertise and knowledge; and the MICCAI society for the general support.

August 2016

Sotirios A. Tsaftaris
Ali Gooya
Alejandro F. Frangi
Jerry L. Prince

Organization

Workshop Chairs

Sotirios A. Tsaftaris   University of Edinburgh, UK
Ali Gooya   University of Sheffield, UK
Alejandro F. Frangi   University of Sheffield, UK
Jerry L. Prince   Johns Hopkins University, USA

Organizing Committee

Serkan Çimen   University of Sheffield, UK
Ilkay Oksuz   Yale University and IMT Lucca, Italy

E-mail to contact the organizers: sashimi@cistib.org

Program Committee

Leandro Beltrachini   University of Sheffield, UK
Serkan Çimen   University of Sheffield, UK
M. Jorge Cardoso   University College London, UK
Marleen de Brujine   Erasmus University Medical Center, The Netherlands
Mathieu De Craene   Philips Research, France
Herve Delingette   Inria Sophia Antipolis, France
Ivana Drobnjak   University College London, UK
Yong Fan   University of Pennsylvania, USA
Alejandro F. Frangi   University of Sheffield, UK
Orcun Goksel   ETH Zurich, Switzerland
Ali Gooya   University of Sheffield, UK
Daniel Herzka   Johns Hopkins University, USA
Andrada Ianus   University College London, UK
Ender Konukoglu   Martinos Center for Biomedical Imaging, USA
Niels Kuster   IT'IS Foundation ETH Zurich, Switzerland
Hervé Liebgott   CREATIS, France
David Liu   Siemens Medical Solutions, USA
Bryn Lloyd   IT'IS Foundation ETH Zurich, Switzerland
Frederik Maes   University of Leuven, Belgium
Nassir Navab   TU Munich, Germany
Esra Neufeld   IT'IS Foundation and ZMT Zurich MedTech AG, Switzerland
Hien V. Nguyen   Siemens Corporate Research, USA
Ilkay Oksuz   Yale University and IMT Lucca, Italy

Contents

Simulation and Its Applications in Computational Medical Imaging

Software Framework for Realistic MRI Simulations Using the Polyhedral Fourier Transform

Shuo Han and Daniel A. Herzka[✉]

Department of Biomedical Engineering, Johns Hopkins University School of Medicine,
Baltimore, MD, USA
{shan50,daniel.herzka}@jhu.edu

Abstract. This work presents a freely available operating system-independent Matlab software tool for simulation of magnetic resonance imaging (MRI) acquisition and image reconstruction using polyhedral phantoms. The tool is based on an efficient implementation of the closed form solution of the polyhedral Fourier transform (FT). The software tool, named "PolyFT", can be applied to polyhedral surface and tetrahedral volume meshes. The tool enables the calculation of the Fourier domain representation of physiologically relevant objects with spatially varying intensities, permitting accurate simulation of slice selection and parallel imaging techniques that require coil sensitivity profiles. Several examples of applications are given. Though more computationally intense than the FT, the polyhedral FT allows relevant simulation of both MRI sampling and reconstruction processes. The freely-available software tool should be useful in the same situations in which the standard Shepp-Logan phantom is used, and additionally when analytical Fourier representations of objects with non-uniform intensities are needed.

1 Introduction

Analytical phantoms that have closed-form Fourier Transform (FT) expressions are used throughout magnetic resonance imaging (MRI) to simulate the process of image acquisition in Fourier space. Most existing phantoms in 2D and 3D are restricted to simple shapes such as the ellipses or ellipsoids used in the various implementations of the Shepp-Logan phantoms [1, 2]. Recently, analytical expressions for the FTs of additional shapes such as polygons and spline and Bézier contours in 2D, and polyhedra in 3D have been used in the simulation of the MRI data acquisition process [3, 4]. In 2D, the incorporation of polynomial or sinusoidal coil sensitivity profiles has been demonstrated for use in simulations of MRI reconstruction with parallel imaging [3].

Despite the attractiveness of digital phantoms for simulations, the availability of tools that use more desirable yet complex shapes beyond ellipsoids used in the Shepp-Logan phantom, is limited. Furthermore, to date, there is no freely-available tool for simulation in 3D incorporating coil sensitivity profiles. In this work, we present a freely-available software platform for simulation of both acquisition and reconstruction processes in MRI. The software tool extends the original formulation in [4] to include objects with non-uniform intensity which enables the use of non-ideal slice selection as well as simulation of parallel imaging approaches that require coil sensitivity maps.

© Springer International Publishing AG 2016
S.A. Tsaftaris et al. (Eds.): SASHIMI 2016, LNCS 9968, pp. 3–12, 2016.
DOI: 10.1007/978-3-319-46630-9_1

2   Theory

The polyhedral FT was proposed by Komrska in the field of x-ray crystallography [5]. The closed form expressions of the polyhedral FT seen in Eqs. (1–4). Vector quantities are displayed in bold, scalars in plain typeface. If both bold and plain symbols exist ($\boldsymbol{k}$ and k) the former represents the vector, the latter the magnitude of the vector. In Eqs. (1–4) we follow the representation in [4]. Table 1 defines the symbols in these equations.

$$
S_{3D}(\boldsymbol{k}) = \begin{cases} -\dfrac{1}{(2\pi k)^2} \sum_{f=1}^{F} S_f^*(\boldsymbol{k}) & k \neq 0, \\[2ex] \dfrac{1}{3} \sum_{f=1}^{F} \boldsymbol{r}^{(V_{f,1})} \cdot \hat{\boldsymbol{N}}_f P_f & k = 0. \end{cases} \tag{1}
$$

$$
S_f^*(\boldsymbol{k}|\boldsymbol{k} \neq k\hat{\boldsymbol{N}}_f) = \frac{\boldsymbol{k} \cdot \hat{\boldsymbol{N}}_f}{k^2 - (\boldsymbol{k} \cdot \hat{\boldsymbol{N}}_f)^2} \sum_{e=1}^{E_f} (L_{f,e} \boldsymbol{k} \cdot \hat{\boldsymbol{n}}_{f,e} \operatorname{sinc}(\pi \boldsymbol{k} \cdot \boldsymbol{L}_{f,e}) \exp(-2\pi i \boldsymbol{k} \cdot \boldsymbol{r}^{(C_{f,e})})). \tag{2}
$$

$$
S_f^*(\boldsymbol{k}|\boldsymbol{k} = k\hat{\boldsymbol{N}}_f) = -2\pi i \boldsymbol{k} \cdot \hat{\boldsymbol{N}}_f \exp(-2\pi i \boldsymbol{k} \cdot \boldsymbol{r}^{(V_{f,1})}) P_f. \tag{3}
$$

$$
P_f = \frac{1}{2} \left| \hat{\boldsymbol{N}}_f \cdot \sum_{e=1}^{E_f} (\boldsymbol{r}^{(V_{f,e})} \times \boldsymbol{r}^{(V_{f,e+1})}) \right|. \tag{4}
$$

Table 1. Nomenclature used in Eqs. 1 through 9.

Symbol	Definition
$S_{3D} \in \mathbb{C}$	MR signal in Fourier domain
$S_f^* \in \mathbb{C}$	Contribution of the fth face to S_{3D}
$\boldsymbol{k} \in \mathbb{R}^3$	k-Space sample vector (3D)
$k \in \mathbb{R}$	Norm of $\boldsymbol{k}$
$F \in \mathbb{N}$	Total number of faces in the surface or volume mesh
$f, e \in \mathbb{N}$	Index of the fth face or e^{th} edge
$E_f \in \mathbb{N}$	Number of edges in the fth face
$\hat{\boldsymbol{N}}_f \in \mathbb{R}^3$	Outward pointing normal vector of the fth face
$\boldsymbol{r}^{(V_{f,e})} \in \mathbb{R}^3$	e^{th} vertex of the fth face
$\boldsymbol{L}_{f,e} \in \mathbb{R}^3$	$\boldsymbol{r}^{V_{f,e}} - \boldsymbol{r}^{V_{f,e+1}}$, the vector of the eth edge of the fth face
$\boldsymbol{r}^{(C_{f,e})} \in \mathbb{R}^3$	$(\boldsymbol{r}^{V_{f,e}} + \boldsymbol{r}^{V_{f,e+1}})/2$, mid-point of the eth edge of the fth face
$\hat{\boldsymbol{t}}_{f,e} \in \mathbb{R}^3$	$\boldsymbol{L}_{f,e} / \left\| \boldsymbol{L}_{f,e} \right\|_2$, direction vector of the eth edge of the fth face
$\hat{\boldsymbol{n}}_{f,e} \in \mathbb{R}^3$	Normal vector of the eth edge of the fth face and in this face plane
$P_f \in \mathbb{R}$	Area of the fth polygonal face
$\Delta d_f \in \mathbb{R}$	Intensity difference between inside and outside of f_{th} polygonal face

Equations (1) and (2) show that the signal at a given point in the 3-dimensional (3D) FT or k-space of a polyhedron, $S_{3D}(\boldsymbol{k})$, includes a summation over the contribution of each polygonal face of the polyhedron, $S_f^*(\boldsymbol{k})$. This term includes, for the majority of faces, a summation over the contribution from each edge. Though an analytical solution is achieved, it is computationally intensive particularly during the calculation of the polyhedral FT of complex polyhedral meshes with the relatively large number of faces that are required to represent physiologically relevant structures. Furthermore, evaluation of the polyhedral FT equations yields only a single point in k-space. This problem is compounded when a large number of k-samples are used to represent objects with high resolution. Nevertheless, by sampling data from the analytical k-space, errors that result when using simulated data to solve a direct fitting or reconstruction problem when the identical method used to generate the simulated data (i.e. generating image data in a Cartesian coordinate system, upsampling and Fourier-transforming to k-space, and sampling in a k-space Cartesian coordinate system, only to reconstructed via inverse Fourier Transform, a.k.a the "inverse crime" or perfect data methods) are avoided. [3] This type of error produces overly optimistic results.

2.1 Simulating Objects of Varying Spatial Intensity

The polyhedral FT assumes unit intensity within the polyhedron. To achieve simulations with arbitrary uniform intensity, unit intensity is assumed and scaling of k-space is applied after sampling. To simulate objects with non-uniform intensity, two relatively simple approaches are available. Both options require conversion of the surface mesh of the polyhedral shape to be simulated into a volumetric tetrahedral mesh using readily available software libraries (i.e. iso2mesh, [6]) Each tetrahedron is then assumed to have uniform intensity whose value is approximated by the desired intensity at the location of the center of mass of the tetrahedron.

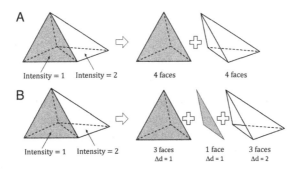

Fig. 1. Example of a simple polyhedral phantom composed of two tetrahedrons with a single step in intensity. (**A**) The contribution of each tetrahedron to the polyhedral FT can be calculated separately and summed using Eqs. (1-4). However, the contribution of the shared face is calculated twice. (**B**) By rephrasing the equations of the polyhedral FT in terms of face contributions weighted by intensity differences (Eqs. (5-9)), efficiency is improved. The intensity outside the polyhedron is assumed to be zero.

With the first approach, the desired k-space samples can be approximated by the summation of the k-space samples calculated each individual tetrahedron (Fig. 1A), taking advantage to the linearity of the FT. Equations (1–4) can be modified to include an additional summation for each tetrahedral element of the volume mesh. Increased accuracy and smoother gradients in intensity can be achieved by increasing the number of tetrahedrons in the volumetric tetrahedral mesh.

With the first option, the contribution to the signal of a face shared by two adjacent tetrahedrons is calculated twice. However, if the shared faces are weighted by the intensity difference between the two sides of the faces, Δd_f, duplicate calculation is avoided (Fig. 1B). Equations (5–9), which are derived from Eqs. (1–4) can therefore be used to achieve higher computational efficiency and were therefore implemented in the presented software tool. Note that in these equations the face index F includes all faces of all tetrahedrons in the volume mesh.

$$S_{3D}(k) = \sum_{f=1}^{F} \Delta d_f \cdot S_f^*(k). \tag{5}$$

$$S_f^*\left(k|k \neq k\hat{N}_f\right) = \frac{-k \cdot \hat{N}_f}{(2\pi k)^2 \left(k^2 - \left(k \cdot \hat{N}_f\right)^2\right)} \cdot \sum_{e=1}^{E_f} L_{f,e} k \cdot \hat{n}_{f,e} \mathrm{sinc}\left(\pi k \cdot L_{f,e}\right) \exp\left(-2\pi i k \cdot r^{(C_{f,e})}\right). \tag{6}$$

$$S_f^*\left(k|k = k\hat{N}_f, k \neq 0\right) = \frac{i}{2\pi k^2} k \cdot \hat{N}_f \exp\left(-2\pi i k \cdot r^{(V_{f,1})}\right) P_f. \tag{7}$$

$$S_f^*(k|k = 0) = \frac{1}{3} P_f r^{(V_{f,1})} \cdot \hat{N}_f. \tag{8}$$

$$P_f = \frac{1}{2} \left| \hat{N}_f \cdot \sum_{e=1}^{E_f} \left(r^{(V_{f,e})} \times r^{(V_{f,e+1})}\right) \right|. \tag{9}$$

3 Methods

3.1 Platform-Independent Implementation in Matlab

The goals for the implementation of the software platform for MRI simulations based on the polyhedral FT included: (1) operating system independence, (2) efficient computation, and (3) integration of parallelization where possible. To maximize portability and widespread usability of the software platform, the polyhedral Fourier transform was implemented in Matlab (The Mathworks, Natick, MA) with both precompiled *mex* functions and m-file-only implementations. By providing both alternatives, users can opt for the approach that best suits their particular operating system.

For a given k-space point, the polyhedral FT is more computationally intense than other digital phantoms and significantly more computationally intense than Fast Fourier Transform (FFT) based methods (that incur errors at high frequency components [3]).

Also, Eqs. (1–4) and (5–9) need to be evaluated per k-point. Finally, for volumetric meshes, which are required for simulations involving objects with non-uniform intensity, the number of effective polygonal faces in the mesh increases can increase drastically, especially if smooth variations in intensity are desired. Therefore, efficient implementation was a central goal in this work.

To increase computational efficiency, the software platform takes advantage of the innate parallelization in Matlab. Depending on the task, computation of the polyhedral FT could be parallelized along two dimensions: (1) the 'k-point' dimension: calculation of the contribution of one face to all k-points in parallel and repeating for (looping) through all faces, or (2) the 'faces' dimension: calculation of the contributions of all faces to one k-point and repeating for (looping) for all k-points. For simple objects such as an ellipsoid with a ~50 faces (Fig. 2) but requiring a full 256^3 k-space matrix, it is more computationally efficient to parallelize along k-points, and calculate the contribution of each face via standard *for*-loop. However, for complex objects such as a brain with ~350,000 faces (Fig. 3), it more efficient to parallelize the calculation of the contribution of each face, and loop per k-point. Both options were included in the software platform, and the direction of parallelization is chosen automatically though manual configuration is possible.

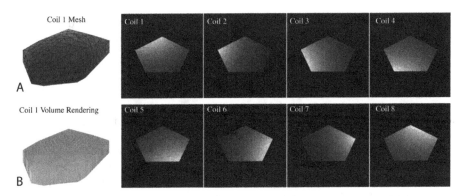

Fig. 2. Demonstration of the application of coil sensitivity profiles as used in parallel imaging to a simple polyhedron.

Matlab provides the ability to interface with C or C++ libraries through its *mex* application program interface (API). Using pre-compiled code can result in a significant decrease in computational time, especially for looping structures that can be slower in execution in scripted (non-compiled) languages. As an initial attempt, we incorporated *mex* functionality that calculated the contribution of either one face or one k-point. Though it is possible to implement the complete computation including all summations (for-loops) within a *mex* function, the lack of support for operating system-independent parallelization within the *mex* API hindered its implementation in this work.

To provide additional flexibility, the software platform includes functionality to maintain computational efficiency when using both regular meshes with a constant number of edges polygonal faces (e.g. triangular surface meshes and tetrahedral volume

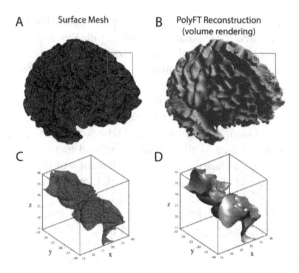

Fig. 3. Brain surface meshes with uniform intensities (A, C) and the volume rendered 3D inverse FFT reconstruction of the k-space sampled data (B, D).

meshes), or when using irregular meshes. The software platform was tested in several operating systems, though execution time is reported for one platform. The software platform was named "PolyFT".

3.2 Demonstrations of PolyFT

Several examples of the potential uses of the PolyFT software platform are presented.

Brain Mesh. To demonstrate the feasibility of using PolyFT to simulate the acquisition of a physiologically-relevant complex structure, a set of MRI images of a brain were downloaded from the OASIS dataset [7], segmented by TOADS algorithm [8], and meshed by the CRUISE algorithm [9] to generate a triangular surface mesh composed of 354,908 faces with uniform intensity (Fig. 3). This data was sampled using a Cartesian 256^3 k-space matrix. The resulting matrix underwent 3D inverse FFT and an isointense surface was volume rendered for display.

Slice Selection with Ideal and Non-ideal Slice Thickness. To demonstrate the feasibility of simulation complex acquisition, the process of non-ideal slice selection carried out. A very thin (0.1 mm) and a thick (10 mm) plane were used, and these were intersected with the volume mesh. The $k_z = 0$ plane of the analytical k-spaces of the 3D polyhedra were then sampled using using 1024^2 k-points. Sampling this plane is equivalent to sampling the projection of the volume on the the k_z-plane as is done during slice selection in 2D MRI. [4] Images were reconstructed through inverse FFT.

Parallel Imaging with Sparsity-Driven Reconstruction. To demonstrate the feasibility of simulating both acquisition and reconstruction processes, a sparsity-driven parallel imaging experiment was performed using a simple polyhedral shape. Coil sensitivity profiles derived from MRI of a homogeneous gel phantom using a standard 8-channel head coil were used. First, a tetrahedral volume mesh was generated (Fig. 2A).

Then, individual coil volume meshes were sampled with a Cartesian grid (128^3 k-points) and the k-space of each tetrahedral element was weighted by the relative intensity of the coil sensitivity profile at that coordinate before summation into a single k-space (Fig. 2, right). Complex zero-mean Gaussian noise with $\sigma = 0.2 \times 10^{-4}$ (0.55 % of the DC signal) was added to the k-space data. The central horizontal slice ($z = 0$) of each coil displaying intensity variation is shown. The volume rendered image for coil 1 is displayed as as reference.

Next, the individual coils k-spaces were undersampled using a Poisson disk-derived pattern well suited for sparsity-driven MRI reconstruction. [10] An undersampling rate of ~6 was used. A freely-available software package (Berkley Advanced Reconstruction Toolbox, BART, http://www.eecs.berkeley.edu/~mlustig/Software.html) was used for sparsity-driven reconstruction of the undersampled k-space data.

4   Results

4.1   Computational Time

Computational times for the polyFT software platform for three different sized meshes and three different k-space sampling resolutions are shown in Table 2. Both software options (m-file + *mex*, m-file-only) were compared. Typically, over the range of number of faces and number of k-points tested, an average of ~95 ns/k-point/triangular face was achieved. The implementation involving *mex* functionality proved more consistent, though not always fastest. The incorporation of *mex* files maintained performance with larger more complex meshes as seen in Fig. 3.

Table 2. Computational times for the PolyFT software platform measured on a 4-core 2.7 GHz Intel i7 CPU, 16 GB of RAM MacBook Pro laptop.

# triangular faces	# k-points	MATLAB + mex		MATLAB-only	
		Total Time (s)	Time / k-sample / face (ns)	Total Time (s)	Time / k-sample / face (ns)
	4096	1.72 ± 0.00	96.67 ± 0.25	1.65 ± 0.01	93.02 ± 0.64
4332	32768	13.89 ± 0.03	97.82 ± 0.20	13.94 ± 0.39	98.22 ± 2.72
	262144	113.36 ± 0.73	99.82 ± 0.64	162.14 ± 0.92	142.78 ± 0.81
	4096	28.19 ± 0.32	91.90 ± 1.03	27.23 ± 0.19	88.76 ± 0.62
74892	32768	225.11± 3.49	91.73 ± 1.42	237.47 ± 16.87	96.77 ± 1.44
	262144	1863.63 ± 36.53	94.93 ± 1.86	2767.04 ± 16.87	140.94 ± 0.86
	4096	113.70 ± 0.24	91.50 ± 0.19	111.18 ± 0.26	89.47 ± 0.21
303372	32768	911.50 ± 12.35	91.69 ± 1.24	972.08 ± 21.10	97.79 ± 2.12
	262144	7381.92 ± 133.28	92.82 ± 1.68	11317.69 ± 95.26	142.31 ± 1.20

4.2 Brain Mesh

The brain mesh and the volume rendering of IFFT reconstruction of the PolyFT-sampled 3D k-space can be seen in Fig. 2. The volume rendering was generated by thresholding the resulting 3D Cartesian matrix and display an isointense surface. The computation of this mesh took approximately 6.4 days on a standard laptop due to the large number of faces in the mesh, and the large number of k-space samples.

4.3 Slice Selection with Ideal and Non-ideal Slice Thickness

Figure 4 shows the comparison of ideally thin slice and a 10 mm thick slice meshes and image reconstructions. The effects of partial volume averaging typical with slice selection are readily observed. Note that if the thicker slice mesh was turned into a volume mesh, a non-ideal slice selection profile such as those obtained with sinc-shaped excitation pulses could be applied.

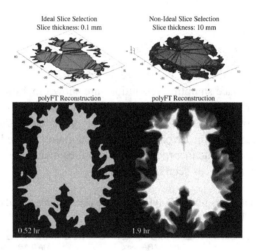

Fig. 4. Comparison of surface meshes (top) and reconstructions (bottom) that represents and the volume rendered 3D inverse FFT reconstruction of the k-space sampled data.

4.4 Parallel Imaging with Sparsity-Driven Reconstruction

Figure 5 shows the feasibility of simulating parallel imaging reconstructions as used in MRI. After undersampling of k-space data, the reconstruction is noisier, though since the object is truly sparse and the SNR of the underlying data is relatively high, no residual artifact is observed beyond the standard nose amplification.

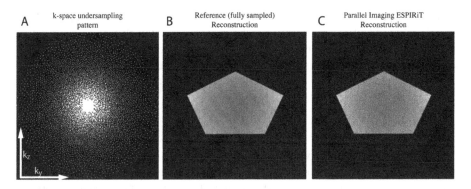

Fig. 5. (A) Poisson Disk undersampling pattern applied to analytical k-space data. (B) Reference central place (z = 0) from 3D reconstruction using fully sampled data. (C) Central plane from 3D reconstruction using undersampled k-space data. The ESPIRiT technique was used for reconstruction.

5   Discussion

The software tol produced consistent results, with a typical speed of 95 ns/k-point/triangular face on a standard MacBook Pro laptop. Performance could be improved with a larger number of CPU cores. Furthermore, the current implementation uses *mex* functionality for the calculation of the contribution of one face or one k-point. When placed inside a parallelized for-loop, performance may have been compromised due to the need to copy large data arrays containing the face and vertex information. Placing all looping structures inside the *mex* functions could also result in significant computational performance improvement, at a loss of parallelization since Matlab currently does not have capability to execute parallelized *mex* functions in a platform-independent manner.

The software tool was able to use surface and volume meshes for realistic simulation of typical MRI phenomena such as slice selection. Additionally, the platform enabled the incorporation of objects with non-uniform intensity such as that induced by coil sensitivity profiles. The behavior of the coil-weighted k-space data was equivalent to that in standard scanning, responding to highly accelerated reconstruction in an expected manner yielding noise amplification.

PolyFT is uses a closed-form analytical solution to find the exact value (within numerical precision of the IEEE floating point representation, [4]) at a k-point and does not rely on approximation as do methods that upsample digitized images before FT into k-space. At the same time, PolyFT could be paired with a Bloch simulator to weight the signal at a k- point and simulate modulation transfer and point spread functions.

5.1   Limitations

The current implementation of the polyhedral FT is unlikely to be the most efficient, as using compiled language (e.g. C or C++) should improve performance. However, the goal of PolyFT was to provide a software tool within the Matlab environment while maintaining operating-system independence. Due to the structure of the problem, where k-points independent of each other, and the contribution of each face is independent from that of all other faces, it is likely that GPU implementations could significantly accelerate processing, albeit in a platform dependent manner. Further work is needed to develop this approach.

6 Conclusion

The presented MATLAB software library allows for more realistic MRI simulations in any scenario in which the Shepp-Logan phantom has been used in the past. Additionally, it allows for the inclusion of non-uniform intensities. PolyFT provides a platform to evaluate and compare both acquisition and reconstruction algorithms of complex physiologically relevant shapes. Though computationally intensive, effective parallelization in MATLAB reduces computation time to ~95 ns/k-space point/triangular face for surface meshes. This could be further reduced by more aggressive parallelization involving GPUs. The presented library is now available to public.

References

1. Shepp, L.A., Logan, B.F.: The Fourier reconstruction of a head section. IEEE Trans. Nucl. Sci. **21**(3), 21–43 (1974)
2. Koay, C.G., Sarlls, J.E., Ozarslan, E.: Three-dimensional analytical magnetic resonance imaging phantom in the Fourier domain. Magn. Reson. Med. **58**(2), 430–436 (2007)
3. Guerquin-Kern, M., Lejeune, L., Pruessmann, K.P., Unser, M.: Realistic analytical phantoms for parallel magnetic resonance imaging. IEEE Trans. Med. Imaging **31**(3), 626–636 (2012)
4. Ngo, T.M., Fung, G.S., Han, S., Chen, M., Prince, J.L., Tsui, B.M., McVeigh, E.R., Herzka, D.A.: Realistic Analytical Polyhedral MRI Phantoms. Magn. Reson. Med. (2015)
5. Komrska, J.: Algebraic expressions of shape amplitudes of polygons and polyhedra. Optik **80**(4), 171–183 (1988)
6. Fang, Q., Boas, D.: Tetrahedral mesh generation from volumetric binary and gray-scale images. In: IEEE International Symposium on Biomedical Imaging, pp. 1142–1145 (2009)
7. Marcus, D.S., Wang, T.H., Parker, J., Csernansky, J.G., Morris, J.C., Buckner, R.L.: Open access series of imaging studies (OASIS): cross-sectional MRI data in young, middle aged, nondemented, and demented older adults. J. Cogn. Neurosci. **19**(9), 1498–1507 (2007)
8. Bazin, P.L., Pham, D.L.: Topology correction of segmented medical images using a fast marching algorithm. Comput. Methods Programs Biomed. **88**(2), 182–190 (2007)
9. Han, X., Pham, D.L., Tosun, D., Rettmann, M.E., Xu, C., Prince, J.L.: CRUISE: cortical reconstruction using implicit surface evolution. Neuroimage **23**(3), 997–1012 (2004)
10. Uecker, M., Lai, P., Murphy, M.J., Virtue, P., Elad, M., Pauly, J.M., Vasanawala, S.S., Lustig, M.: ESPIRiT–an eigenvalue approach to autocalibrating parallel MRI: where SENSE meets GRAPPA. Magn. Reson. Med. **71**(3), 990–1001 (2014)

Covering Population Variability: Morphing of Computation Anatomical Models

Bryn Lloyd[1,2(✉)], Emilio Cherubini[3], Silvia Farcito[1], Esra Neufeld[1,2], Christian Baumgartner[1], and Niels Kuster[1,4]

[1] IT'IS Foundation for Research on Information Technologies in Society,
Zürich, Switzerland
lloyd@itis.ethz.ch
[2] Zurich MedTech, Zürich, Switzerland
[3] SPEAG, Zürich, Switzerland
[4] ETH-Zurich, Zürich, Switzerland
http://www.itis.ethz.ch

Abstract. We present a method to change the volume of organs or tissues in computational anatomical models by simulating the human body as a biomechanical solid with initial strains causing local volume shrinkage or expansion. The non-linear hyperelastic material behavior is solved with the finite element method. The bone positions are prescribed and treated as rigid bodies surrounded by elastic soft tissue. A multi-domain mesh defines individual bones and at least one soft tissue region. Each region can have different material properties, volume growth rates or mesh settings. The method can be used to deform complex anatomical models, such as the Virtual Population models. The proposed strategy has been used to parametrize models by different BMI levels, change the volume of selected organs, and modify the posture of anatomical models.

Keywords: Anatomical model · Simulation · Population variability · Obesity · Parametrization · BMI

1 Introduction

Computational anatomical phantoms are increasingly important in academic research and regulatory compliance certification processes. Virtual anatomical models are used to study a variety of scenarios, including, for instance, magnetic resonance imaging (MRI) exposure [9,17], active and passive implant safety, electromagnetic (EM) field interactions with the peripheral nervous system [18], or passive car safety [24]. Anatomical models have also been used for virtual imaging, for instance to simulate the processes and hardware involved in MRI for designing gradient and radio frequency (RF) coils or pulse sequences [8, 12]. Virtual positron emission tomography (PET) and single-photon emission computed tomography (SPECT) imaging can be performed, e.g., with open-source software and plays a key role in the design of new medical imaging devices, acquisition algorithms, and protocols [20].

© Springer International Publishing AG 2016
S.A. Tsaftaris et al. (Eds.): SASHIMI 2016, LNCS 9968, pp. 13–22, 2016.
DOI: 10.1007/978-3-319-46630-9_2

The Virtual Population (ViP) [7,11] is a set of highly detailed computational anatomical models based on MRI data from healthy volunteers segmented at a resolution of $0.5 \times 0.5 \times 0.5$ mm. High quality surface meshes enclosing each of the more than 300 tissues and organs were generated from the segmented label fields [11]. The ViP models already cover important parts of the population variability, including children at different ages, adults, an elderly man, an obese man, and a pregnant woman. However, certain applications require personalized or parametrized models to investigate relationships between differences in morphology or gross anatomical descriptors such as body mass index (BMI), weight, height, or sex. The creation of additional models from new image data could fill some gaps in the population coverage, but would require a significant amount of work to develop. Therefore, strategies are needed to extrapolate from or morph existing models.

Morphing of surface models by means of freeform deformation, e.g., with a control grid, cage-based technique, or thin-plate splines, has been studied in the computer graphics community [19]. Finite element method (FEM) deformable models have been used in virtual reality surgery simulators [23]. Methods to simulate as-rigid-as-possible deformation without a volumetric mesh have been presented in [16,21] these models are based on assumed homogeneous (tissue) deformation properties with no internal structures such as bones or organs inside the skin surface. Skeleton-based techniques typically allow a human body model to be animated by positioning individual bones that are linked in a hierarchical structure, connected via joints. Bones can be transformed relative to their parents, with their transformations propagated to all children [6], but typically allow only posture to be changed with no alteration to tissue size and shape. Fonseca et al. [10] used MakeHuman [3] and other tools to change the fat volume and posture of a simple human body model consisting of an outer surface and two internal organs for dosimetry evaluations. MakeHuman is open-source software for modeling human characters for computer games and animations [3]. Simple scaling and rigid transformation were used to scale organ surfaces to reference sizes (weights) published by the International Commission on Radiological Protection (ICRP) [4,15], and similar approaches have been used by others [13]. Ali-Hamadi et al. [1] presented a method to register an anatomical model to a target skin surface while prescribing a fat distribution. The approach is based on registering the surface below the subcutaneous fat between characters using a nonlinear iterative closest point algorithm. The thickness of the subcutaneous fat layer in the target character is assumed to be approximately constant around each bone. While these techniques allow generic deformation of surface models, they deal with homogenous models that are relatively simple compared to the ViP or do not provide strategies for changing, e.g., the volume of specific tissues of anatomical surface meshes in a physiologically realistic way.

In this work, we describe an approach for extending the population coverage of existing models. The method allows an anatomical model to be parameterized, e.g., to high level descriptors such as BMI, weight, or the volume of individual tissues. It is an extension of previous work to change the posture of anatomical models [6,14,22] in which a biomechanical finite element model is used to morph the anatomy on the basis of a set of physically realistic constraints.

2 Methods

We have developed a technique to shrink or expand tissues locally, allowing changes to be made in, e.g., the size of the liver or even the entire subcutaneous fat layer by a specified percentage. The approach treats the body as a deformable hyper-elastic material with rigid bones. Specific tissues can be parametrized by locally prescribing initial strain [22,25] and thereby controlling the volume. The tissue deformation is constrained by nearby rigid bones and regularized by the surrounding soft elastic tissue. This method can be combined with an approach to change the posture of anatomical models [14]. Bones are moved by prescribing rotations around articulated joints. The bone hierarchy allows relative transformations to be propagated from a parent bone to all children, and the new bone positions are applied as constraints to the biomechanical finite element simulation.

2.1 Hyperelastic Material

A hyperelastic material is defined by its elastic strain energy density W, which is a function of the elastic strain state. It is usually referred to as the energy density and determines the linear or non-linear stress-strain relation and geometric non-linearities. The strain state is often formulated via the right Cauchy-Green deformation tensor $\mathbf{C}$. For isotropic materials, any state of strain can be described by three independent variables - typically the invariants of the Cauchy-Green tensor.

The strain tensor $\mathbf{C}$ is defined via the deformation gradient $\mathbf{F}$. In the Lagrangian formulation, the deformation gradient $\mathbf{F}$ can be computed as the displacement vector $\mathbf{u}$ relative to the reference coordinates $\mathbf{X}$

$$\mathbf{F} = \frac{\partial \mathbf{x}}{\partial \mathbf{X}} = \mathbf{I} + \frac{\partial \mathbf{u}}{\partial \mathbf{X}} \tag{1}$$

where $\mathbf{x}$ is the deformed position, which can be formulated as $\mathbf{x} = \mathbf{X} + \mathbf{u}$. In general the total deformation gradient can be decomposed into elastic and inelastic parts

$$\mathbf{F} = \mathbf{F}_{el}\mathbf{F}_{in} \tag{2}$$

where the inelastic part could be due to initial strain, thermal expansion, or, e.g., plastic deformation. The elastic Cauch-Green tensor is defined as

$$\mathbf{C}_{el} = \mathbf{F}_{el}^{T}\mathbf{F}_{el} \tag{3}$$

We use this formulation to introduce a local change in volume, in analogy to thermal expansion, by defining

$$\mathbf{F}_{in} = \mathbf{F}_{vol} = \mathbf{I}\lambda \tag{4}$$

resulting in a volume scale factor of

$$det(\mathbf{F}_{vol}) = \lambda^3 \tag{5}$$

Accordingly, we can implement different material models with local volume changes by inserting Eqs. 2 and 3 into the strain energy density function, which now depends on an inhomogeneous distribution of $\lambda(\mathbf{X})$, i.e. $W(\lambda(\mathbf{X}))$.

2.2 · Numerical Procedure

A variety of hyperelastic material models exist, and each defines a different stress-strain relationship. Currently, we have implemented St. Venant-Kirchhoff, Neo-Hookean, or Mooney-Rivlin material models. We solve for static equilibrium by a non-linear finite element method. The main application of the presented approach is to change the size and shape of individual organs or tissues, e.g., to increase or decrease the amount of subcutaneous adipose tissue (SAT). In this case, we can assume the bones undergo no deformation (the bones are rigid) and define a Dirichlet boundary condition on the surface of the bones. In the simplest case, the displacement of the bones can be set to zero. However, we have developed a more powerful approach, which allows us to move the bones to change the posture of the anatomical model while simultaneously morphing (expanding or shrinking) specific tissue regions.

To solve the deformation on a regular workstation in a reasonable time, the human body model is meshed as coarsely as possible. The use of a tetrahedral mesh with approximately 500K–1.5M elements results in a computation time in the range of 1–5 min. Larger meshes quickly increase the memory consumption and take longer to solve. Obtaining a high quality coarse volumetric mesh is challenging when dealing with complex anatomical models, such as the ViP models [11]. As an example, the SAT surface of the obese model "Fats" contains more than 300K triangles alone, and represents a complex geometry with fine details and thin regions. Directly remeshing the SAT surface frequently introduces self-intersections, which subsequently prevent the tetrahedral mesher from generating a computational mesh. Our current implementation allows us to create a multi-domain (multiple material) tetrahedral mesh by a combination of the following strategies:

- reconstruct tissue surface [5] to remove small features
- simplify the geometry, e.g. replacing a bone surface by a cylinder
- repair self-intersections with heuristics [2] that involve iterative removal of intersecting triangles and closing holes
- locally refine tetrahedral mesh and snapping or smoothing nodes to improve geometric approximation of tissue region.

The displacement field calculated by the FEM on the coarse tetrahedral mesh is interpolated to the vertices of the high resolution surface model. This interpolation or projection step is reasonable, since it can be assumed that the deformation is fairly smooth. The interpolation weights used to interpolate the coarse displacement field on the vertices of the surface mesh are precomputed and stored in the model to further improve the performance of the method.

3   Results

3.1   Parametrization of Subcutaneous Tissue

The morphing method is demonstrated here with the obese ViP model "Fats" (37 years old, 119.5 kg [11]). The body has been meshed with separate SAT, soft (non-SAT) tissue, and rigid bones by means of an adaptive Delaunay mesh generation method with approximately 1.5 million tetrahedral elements. Two different initial strains are simulated, reducing the SAT volume by approximately 60 % ($\lambda = 0.7$) and increasing it by approximately 120 % ($\lambda = 1.3$). Figure 1 depicts "Fats" morphed to different obesity levels.

3.2   Scaling of Organ Sizes

As a second example of the approach, we parametrize an anatomical model by organ volume. Specific organs of the ViP model "Duke" shown in Fig. 2 (34 years old, 70.2 kg) have been morphed to match the values for the adult male referenced in the ICRP Publication 110 [15]. The volume of the heart muscle was scaled by a factor of 1.45, the heart lumen by a factor of 0.5 and the lungs by a factor of 1.27. Figure 3 shows the resulting deformation. Due to the confinement

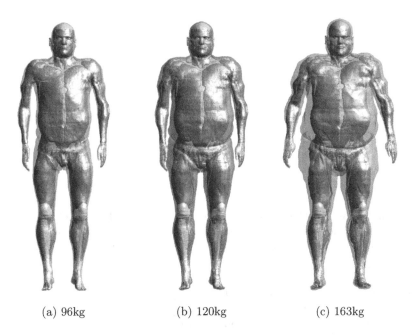

(a) 96kg   (b) 120kg   (c) 163kg

Fig. 1. ViP model "Fats" morphed to different weights and BMI values. The standard "Fats" model is depicted in (b) and weighs approximately 120 kg. The version in Figure (c) was posed slightly to avoid self-intersection of groin and arm regions resulting from the significant increase in adipose tissue. The subcutaneous adipose tissue and skin layer is rendered transparently. The BMI from left to right is 29, 36 and 49

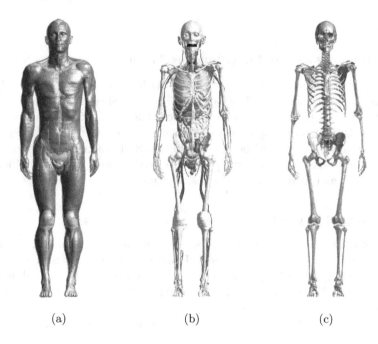

(a)   (b)   (c)

Fig. 2. The ViP model "Duke"

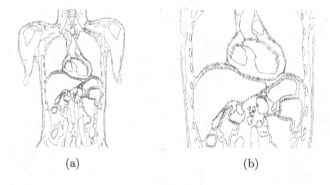

(a)   (b)

Fig. 3. The ViP model "Duke" with modified organ volumes. The model has been cut to show tissue boundaries with displacement field vectors overlayed. A close-up of the torso section (a) is shown in image (b).

of the rib-cage, the change in volume of the lungs pushes other organs and tissues down. The overall shape of the heart does not change much, because the volume reduction of the lumen is compensated by the increased volume of the heart muscle tissue. The tetrahedral mesh contained approximately 1.2 million elements and is shown in Fig. 4.

Fig. 4. The adaptive tetrahedral mesh used to morph lung and heart tissues to weights referenced in the ICRP Publication 110 [15].

Fig. 5. Image depicting ViP model "Fats" in sitting position. The biomechanical finite element model was used to change the relative position of the bones and simulate the resulting soft tissue deformation. The subcutaneous adipose tissue and skin layer is rendered transparently to show internal structures.

3.3 Posing of Anatomical Model

The biomechanical formulation can also be used to change the posture of the existing model, e.g., for applications in which the safety of humans sitting in a car or at a work place (wireless power transfer, car crash safety, etc.) is investigated. Figure 5 shows "Fats" in a sitting position with arms reaching towards, e.g., a driving wheel. In order to place "Fats" in the driving seet, rotations where prescibed in the hip and knee joint. Similarly the arms and hands/fingers where positioned on the steering wheel by user defined rotations of the humerus and various joints in the hand and fingers. The whole skeleton was posed interactively in a few minutes before the actual deformed model was computed in approximately one minute.

4   Conclusions and Future Work

We have presented a method to parametrize existing detailed anatomical models by treating the human body as being composed of rigid bones and soft elastic tissue, with deformation to balance stresses caused by prescribed spatially varying and tissue-specific initial strains. The method can be used to shrink and expand existing tissues, e.g., fat layers, in a physically realistic way. The various examples described illustrate how the method can be applied to parametrize BMI and the size of individual organs, and how to change the posture of Virtual Population models.

For the BMI parametrization example, we assume isotropic homogenous strains for the SAT, which is clearly a simplification. A detailed literature survey or database of MRI data with good fat contrast is likely to provide more insight into physiologically realistic population distributions of fat tissue, which could be used to define a strain map. The BMI is not only influenced by the SAT distribution but also by the amount of visceral fat. Naturally, the presented method can also scale visceral fat.

A limitation of the current method is that only existing tissue structures can be morphed. For instance, in regions where the adipose tissue is so thin that it was not included in the segmentation, the current approach does not provide a way to create new adipose tissue. Inserting a very thin fat layer between skin and adjacent tissues surfaces might allow us to resolve this issue.

Acknowledgements. The research leading to these results has received funding and support from the Swiss Commission for Technology and Innovation (Project: S4L-CAPITALIS CTI 14930.1 PFLS-LS), COST Action BM1309 and from the European Union's Seventh Framework Programme (FP7/2007–2013) under grant agreement no. 282891.

References

1. Ali-Hamadi, D., Liu, T., Gilles, B., Kavan, L., Faure, F., Palombi, O., Cani, M.P.: Anatomy transfer. ACM Trans. Graph. (TOG) **32**(6), 188 (2013)
2. Attene, M.: A lightweight approach to repairing digitized polygon meshes. Vis. Comput. **26**(11), 1393–1406 (2010)
3. Bastioni, M.: The makehuman applicationopen source tool for making 3d characters (2011). www.makehuman.org

4. Broggio, D., Beurrier, J., Bremaud, M., Desbree, A., Farah, J., Huet, C., Franck, D.: Construction of an extended library of adult male 3d models: rationale and results. Phys. Med. Biol. **56**(23), 7659 (2011)
5. Calakli, F., Taubin, G.: SSD: smooth signed distance surface reconstruction. In: Computer Graphics Forum, vol. 30, pp. 1993–2002. Wiley Online Library (2011)
6. Cherubini, E., Chavannes, N., Kuster, N.: Realistic skeleton based deformation of high-resolution anatomical human models for electromagnetic simulations. In: The 31st Annual Meeting of the Bioelectromagnetics Society (2009)
7. Christ, A., Kainz, W., Hahn, E.G., Honegger, K., Zefferer, M., Neufeld, E., Rascher, W., Janka, R., Bautz, W., Chen, J., Kiefer, B., Schmitt, P., Hollenbach, H.P., Shen, J., Oberle, M., Szczerba, D., Kam, A., Guag, J.W., Kuster, N.: The virtual family—development of surface-based anatomical models of two adults and two children for dosimetric simulations. Phys. Med. Biol. **55**(2), N23 (2010)
8. Collins, C.M., Wang, Z.: Calculation of radiofrequency electromagnetic fields and their effects in MRI of human subjects. Magn. Reson. Med. **65**(5), 1470–1482 (2011)
9. Corcoles, J., Zastrow, E., Kuster, N.: Convex optimization of MRI exposure for mitigation of RF-heating from active medical implants. Phys. Med. Biol. **60**(18), 7293 (2015)
10. Fonseca, T.F., Bogaerts, R., Hunt, J., Vanhavere, F.: A methodology to develop computational phantoms with adjustable posture for WBC calibration. Phys. Med. Biol. **59**(22), 6811 (2014)
11. Gosselin, M.C., Neufeld, E., Moser, H., Huber, E., Farcito, S., Gerber, L., Jedensjo, M., Hilber, I., Gennaro, F., Lloyd, B.A., Cherubini, E., Szczerba, D., Kainz, W., Kuster, N.: Development of a new generation of high-resolution anatomical models for medical device evaluation: the Virtual Population 3.0. Phys. Med. Biol. **59**(18), 5287 (2014)
12. Harris, C.T., Handler, W.B., Chronik, B.A.: Electromagnet design allowing explicit and simultaneous control of minimum wire spacing and field uniformity. Concepts Magn. Reson. Part B: Magn. Reson. Eng. **41**(4), 120–129 (2012)
13. Hynčík, L., Nováček, V., Bláha, P., Chvojka, O., Krejčí, P.: On scaling of human body models. Appl. Comput. Mech. **1**, 63–76 (2007)
14. Lloyd, B., Cherubini, E., Chavannes, N., Kuster, N.: Realistic physics-based posing of anatomical models for safety evaluations and computational life science in various configurations. In: BioEM 2016, June 2016
15. Menzel, H., Clement, C., DeLuca, P.: ICRP publication 110. Realistic reference phantoms: an ICRP/ICRU joint effort. A report of adult reference computational phantoms. Ann. ICRP **39**(2), 1 (2009)
16. Müller, M., Heidelberger, B., Teschner, M., Gross, M.: Meshless deformations based on shape matching. ACM Trans. Graph. (TOG) **24**, 471–478 (2005)
17. Murbach, M., Neufeld, E., Capstick, M., Kainz, W., Brunner, D.O., Samaras, T., Pruessmann, K.P., Kuster, N.: Thermal tissue damage model analyzed for different whole-body SAR and scan durations for standard MR body coils. Magn. Reson. Med. **71**(1), 421–431 (2014)
18. Neufeld, E., Cassara, A., Montanaro, H., Kuster, N., Kainz, W.: Functionalized anatomical models for EM-neuron interaction modeling. Phys. Med. Biol., February 2016
19. Nieto, J.R., Susin, A.: Cage based deformations: a survey. In: Hidalgo, M.G., Torres, A.M., Gmez, J.V. (eds.) Deformation Models. Lecture Notes in Computational Vision and Biomechanics, vol. 7, pp. 75–99. Springer, Heidelberg (2013)

20. Santin, G., Staelens, S., Taschereau, R., Descourt, P., Schmidtlein, C., Simon, L., Visvikis, D., Jan, S., Buvat, I.: Evolution of the GATE project: new results and developments. Nucl. Phys. B Proc. Suppl. **172**, 101–103 (2007)
21. Sorkine, O., Alexa, M.: As-rigid-as-possible surface modeling. In: Proceedings of the Fifth Eurographics Symposium on Geometry Processing, SGP 2007, pp. 109–116. Eurographics Association, Aire-la-Ville (2007)
22. Szczerba, D., Neufeld, E., Zefferer, M., Bhlmann, B., Kuster, N.: FEM based morphing of whole body human models. In: 2011 XXXth URSI of General Assembly and Scientific Symposium, pp. 1–3. IEEE (2011)
23. Szekely, G., Brechbhler, C., Dual, J., Enzler, R., Hug, J., Hutter, R., Ironmonger, N., Kauer, M., Meier, V., Niederer, P., Rhomberg, A., Schmid, P., Schweitzer, G., Thaler, M., Vuskovic, V., Tröster, G., Haller, U., Bajka, M.: Virtual reality-based simulation of endoscopic surgery. Presence: Teleoperators Virtual Environ. **9**(3), 310–333 (2000)
24. Vezin, P., Verriest, J.P.: Development of a set of numerical human models for safety, June 2005
25. Zienkiewicz, O.C., Taylor, R.L.: The Finite Element Method for Solid and Structural Mechanics. Butterworth-Heinemann, August 2005

Image-Based PSF Estimation for Ultrasound Training Simulation

Oliver Mattausch[(✉)] and Orcun Goksel

Computer-Assisted Applications in Medicine Group, ETH Zurich, Zürich, Switzerland
`oliver.mattausch@vision.ee.ethz.ch`

Abstract. A key aspect for virtual-reality based ultrasound training is the plausible simulation of the characteristic noise pattern known as ultrasonic speckle. The formation of ultrasonic speckle can be approximated efficiently by convolving the ultrasound point-spread function (PSF) with a distribution of point scatterers. Recent work extracts the latter directly from ultrasound images for use in forward simulation, assuming that the PSF can be known, e.g., from experiments. In this paper, we investigate the problem of automatically estimating an unknown PSF for the purpose of ultrasound simulation, such as to use in convolution-based ultrasound image formation. Our method estimates the PSF *directly* from an ultrasound image, based on homomorphic filtering in the cepstrum domain. It robustly captures *local* changes in the PSF as a function of depth, and hence is able to reproduce *continuous* ultrasound beam profiles. We compare our method to numerical simulations as the ground truth to study PSF estimation accuracy, achieving small approximation errors of $\leq 15\%$ FWHM. We also demonstrate simulated in-vivo images, with beam profiles estimated from real images.

1 Introduction

Ultrasound is a relatively low-cost and risk-free medical examination modality. The existence of various ultrasound-specific artifacts necessitate extensive training of sonographers, since standard examination procedures like the assessment of the gestational age of an embryo can lead to a life or death decision in the face of a possible abortion. It was suggested that medical students have a chance to learn only 80% of the important pathologies after one year of education [17]. This shows the enormous untapped potential of virtual-reality based simulation of ultrasound examination to boost the success rate of medical procedures, where arbitrary scenes, pathologies, and embryo instances can be simulated.

One aspect of ultrasound (US) interaction with tissue is through its scattering by sub-wavelength tissue structures and particles, herein called *scatterers*. This interaction creates the typical interference patterns known as ultrasonic speckle. Speckles can be efficiently approximated by convolving a point-spread-function (PSF) with said scatterers [2,5,13]. The interactions of the US beam with macro-level surfaces (comparable or larger than wavelength) can be simulated, e.g., using fast ray-tracing methods at interactive rates [4]. An inverse-problem approach of reconstructing scatterer parametrizations based on speckle

© Springer International Publishing AG 2016
S.A. Tsaftaris et al. (Eds.): SASHIMI 2016, LNCS 9968, pp. 23–33, 2016.
DOI: 10.1007/978-3-319-46630-9_3

observations was proposed [11], such that plausible images of the observed tissue can be generated in simulations from its a-priori imaging examples. One of the major standing issues with inverse-problem scatterer reconstruction, however, is the point-spread-function (PSF) being unknown in general. The same is true for convolution-based image simulation, where the knowledge of PSF is also required as a fundamental input parameter.

While PSF estimation has been studied thoroughly in the context of blind deconvolution for improving US image fidelity, to the best of our knowledge it has not been investigated before in the context of ultrasound image simulation for training. Currently, the state-of the-art [2,4,5,11,13] is to manually define and hand-craft a PSF, which is tedious technique, also not generalizable for changing imaging parameters. A PSF estimation method for the limited case of 1D deconvolution and minimum phase signals in the *cepstrum domain* has been introduced for ultrasound by Jensen et al. [8] and applied to in-vivo data [7]. The more general case of non-minimal signals typically require the solution of an ill-posed phase unwrapping problem [18–20]. Luckily for these methods, locality is not required for the purpose of deconvolution, and hence constant kernels suffice as input for the Wiener filter [18].

For our purpose of 2D US simulation, however, these methods do not work well. Convolution-based US simulation demands a smoothly-varying PSF to achieve the realism of an actual ultrasound image, and to teach aspiring sonographers the subtleties and effects of ultrasound beamforming on the image formation. The PSF varies not only with transducer geometry and acquisition settings, but it also changes locally as a function of depth (e.g., for a focused beam), and on a point-per-point basis as an effect of the underlying tissue. Hence a globally constant, or even a piece-wise constant PSF does not capture the complexity of a real continuous PSF distribution as a function of position.

We herein introduce a novel cepstrum-domain algorithm to approximate the PSF *locally* from an input US image to be used in simulations. Our goal is to (robustly) estimate *beam profiles* from actual images in order to use those later in common convolution-based (similarly, as well, in ray-tracing based) image simulation for training. Assuming separability of the PSF, our algorithm avoids the challenging problem of cepstrum-based estimation in 2D. Instead, we achieve robustness by sampling and combining many 1D cepstrum measurements via filtering in cepstrum domain. Our estimated PSF can be subsequently used for simulation, without any manual modeling effort needed for this important aspect of ultrasound imaging. We demonstrate this in simulated and in-vivo images.

2   PSF Estimation from Image Data

In the typical convolution model of ultrasound speckle [2,12,13], the reflective image intensity $r(x, y)$ results from the convolution of a tissue model $g(x, y)$ with PSF $h(x, y)$ given noise n, i.e.,

$$r(x, y) = g(x, y) * h(x, y) + n \tag{1}$$

where x denotes the lateral and y the axial transducer axes. Without loss of generality we omit the additive noise term n in the following, assuming that it can be handled using standard filtering techniques. Commonly, $h(x, y)$ is approximated by a periodic signal of acquisition center-frequency f_c modulated by a Gaussian [4,5]. The PSF is then of the form

$$h(x, y) = e^{-\frac{x^2}{\sigma_x^2} - \frac{y^2}{\sigma_y^2}} \cos(2\pi f_c), \tag{2}$$

which is a function separable to lateral and axial components. We use separability to efficiently estimate the axial and lateral h components *directly* from an US image, given as a spatial discretization $r[x, y]$ of radio-frequency (RF) data. Finding the PSF from an image of reflective intensities r requires the contribution of PSF h to be separated from the reflected echo of the tissue g.

Homomorphic filtering is a signal processing technique [9] for separating a Fourier domain signal into its components. Using this, the signals h and g in Eq. 1 can be decoupled in Fourier space as follows:

$$\log(\mathcal{F}(h * g)) = \log(H \cdot G) = \log H + \log G, \tag{3}$$

where $\mathcal{F}$ denotes the Fourier transform and the capitals represent Fourier transforms of signals. Since a given signal is not necessarily minimum phase, the complex logarithm is employed [3], i.e. $\log H \cdot G = \log(R) = \log(|R|e^{j\phi R}) = \log|R| + j\phi(R)$, where $\phi(R)$ denotes the unwrapped phase of the signal.

The main assumption of homomorphic filtering is that H is a relatively smooth function in Fourier space, in comparison to the typically highly varying and discontinuous nature of tissue G. As such, the components of H can be separated from the components of G by using lowpass filtering in the so-called *cepstrum* domain. The cepstrum is defined as $c = \mathcal{F}^{-1}(\log R)$, and constitutes a complex function $c(n)$ of the so-called *quefrencies*. Ideally, the first few components of c (up to a cutoff) contain only the PSF components of the input image. Using inverse cepstrum transformation on this truncated cepstrum c' then gives an estimation of PSF, i.e.,

$$h \approx \mathcal{F}^{-1}(\exp(\mathcal{F}(c'))). \tag{4}$$

In practice, a perfect separation between components is often not achieved. Several strategies have been proposed to improve robustness by increasing the separation between H and G in the Fourier domain. We adopt the strategy of *exponential pixel weighting* [9,23]. For each measurement location, each data point within a surrounding window is multiplied by a factor $w = \alpha^d$, where $\alpha < 1$ and d is the distance from the upper left corner. This ensures a monotonically lower influence of farther signal values to a measurement in Eq. 3. This windowing technique is used herein to compute localized but spatially-smooth cepstrum measurements.

For ultrasound, homomorphic filtering has been used in the context of US deconvolution for *image restoration* in 1D, 2D, and 3D [6,18–20]. These methods

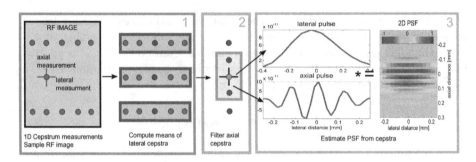

Fig. 1. Our method for robust estimation of a smoothly varying PSF (Color figure online)

face several challenges, however, since in-vivo tissue and clinical scans are corrupted by noise and contain artifacts and strong specular reflections hindering above approaches. For instance, a major challenge is due to the high sensitivity of phase unwrapping to noise, even more so in higher dimensions [10,14,19,20]. Alternatives to phase unwrapping based on logarithmic derivatives exist [16,18], but these are prone to severe aliasing artifacts. Instead, we propose the following.

3   Proposed Technique for Local PSF Estimation

As input to our method we use the raw radio-frequency (RF) data from a US scan. From an RF image $r[x, y]$, our algorithm computes a PSF $h[y]$ as a function of axial position y, while smaller lateral variations in x are ignored to employ averaging to increase estimation SNR. We describe below the three steps of our PSF estimation algorithm, which are also depicted in Fig. 1.

Robust cepstrum estimation. The purpose of Step 1 in Fig. 1 is to avoid instability and improve the SNR of homomorphic filtering. Assuming a *separable* PSF, Eq. 3 is used twice per sample location to separately find the axial and lateral components of the cepstrum, respectively. Phase unwrapping can then be reduced to a 1D problem in either direction, which can be solved efficiently. Noise-corrupted phase unwrapping in 1D can still cause a corrupted cepstrum measurement, which would negatively influence the following steps. Fortunately, a potentially corrupted measurement can be detected from cepstrum values $c(n)$ as follows: While $c(1)$ encodes the overall image brightness similar to a DC component [10], $c(2)$ and $c(3)$ influence the shape of the estimated pulse. Suggestions for plausible cepstrum values and their interpretation are described in detail in the cepstrum literature, e.g. for $c(2)$ [20]. Based on these, we empirically defined valid cepstrum measurements as $2 \leq |c(2)| \leq 6$ and $|c(2)| \leq |c(3)|$. We use these constraints as an outlier test, such that only the cepstra $\bar{c}$ that pass this test are employed in the following steps.

For each axial index y we compute a set of *local* cepstrum measurements $c\{[y_i]\}$, separated by lateral sampling distance δ (in our implementation $\delta = 4$

RF lines/pixels), depicted as red dots in Fig. 1. We then compute both axial and lateral cepstra for each such sample point y_i, by giving importance only to local neighborhood via exponentially weighted windowing.

Computing a globally constant or piecewise-constant PSF from cepstra was proposed in previous works [6, 18–20]. A global PSF is no viable option for simulation, since real PSFs vary significantly w.r.t. image depth, and mimicking this is essential for a plausible simulation. A piecewise-constant (PWC) PSF approximation leads to discontinuities in the simulated image. Instead, we compute a cepstrum value $c[y]$ per axial position y as the arithmetic mean over valid cepstra $\bar{c}\{[y_i]\}$ (those surrounded by a blue box in Fig. 1). By computing averaged cepstra $c[y]$ (depicted as blue dots in Fig. 1), we remove lateral PSF variation for robustness while preserving and estimating its axial variation.

Axial filtering in cepstrum domain. In Step 2 of Fig. 1, the axial cepstra $c[y]$ have been averaged laterally, but may exhibit strong variations in axial direction, leading to discontinuities in the corresponding PSF kernels. A simple interpolation of discrete PSF kernels $h[y]$ in the *spatial* domain would not give a properly defined PSF, due to the frequency component of h. Varray et al. [21] avoid image discontinuities due to discrete PSF kernels by running several simulations using different PSFs and merging resulting images in a weighting schem. Alternatively, we use a filtering of axial cepstra $c[y]$ to obtain a smoothly varying function in the cepstrum domain, which subsequently can be transformed into a smoothly varying $h[y]$. A Gaussian window of standard deviation σ is applied on $c[y]$ (depicted as green box in Fig. 1), where σ corresponds to an empirically set scale of expected PSF variation. Each value is then weighted by the number of valid cepstra $\bar{c}\{[y_i]\}$. The filter width n was set to 256 samples in our implementation, corresponding to $\approx 5\,\mathrm{mm}$ for given sampling frequency. A $\sigma = 80$ RF samples (corresponding to a 3σ range of $\approx 4.6\,\mathrm{mm}$) results in a successful trade-off between smoothing and variations.

PSF estimation from cepstrum. In third step the PSF $h[y]$ is computed from $c[y]$ as follows. For each $h[a]$, we recover the lateral and axial pulse profiles by applying the inverse transformation from Eq. 4 to the truncated cepstrum $c'[a]$ after cutoff. The separable 2D PSF for each y is computed from the 1D pulses by convolution. A remaining problem is that Eq. 4 aligns h with the upper left corner of the image and hence does not constitute a proper impulse response. Assuming a pulse similar to Eq. 2, to get a centered PSF we first compute the envelope $E = \max(|\mathcal{H}(h)|)$ to remove the frequency component, and then center the maximum intensity $\max(E)$ in the lateral and axial directions. Since the envelope of an idealized PSF corresponds to a Gaussian, centering the maximum intensity also corresponds to centering the mean of the signal.

4   Results and Discussion

To find the ideal value of the cepstrum cutoff, using $1/6^{th}$ of the PSF *Full-Width at Half-Maximum* (FWHM) was recommended as a rule of thumb in the

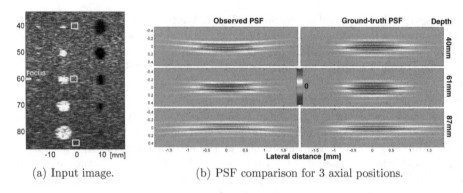

(a) Input image.   (b) PSF comparison for 3 axial positions.

Fig. 2. Comparison of FieldII-simulated PSF and estimated PSF for cyst phantom. (a) Input image. (b) PSF comparison for 3 axial positions.

literature [18]. FWHM is the extent of a pulse where its intensity is half of its maximum value. In our implementation, we permanently fixed the lateral and axial cutoff to the first 4 and 5 quefrencies of c, respectively. The parameter α for exponential weighting, typically in the range of $[0.965, 0.995]$ [23], was set to 0.975 for all experiments. Figure 2 demonstrates local PSF estimation from a FieldII-simulated image (a) as input. For simulation, a 6.6 MHz linear transducer with sampling frequency of 40 MHz and a width of 40 mm was used with a single transmit focus. To illustrate axial PSF variation, fixed receive focus points were used. A qualitative comparison of the FieldII PSF with the PSF estimated by our method in Fig. 2(b) demonstrates an excellent agreement. Table 1 gives a numerical comparison of FWHM from simulated and estimated PSF at the illustrated three depths, which shows that the estimated values are in good agreement with the FWHM of the FieldII PSF, with differences <15%. Added Gaussian noise affects our method minimally; up to a noise level of 40 dB, where significant errors are observed.

Table 1. FWHM of estimated and FieldII-simulated PSFs, and the normalized errors.

Depth [mm]	40.4	60.6	86.6	40.4	60.6	86.6	40.4	60.6	86.6	40.4	60.6	86.6
FWHM	Lateral [mm]			Axial [mm]			Lat. error [%]			Ax. error [%]		
Noise-free	1.38	1.18	1.90	.262	.263	.258	0	7	0	6	**11**	5
70 dB noise	1.36	1.18	1.89	.263	.263	.257	1	7	0	1	**11**	4
50 dB noise	1.23	1.11	1.55	.244	.240	.210	**21**	1	13	1	2	19
40 dB noise	0.52	0.62	0.48	.194	.185	.142	**167**	79	291	26	27	73
Ground-truth	1.38	1.11	1.89	.246	.234	.246	0	0	0	0	0	0

Figure 3(a) visually compares FWHM for different values of axial filtering parameter σ. This illustrates our method in the case of PSF discontinuities in the original beam profile, which are caused by using multiple receive focus points equally-spaced with 20 mm separations. Despite the discontinuities, our method can faithfully approximate the original FHWM values and the general shape of the curve. While there is certain variation among the methods, they all converge to similar values in the far field. The lateral spread of local PSF, obtained as the aggregation of a fine discretization of local PSF envelopes placed along a vertical line, is shown in Fig. 3(b) and called herein *beam shape*. It demonstrates that the estimated PSF is a smoothly varying function and in good agreement with FieldII simulation. Figure 3(c) and (d) show results for dynamic receive focusing, where PSF variations are smaller. In this case, a better estimation accuracy is indicated by our results.

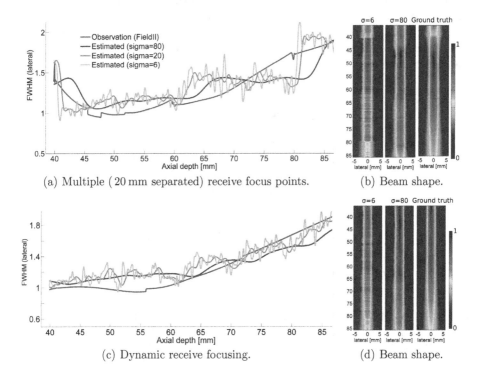

(a) Multiple (20 mm separated) receive focus points.   (b) Beam shape.

(c) Dynamic receive focusing.   (d) Beam shape.

Fig. 3. Full-Width-at-Half-Maximum (FWHM) of PSF over entire axial range of cyst phantom for 3 levels of axial filtering and two types of receive beam-forming; together with corresponding (lateral) beam shapes. The transmit focus is fixed at 60 mm in both cases. (a) Multiple (20 mm separated) receive focus points. (b) Beam shape. (c) Dynamic receive focusing. (d) Beam shape.

Figure 4 uses the estimated PSF for convolution-based simulation. In this example, the continuous set of $100K$ scatterers from a FieldII cyst phantom was discretized on a scatterer grid of 2701×1024 pixels (Fig. 4(a)). This map was convolved with the PSF estimated from FieldII simulation, where the simulated image should ideally be equivalent to the FieldII image. As baseline comparison, we used a technique from deconvolution literature, in which PSF estimation has most commonly been investigated. In particular, we approximate the PSF by piecewise-constant (PWC) kernels; two in our case for the near and the far fields, c.f. Fig. 4(b). The discontinuity between the two PSF kernels can be seen clearly as artifacts in the speckle pattern around 60 mm depth, making this method a poor choice for simulation. Conversely, the proposed PSF estimation method in Fig. 4(c) exhibits a smoothly varying speckle appearance. Our method is visually in good agreement with the original image in Fig. 4(d), with a focus sharper near 60 mm. For the anechoic cyst at 60 mm, we computed contrast-to-noise ratio (CNR) as an indicator for visibility of pathology. Using $\mathrm{CNR} = \frac{|\mu_{I_1} - \mu_{I_2}|}{\sigma_{I_1} + \sigma_{I_2}}$, where I_1 and I_2 denote B-Mode pixel intensity values of the cyst and the surrounding tissue, respectively, resulted in 1.05 dB for piecewise-constant PSF estimation and 1.16 dB for our local PSF estimation, which is closer to the observed value of 1.15 dB and indicates a contrast drop (and hence potential mis-training) in the case of inadequate PSF.

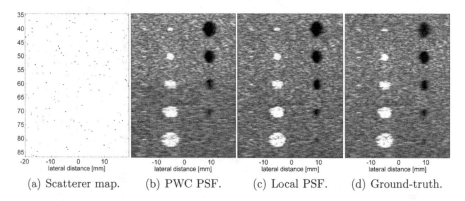

(a) Scatterer map.   (b) PWC PSF.   (c) Local PSF.   (d) Ground-truth.

Fig. 4. Convolution-based simulation for the cyst phantom: (a) Discretized scatterers, $100\times$ downsampled; (b) using 2-part piecewise-constant PSF with near- and far-field parts; (c) proposed local PSF estimation with $\sigma = 80$; (d) ground-truth FieldII image. (a) Scatterer map. (b) PWC PSF. (c) Local PSF. (d) Ground-truth.

Figure 5 shows the example of an in-vivo liver scan. The input image (shown as *envelope* image on the left without dynamic compression) was captured with a SonixTouch $4DC7$-3/40 convex probe operating at 4.5 MHz with 20 MHz sampling frequency and a transmit focus placed at 80 mm. The middle image shows the estimated PSF at four depths marked in the left image. Note that since the estimation is performed in the pre-scan-converted RF data, convex images are also handled easily. The rightmost image depicts the continuous beam shape. As expected for a convex probe, it exhibits an almost linear increase of the beam

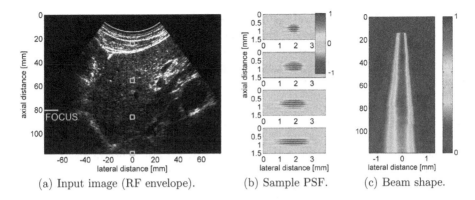

(a) Input image (RF envelope).   (b) Sample PSF.   (c) Beam shape.

Fig. 5. (a) Liver scan acquired with a convex probe. (b) Samples of the estimated PSF at 4 depths. (c) Beam shape as the smooth (lateral) variation of local PSFs.

width, where the focus is also discernible. The run time of the PSF estimation for this image was 13 min, in MATLAB with an Intel i7-4900MQ 2.8 GHZ CPU with 24 GB memory.

Discussion. Compared to earlier PSF estimation works such as [14,18], our 3-stage approach has the most similarities to methods on separable deconvolution [1,22], with some important differences: In contrast to our method, these methods make a single axial/lateral cepstrum measurement per axial/lateral scanline. As a result, they can capture lateral variation of the PSF w.r.t. image depth, but *not* the axial variation. Although the latter is potentially less pronounced than the former, it nevertheless still influences speckle statistics [15]. Instead, our algorithm first employs averaging in lateral direction followed by axial filtering, hence taking into account both lateral and axial components for each axial position. This allows us to robustly capture variation in *both* lateral and axial PSF components. For the actual deconvolution, these earlier works simply use a global PSF averaged over local measurements, whereas we make use of the additional local information for the subsequent simulation task. A potential limitation of our method is that RF images are not accessible on most commercial ultrasound systems. Furthermore, to achieve simulation realism, not only the PSF but also the (proprietary) image post-processing steps should match those of a commercial system.

5   Conclusions

We have hereby presented a method to estimate PSF and its spatial variation from ultrasound images. This is to be used in US training simulation of linear and convex transducers. Despite several studies on both PSF estimation and convolution-based simulation, these fields have not been fused yet. We believe that both (convolution-based) US simulation and other potential uses of US PSF are of significant interest to medical ultrasound community. As evaluation, we presented visual and numerical comparisons of the acquired PSF with the PSF from numerical simulations. We also demonstrated an example of estimating PSF and the beam shape from a 2D in-vivo image. A 3D extension is to be studied in future work. This work was supported by the Swiss Commission for Technology and Innovation (CTI).

References

1. Abeyratne, U.R., Petropulu, A.P., Reid, J.M.: Higher order spectra based deconvolution of ultrasound images. IEEE Trans. Ultrason. Ferroelectr. Freq. Control **42**(6), 1064–1075 (1995)
2. Bamber, J.C., Dickinson, R.J.: Ultrasonic b-scanning: a computer simulation. Phys. Med. Biol. **25**(3), 463 (1980)
3. Bhanu, B., McClellan, J.H.: On the computation of the complex cepstrum. IEEE Trans. Acoust. Speech Signal Process. **28**(5), 583–585 (1980)
4. Bürger, B., Bettinghausen, S., Rädle, M., Hesser, J.: Real-time GPU-based ultrasound simulation using deformable mesh models. IEEE Trans. Med. Imaging **32**(3), 609–618 (2013)
5. Gao, H., Choi, H., Claus, P., Boonen, S., Jaecques, S., Van Lenthe, G., Van der Perre, G., Lauriks, W., D'hooge, J.: A fast convolution-based methodology to simulate 2-d/3-d cardiac ultrasound images. IEEE Trans. Ultrason. Ferroelectr. Freq. Control **56**(2), 404–409 (2009)
6. Jensen, J., Leeman, S.: Nonparametric estimation of ultrasound pulses. IEEE Trans. Biomed. Eng. **41**(10), 929–936 (1994)
7. Jensen, J., Mathorne, J., Gravesen, T., Stage, B.: Deconvolution of in vivo ultrasound b-mode images. Ultrason. Imaging **15**(2), 122–133 (1993)
8. Jensen, J.A.: Deconvolution of ultrasound images. Ultrason. Imaging **14**(1), 1–15 (1992)
9. Kobayashi, T., Imai, S.: Spectral analysis using generalized cepstrum. IEEE Trans. Acoust. Speech Signal Process. **32**(5), 1087–1089 (1984)
10. Lee, J.K., Kabrisky, M., Oxley, M.E., Rogers, S.K., Ruck, D.W.: The complex cepstrum applied to two-dimensional images. Pattern Recognit. **26**(10), 1579–1592 (1993)
11. Mattausch, O., Goksel, O.: Scatterer reconstruction and parametrization of homogeneous tissue for ultrasound image simulation. In: IEEE EMBC, pp. 6350–6353, August 2015
12. Meunier, J., Bertrand, M.: Ultrasonic texture motion analysis: theory and simulation. IEEE Trans. Med. Imaging **14**(2), 293–300 (1995)
13. Meunier, J., Bertrand, M., Mailloux, G.: A model for dynamic texture analysis in two-dimensional echocardiograms of the myocardium. In: SPI 0768, pp. 193–200 (1987)
14. Michailovich, O., Adam, D.: Phase unwrapping for 2-d blind deconvolution of ultrasound images. IEEE Trans. Med. Imaging **23**(1), 7–25 (2004)
15. Oosterveld, B., Thijssen, J., Verhoef, W.: Texture of b-mode echograms: 3-d simulations and experiments of the effects of diffraction and scatterer density. Ultrason. Imaging **7**(2), 142–160 (1985)
16. Oppenheim, A.V., Schafer, R.W., Buck, J.R., et al.: Discrete-Time Signal Processing, vol. 2. Prentice-Hall, Englewood Cliffs (1989)

17. Reis, G., Lappe, B., Kohn, S., Weber, C., Bertram, M., Hagen, H.: Towards a virtual echocardiographic tutoring system. In: Linsen, L., Hagen, H., Hamann, B. (eds.) Visualization in Medicine and Life Sciences, pp. 99–119. Springer, Heidelberg (2008)
18. Taxt, T.: Restoration of medical ultrasound images using two-dimensional homomorphic deconvolution. IEEE Trans. UFFC **42**(4), 543–554 (1995)
19. Taxt, T.: Three-dimensional blind deconvolution of ultrasound images. IEEE Trans. UFFC **48**(4), 867–871 (2001)
20. Taxt, T.: Comparison of cepstrum based methods for radial blind deconvolution of ultrasound images. IEEE Trans. UFFC **1417**(44), 666–674 (1997)
21. Varray, F., Liebgott, H., Cachard, C., Vray, D.: Fast simulation of realistic pseudo-acoustic nonlinear radio-frequency ultrasound images. In: 2014 IEEE International Ultrasonics Symposium, pp. 2217–2220, September 2014
22. Wan, S., Raju, B.I., Srinivasan, M.A.: Robust deconvolution of high-frequency ultrasound images using higher-order spectral analysis and wavelets. IEEE Trans. Ultrason. Ferroelectr. Freq. Control **50**(10), 1286–1295 (2003)
23. Yamada, I., Sakaniwa, K.: An optimal design of homomorphic deconvolution system. In: IEEE Symposium on Circuits and Systems. pp. 1344–1349, May 1989

Microstructure Imaging Sequence
Simulation Toolbox

Andrada Ianuş[✉], Daniel C. Alexander, and Ivana Drobnjak

Centre for Medical Image Computing, Department of Computer Science,
University College London, London, UK
a.inaus@ucl.ac.uk

Abstract. This work describes Microstructure Imaging Sequence Simulation Toolbox (MISST), a practical diffusion MRI simulator for development, testing, and optimisation of novel MR pulse sequences for microstructure imaging. Diffusion MRI measures molecular displacement at microscopic level and provides a non-invasive tool for probing tissue microstructure. The measured signal is determined by various cellular features such as size, shape, intracellular volume fraction, orientation, etc., as well as the acquisition parameters of the diffusion sequence. Numerical simulations are a key step in understanding the effect of various parameters on the measured signal, which is important when developing new techniques for characterizing tissue microstructure using diffusion MRI. Here we present MISST - a semi-analytical simulation software, which is based on a matrix method approach and computes diffusion signal for fully general, user specified pulse sequences and tissue models. Its key purpose is to provide a deep understanding of the restricted diffusion MRI signal for a wide range of realistic, fully flexible scanner acquisition protocols, in practical computational time.

1 Introduction

Diffusion MRI (dMRI) has become one of the most important imaging modalities to probe tissue microstructure with many applications in biomedical imaging [1,2]. The dMRI signal measures the displacement of the water molecules inside the tissue and is sensitive to the configuration of cellular membranes, therefore it provides relevant information for characterising tissue properties at the micron level. By developing geometrical models of the tissue and relating them to the acquired dMRI data, it is possible to estimate cellular features such as size, shape, volume fraction, dominant orientation etc. Such estimates provide valuable biomarkers for studying the brain structure or for diagnosing and monitoring diseases. In order to develop fast and reliable acquisition protocols, a good understanding of the most relevant tissue features which affect the dMRI signal as well the influence of different acquisition parameters is very important.

Numerical simulations provide a cheap and powerful tool to investigate the effect of various sequence parameters and tissue features on the measured signal. With synthetic data, we can investigate the ability of various imaging techniques,

S.A. Tsaftaris et al. (Eds.): SASHIMI 2016, LNCS 9968, pp. 34–44, 2016.
DOI: 10.1007/978-3-319-46630-9_4

such as AxCaliber [3], ActiveAx [4], VERDICT [5], to estimate microstructural parameters from the data. We can also analyse the effect of including additional tissue features in the model, e.g. fibre dispersion [6] or size distribution [7], of varying acquisition parameters [8] or introducing novel diffusion sequences [9], in a controlled way with known ground truth.

Diffusion MR data synthesis can be divided into three broad categories:

Analytical models have a closed form solution which approximate the diffusion process in bounded geometries under various assumptions. Such approaches include the Short Pulse Gradient (SGP) approximation [10] or the Gaussian Phase Distribution (GPD) approximation [11–13]. The signal is fast to compute, however it departs from ground truth values when the assumptions are broken and cannot recover some signal features such as diffusion-diffraction patterns.

Semi-analytical models are based on matrix operators to calculate the time evolution of the diffusion signal inside simple geometries. Such approaches include the matrix formalism introduced by Callaghan [14] or the Multiple Correlation Function (MCF) technique [15]. The diffusion signal can be computed for arbitrary gradient waveforms, is accurate and relatively fast to compute, however, these techniques can be used only for simple geometries with known solutions of the diffusion equation (parallel planes, cylinders, spheres [11], spherical shells [12], triangles [16]).

Numerical models simulate the diffusion process either by numerical solutions of the diffusion equation in a known substrate (e.g. [17,18]) or using a Monte-Carlo approach (e.g. [19,20]). Such techniques can represent more complex and realistic diffusion substrates, however, they are computationally demanding and do not provide the same level of mathematical insight as analytical models do.

Analytical approximations of the dMRI signal are fast to compute but not very accurate, while numerical simulations have higher accuracy and can represent complicated geometries but require significantly more computational power. In simple geometries, semi-analytical approaches represent the middle ground, providing accurate signal calculations in a short computational time.

In this work we present the MISST software package, which is based on a semi-analytical approach, namely the 3D extension [21] of the matrix method proposed by Callaghan. MISST simulates the diffusion MRI signal for generalized, user defined, gradient waveforms and a variety of diffusion substrates. The matrix method has been used so far in various research studies to help validate the GPD approximation for oscillating gradients [13], to analyze the sensitivity of pulsed and oscillating gradients to axon diameter [8] as well as to investigate the properties of a newly introduced diffusion sequence, namely double oscillating diffusion encoding [9]. MISST combines a powerful method for simulating diffusion MRI signal with a wide range of diffusion substrates in a flexible, user friendly software package.

2   Theory

This section presents the theory behind the building blocks of MISST.

2.1   Diffusion Contrast

Diffusion MRI contrast is obtained by applying a magnetic field gradient with zero first moment at echo time, i.e. $\int_0^{TE} \mathbf{G}(t) \cdot dt$, where $\mathbf{G}$ denotes the effective gradient after accounting for the effect of inversion pulses from the imaging sequence. Thus, the phase acquired by each spin is $\phi(t) = \gamma \int_0^t \mathbf{G}(t') \cdot \mathbf{r}(t') dt'$ and the measured diffusion signal decay of the spin ensemble $E = \langle \exp(i\phi) \rangle$.

In case of free (Gaussian) diffusion and gradient with a fixed orientation for each measurement, the signal has the well known form:

$$E = \exp(-bD), \quad \text{where } b = \gamma^2 \int_0^{TE} \left| \int_0^t \mathbf{G}(t') dt' \right|^2 dt. \tag{1}$$

For a generalized gradient waveform, Eq. 1 needs to be expanded to a tensor form [22]:

$$E = \exp(- < \mathbf{B}, \mathbf{D} >), \quad \text{where } \mathbf{B} = \gamma^2 \int_0^{TE} \mathbf{F}(t) \mathbf{F}^T(t) dt, \ \mathbf{F}(t) = \int_0^t \mathbf{G}(t') dt', \tag{2}$$

$<, >$ denotes the tensor inner product and $\mathbf{D}$ is the diffusion tensor.

In case of diffusion restricted within closed pores, the solution is not straightforward and the signal depends on the propagator $P(\mathbf{r}_0, t_0 | \mathbf{r}_1, t_1)$ which represents the probability that a particle moves from position $\mathbf{r}_0$ at time t_0 to position $\mathbf{r}_1$ at time t_1 [23].

Matrix Formalism. To simulate restricted diffusion, MISST uses the 3D extension of the matrix method (MM) [14,24], which is based on a multiple propagator approach [25]. MM provides a generic framework for evaluating the restricted diffusion signal E in a closed form under generalised gradient waveforms. The pulse sequence is divided into narrow intervals τ, as illustrated in Fig. 1 and the gradient amplitude $g_0(k\tau)$ is discretized into steps of size g_{step}. Thus, at time $k\tau$ the amplitude of the diffusion vector is $m_k q$ where $q = (2\pi)^{-1} \tau g_{step}$, and $m_k = \lfloor (g_0(k\tau)/g_{step}) \rfloor$.

The signal E is calculated as a product of matrix operators which describe the phase evolution inside the boundaries:

$$E = S(\mathbf{q}) R[A(\mathbf{q})]^{m_2} R...R[A(\mathbf{q})]^{m_{K-1}} R S^T(-\mathbf{q}), \tag{3}$$

where the elements of the matrices S, A and R have the following definitions

$$S_n(\mathbf{q}) = V^{-1/2} \int u_n(\mathbf{r}) \exp(i2\pi \mathbf{q} \cdot \mathbf{r}) d\mathbf{r},$$

$$R_{nn} = \exp(-\lambda_n D \tau),$$

$$A_{nn'}(\mathbf{q}) = \int u_n^*(\mathbf{r}) u_{n'}(\mathbf{r}) \exp(i2\pi \mathbf{q} \cdot \mathbf{r}) d\mathbf{r}; \tag{4}$$

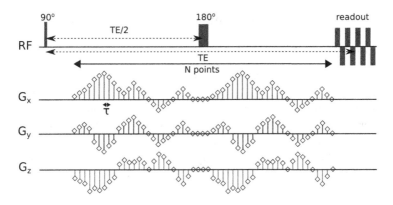

Fig. 1. Schematic representation of a generalized waveform which is repeated before and after the refocusing pulse in a spin-echo sequence. The gradient waveform along each direction is discretized in K steps.

V is the pore volume, $\mathbf{q} = q\hat{\mathbf{g}}$ where $\hat{\mathbf{g}}$ is the unit gradient vector and u_n and λ_n are the eigenfunctions and eigenvalues of the diffusion equation in the given geometry.

The above method has recently been extended for gradients with time varying orientation [24]. In the case of fixed orientation, the vector $\mathbf{q}$ is the same at every time point $k\tau$ which allows the precalculation of matrices $A(\mathbf{q})$ and $S(\mathbf{q})$. However, when the gradient orientation is time-dependant, the vector $\mathbf{q}$ is different at different time points and the matrices also depend on time. Thus Eq. 3 becomes:

$$E = S(q\hat{\mathbf{g}}_1)R[A(q\hat{\mathbf{g}}_2)]^{m_2}R...R[A(q\hat{\mathbf{g}}_{K-1})]^{m_K-1}RS^T(-q\hat{\mathbf{g}}_N), \qquad (5)$$

where $\hat{\mathbf{g}}_k$ denotes the gradient orientation at time $k\tau$.

Calculating the matrices $A(q\hat{\mathbf{g}}_k)$ element-by-element at each time point is too computationally expensive. To decrease computational time, MISST uses an efficient implementation based on the Taylor expansion of the matrices, which has been proposed and validated in [24].

2.2 Tissue Models

MISST simulates the diffusion signal from a variety of multi-compartment tissue models. Thus, the overall signal is computed as a weighted sum over different compartments:

$$E = \sum_{n=1}^{n=N} f_n E_n, \quad \text{with} \quad \sum_{n=1}^{n=N} f_n = 1, \qquad (6)$$

where E_n and f_n are the signal and the volume fraction of the nth compartment and N is the total number of compartments in the model. For compartments exhibiting Gaussian diffusion, the signal is computed according to Eq. 2, while for restricted compartments it is calculated according to Eq. 5.

3   Software Implementation

3.1   General Overview

MISST is implemented in Matlab using a modular design and is schematically represented in Fig. 2. This implementation allows the user to choose between various diffusion sequences which are widely used in the literature and/or to define their own sequences as well as to build a large variety of tissue models by easily combining the diffusion signal from basic compartments. The package is open source and available for download http://mig.cs.ucl.ac.uk/index.php?n=Tutorial.MISST.

3.2   Implementation Details

In order to generate the diffusion signal, the user inputs the parameters of the diffusion sequences and of the tissue model. The simulator outputs the diffusion signal and, optionally, the Jacobian of the signal.

Input parameters

Diffusion sequences: The diffusion measurements are represented as a structure, commonly denoted as "protocol", which stores the information regarding the effective diffusion gradient G and the time discretization τ. The 3D gradient waveform is specified as a M x 3 K matrix, where M is the number of diffusion measurements and K is the number of gradient points in one measurement along each direction. The gradient does not necessarily need to be repeated after the 180 rf pulse, nevertheless, the gradient integral should be zero. We provide a set of examples how to generate the discrete gradient waveforms for several diffusion sequences which are widely used in the literature: pulsed gradient spin echo sequences (PGSE), sinusoidal/square/trapezoidal oscillating gradients (OGSE), double pulsed field gradients, stimulated echo sequences, etc. A detailed descriptions for the parametrization of each sequence can be found in the software documentation.

Tissue models: For the diffusion substrates, MISST provides a flexible design of multi-compartment tissue models by combining basic building blocks which have different diffusion characteristics. The different basic models are illustrated in Fig. 2 and follow the nomenclature presented in [26]. Currently, there are several multi-compartment white matter models available in MISST, nevertheless, other substrates can be easily implemented by combining different compartments. The information related to the diffusion substrate is represented as a structure commonly referred to as "model". The user needs to specify the model name as well as the model parameters such as diffusivity, radius (for cylinders and spheres), volume fractions of different compartments, etc.

Output parameters

MISST outputs a vector of normalized diffusion signals corresponding to each measurement in the protocol, for the diffusion substrate specified by the tissue

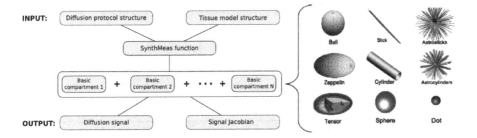

Fig. 2. Schematic representation of MISST, showing the input and output parameters as well as the basic diffusion compartments.

model. Optionally, the simulator can output the signal Jacobian, i.e. the derivatives of the signal with respect to the model parameters. For instance, if the protocol has M measurements and the model has P parameters, the Jacobian is an M × P matrix.

4 Simulations and Results

4.1 Signal Validation

The first set of experiments validate the restricted diffusion signal computed from MISST against the Monte Carlo (MC) diffusion simulator in Camino [19] in a substrate consisting of parallel cylinders with radius R = 3 μm and intrinsic diffusivity $D = 2 \cdot 10^{-9}$ m^2/s, oriented along the z axis, as illustrated in Fig. 3(a).

To show the true potential of MISST, in the first simulation we test a protocol with $M = 50$ fully generalized gradient waveforms, which are generated by random numbers for gradients in x, y and z directions. To ensure a null gradient integral, the waveforms with a duration of 20 ms are repeated before and after the 180 rf pulse, as schematically illustrated in Fig. 3(b). We set the maximum gradient strength to 500 mT/m and we use a time step $\tau = 0.1$ ms. For the MC simulations we used 200000 walkers and the same time step τ. The plot in Fig. 3(c) presents the diffusion signal computed using the two methods. The signal difference between MISST and MC is less than 0.16 % for all data points. The computational time necessary for MISST to generate this data set was 5 s, while the MC simulation took 10 min.

The second simulation investigates an acquisition protocol consisting of double pulsed field gradient sequences (dPFG) which vary the angle between the gradients in the plane perpendicular to the cylinder axis. A schematic representation of the sequence is illustrated in Fig. 3(d). The sequence parameters for this simulation are: gradient strength $G = 500$ mT/m, pulse duration $\delta = 2$ ms, pulse separation $\Delta = 50$ ms, mixing time $\tau_m = \{0, 2, 10\}$ ms and angle φ between the gradient directions from 0 and 2π. The plots in Fig. 3(e) show the dependence of the dPGSE signal as a function of the angle between the gradients for three different mixing times, when the signal was generated either using MISST

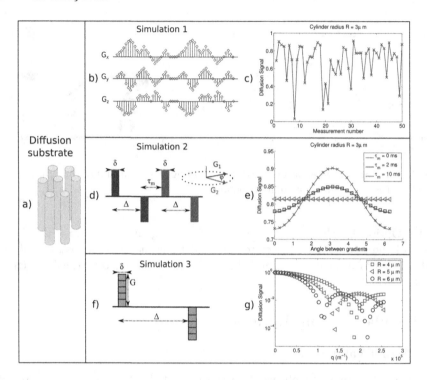

Fig. 3. (a) Schematic representation of the diffusion substrate; Schematic representation of (b) the random gradient waveform and (c) the corresponding diffusion signals obtained using MISST (line) and MC simulations (symbol); Schematic representation of (d) the dPGSE sequence and (e) the corresponding diffusion signals obtained using MISST (line) and MC simulations (symbol); Schematic representation of (f) the PGSE sequence and (g) the corresponding diffusion-diffraction patterns obtained using MISST.

or MC simulations. Similarly to the previous simulations, the signal difference between the two methods is less than 0.3 % for all the data points. In this case, MISST calculations were performed in 10 s, while the MC simulation took 1 h 20 min.

The third analysis shows that MISST can reproduce important features of the restricted diffusion signal which cannot be accurately modelled with simpler analytical approximations like GPD, such as diffusion-diffraction patterns when the wave vector $q = (2\pi)^{-1}\gamma G\delta$ is increased [27,28]. In this simulation we use standard PGSE sequences with $\delta = 3\,\text{ms}$, $\Delta = 100\,\text{ms}$ and $G = \{0, 50, 100, ..., 2000\}\,\text{mT/m}$. The diffusion-diffraction patterns depend on the restriction size, as illustrated in Fig. 3(g) for parallel cylinders with three different radii $R = \{4, 5, 6\}\,\mu\text{m}$.

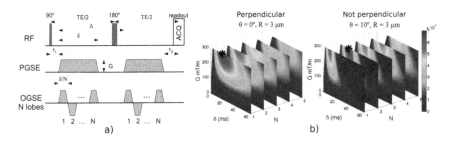

Fig. 4. Sensitivity of PGSE ($N = 1$) and OGSE (N > 1) sequences to cylinder radius for a wide range of sequence parameters. The star denotes the most sensitive sequence.

4.2   Application Example

MISST software can be used for a wide range of applications, from validating analytical approximations [13], to analysing the sensitivity of various diffusion measurements [8] or understanding the contrast of novel sequences [9]. Here we illustrate an example of using MISST to compare the sensitivity of PGSE and OGSE sequences to pore diameter in cylindrical restriction. We investigate two situations: (1) the gradient is orthogonal to the cylinder axis and (2) the gradient is not perfectly perpendicular, deviating by a small angle $\theta = 10°$. We analyse a wide range of practical sequence parameters with gradient strength $G \in [0, 300] \, \mathrm{mT/m}$, $\delta \in [0, 60] \, \mathrm{ms}$, $\Delta = \delta + 10 \, \mathrm{ms}$ and $N = \{1, 2, ..., 5\}$ gradient lobes, as illustrated in Fig. 4(a). In this simulation we use a two-compartment tissue model with parallel cylinders ($R = 3 \, \mu\mathrm{m}$, $D = 1.7 \cdot 10^{-9} \, \mathrm{m}^2/\mathrm{s}$, volume fraction $f = 0.7$) and hindered extracellular space in the tortuosity limit ($D_{\parallel} = 1.7 \cdot 10^{-9} \, \mathrm{m}^2/\mathrm{s}$, $D_{\perp} = (1 - f) \cdot D_{\parallel}$). We account for the effect of T2 decay with a constant $T2 = 70 \, \mathrm{ms}$. An in-depth analysis of PGSE vs. OGSE sensitivity to pore diameter is presented in [8].

Figure 4(b) plots the sensitivity of PGSE ($N = 1$) and OGSE (N > 1) sequences with a wide range of parameters. The results show that in the case when the gradient direction is orthogonal to the cylinder orientation, PGSE sequences have the highest sensitivity, however, if the gradient is no longer perfectly perpendicular or there is fibre dispersion (not shown here), OGSE sequences with low frequency yield the highest sensitivity. This analysis shows the importance of numerical simulations for exploring optimal combinations of sequence parameters in an intuitive way.

5   Discussion

This work introduces MISST, a software package that simulates the diffusion MRI signal from a variety of pulses sequences and diffusion substrates. Being open source, the user can easily tailor the software to explore their own research question, allowing faster development in the field of diffusion MRI.

MISST implements the 3D extension of the matrix method, which allows the computation of restricted diffusion signal for flexible, user defined, gradient waveforms. We provide details of the implementation, as well as examples of tissue models and gradient waveforms. The signal calculation is accurate and preserves important signal features such as diffusion-diffraction patterns, yet it is orders of magnitude faster to compute compared to MC simulations, which makes it practical for many applications.

One limitation of the matrix method is that it can be used to calculate the restricted diffusion signal only for basic geometries with well known solution of the diffusion equation such as parallel planes, cylinders, spheres, spherical shells as well as triangles. Another limitation is the fact that diffusion in extracellular space needs to be computed separately, thus the accuracy of the signal depends on the complexity of the chosen model. Although boundary relaxation effects can be accounted for in the matrix method formalism, the exchange between intra and extracellular spaces cannot be readily incorporated.

Future work aims to provide the template for more diffusion sequences which have been recently developed in the literature (double oscillating diffusion encoding, q-mas and other sequences with isotropic encoding) as well as more diffusion compartments such as cuboids and finite cylinders [7].

The novelty of MISST is that it simulates dMRI signal for any user-defined diffusion gradient waveform, from a standard PGSE to more advanced sequences which are of great interest to the research in this field. Moreover, due to its modular construction, the user can easily combine various diffusion compartments to create models that are representative of various tissue types, such as grey matter, white matter or tumours. All these features are combined in a user-friendly, open source software package.

References

1. Jones, D.K., Diffusion, M.R.I.: Theory, Methods and Application. Oxford University Press, Oxford (2010)
2. Johansen-Berg, H., Behrens, T.E.J.: MRI: Diffusion from Quantitative Measurement to in Vivo Neuroanatomy. Academic Press, San Diego (2009)
3. Assaf, Y., Blumenfeld-Katzir, T., Yovel, Y., Basser, P.J.: AxCaliber: a method for measuring axon diameter distribution from diffusion MRI. Magn. Reson. Med. **59**(6), 1347–1354 (2008)
4. Alexander, D.C., Hubbard, P.L., Hall, M.G., Moore, E.A., Ptito, M., Parker, G.J.M., Dyrby, T.B.: Orientationally invariant indices of axon diameter and density from diffusion MRI. NeuroImage **52**, 1374–1389 (2010)
5. Panagiotaki, E., Walker-Samuel, S., Siow, B., Johnson, S.P., Rajkumar, V., Pedley, R.B., Lythgoe, M.F., Alexander, D.C.: Noninvasive quantification of solid tumor microstructure using VERDICT MRI. Cancer Res. **74**, 1902–1912 (2014)
6. Zhang, H., Hubbard, P.L., Parker, G.J.M., Alexander, D.C.: Axon diameter mapping in the presence of orientation dispersion with diffusion MRI. NeuroImage **56**, 1301–1315 (2011)
7. Ianuş, A., Drobnjak, I., Alexander, D.C.: Model-based estimation of microscopic anisotropy using diffusion MRI: a simulation study. NMR Biomed. **29**, 627–685 (2016)

8. Drobnjak, I., Zhang, H., Ianuş, A., Kaden, E., Alexander, D.C.: PGSE, OGSE, and sensitivity to axon diameter in diffusion MRI: Insight from a simulation study. Magn. Reson. Med. **75**, 688–700 (2016)
9. Shemesh, N., Lanuş, A., Alexander, D.C., Drobnjak, I.: Double oscillating diffusion encoding (DODE) augments microscopic anisotropy contrast. In: Proceedings of ISMRM, p. 952, Toronto, Canada (2015)
10. Stejskal, E.O.: Use of spin echoes in a pulsed magnetic-field gradient to study anisotropic, restricted diffusion and flow. J. Chem. Phys. **43**, 3597–3603 (1965)
11. Neuman, C.H.: Spin echo of spins diffusing in a bounded medium. J. Chem. Phys. **60**, 4508–4511 (1974)
12. Xu, J., Does, M.D., Gore, J.C.: Quantitative characterization of tissue microstructure with temporal diffusion spectroscopy. J. Magn. Reson. **200**, 189–197 (2009)
13. Ianuş, A., Siow, B., Drobnjak, I., Zhang, H., Alexander, D.C.: Gaussian phase distribution approximations for oscillating gradient spin-echo diffusion (MRI). J. Magn. Reson. **227**, 25–34 (2013)
14. Callaghan, P.T.: A simple matrix formalism for spin echo analysis of restricted diffusion under generalized gradient waveforms. J. Magn. Reson. **129**, 74–84 (1997)
15. Grebenkov, D.: Laplacian eigenfunctions in NMR. I. A numerical tool. Concepts Magn. Reson. Part A **32**, 277–301 (2008)
16. Kuder, T.A., Laun, F.B.: NMR-based diffusion pore imaging by double wave vector measurements. Magn. Reson. Med. **70**, 836–841 (2013)
17. Xu, J., Does, M.D., Gore, J.C.: Numerical study of water diffusion in biological tissues using an improved finite difference method. Phys. Med. Biol. **52**, N111–N126 (2007)
18. Li, J.-R., Calhoun, D., Poupon, C., Le Bihan, D.: Numerical simulation of diffusion mri signals using an adaptive time-stepping method. Phys. Med. Biol. **59**, 441–454 (2014)
19. Hall, M.G., Alexander, D.C.: Convergence and parameter choice for Monte-Carlo simulations of diffusion MRI. IEEE Trans. Med. Imaging **28**, 1354–1364 (2009)
20. Yeh, C.H., Schmitt, B., Le Bihan, D., Li-Schlittgen, J.R., Lin, C.P., Poupon, C., Diffusion microscopist simulator: a general monte carlo simulation system for diffusion magnetic resonance imaging. In: PLoS ONE (2013)
21. Drobnjak, I., Alexander, D.C.: Optimising time-varying gradient orientation for microstructure sensitivity in diffusion-weighted MR. J. Magn. Reson. **212**, 344–354 (2011)
22. Westin, C.-F., Szczepankiewicz, F., Pasternak, O., Özarslan, E., Topgaard, D., Knutsson, H., Nilsson, M.: Measurement tensors in diffusion MRI: generalizing the concept of diffusion encoding. In: Golland, P., Hata, N., Barillot, C., Hornegger, J., Howe, R. (eds.) MICCAI 2014, Part III. LNCS, vol. 8675, pp. 209–216. Springer, Heidelberg (2014)
23. Callaghan, P.T.: Principles of Magnetic Resonance Microscopy. Oxford Science Publications, Oxford (1991)
24. Drobnjak, I., Zhang, H., Hall, M.G., Alexander, D.C.: The matrix formalism for generalised gradients with time-varying orientation in diffusion NMR. J. Magn. Reson. **210**, 151–157 (2011)
25. Caprihan, A., Wang, L.Z., Fukushima, E.: A multiple-narrow-pulse approximation for restricted diffusion in a time-varying field gradient. J. Magn. Reson. Ser. A **118**, 94–102 (1996)
26. Panagiotaki, E., Schneider, T., Siow, B., Hall, M.G., Lythgoe, M.F., Alexander, D.C.: Compartment models of the diffuison MR signal in brain white matter: a taxonomy and comparison. NeuroImage **59**, 2241–2254 (2012)

27. Callaghan, P.T., Coy, A., MacGowan, D., Packer, K.J., Zelaya, F.O.: Diffraction-like effects in NMR diffusion studies of fluids in porous solids. Nature **351**, 467–469 (1991)
28. Balinov, B., Jonsson, B., Linse, P., Soderman, O.: The NMR self-diffusion method applied to restricted diffusion. simulation of echo attenuation from molecules in spheres and between planes. J. Magn. Reson. **104**, 17–25 (1993)

From Image-Based Modeling to the Modeling of Imaging with the Virtual Population

Esra Neufeld[1($\boxtimes$)], Bryn Lloyd[1], and Niels Kuster[1,2]

[1] IT'IS Foundation for Research on Information Technologies in Society,
8004 Zurich, Switzerland
neufeld@itis.ethz.ch
[2] Swiss Federal Institute of Technology (ETHZ), 8092 Zurich, Switzerland
http://www.itis.ethz.ch/

Abstract. Image data has been used to create the Virtual Population models, a range of highly detailed anatomical models (male/female, neonates/children/adults/elderly, average build/obese) which have been found to be useful for a wide range of computational life sciences applications. They are at the core of the Sim4Life simulation platform. Different image modalities provide a wealth of information enabling model functionalization by facilitating anatomy parameterization and animation, consideration of tissue inhomogeneity, imposition of realistic boundary conditions, and integration of dynamic physiological models. Closing the circle, these functionalized anatomical models have also been used to generate virtual image data, particularly by simulating MR imaging. Thus, image data can be produced under controlled conditions and with known base-anatomy for different pulse sequences. Virtual imaging has been used to study different imaging artefacts.

Keywords: Virtual Population · Anatomical phantoms · Image-based modeling · Model functionalization · MRI simulation

1 Introduction

The human body, its anatomy and physiology, are at the center of life sciences applications. Thus, computational life sciences frequently require virtual models of the human anatomy and physiology. The Virtual Population (ViP) models are a range of highly detailed human anatomical models, which have been segmented from magnetic resonance images of volunteers (Fig. 1). Using different image modalities and other sources of information they have been functionalized to go beyond static representations of the human anatomy, including tissue material property distributions and dynamic behavior. The ViP models have been employed to investigate a wide range of life sciences applications, including issues related to magnetic resonance imaging (MRI). MRI modeling has been used for imaging optimization and safety assessment. Imaging optimization includes hardware modeling and optimization, as well as pulse sequence-related

© Springer International Publishing AG 2016
S.A. Tsaftaris et al. (Eds.): SASHIMI 2016, LNCS 9968, pp. 45–54, 2016.
DOI: 10.1007/978-3-319-46630-9_5

modeling and optimization of the imaging-process - virtual MRI imaging. Virtual MR imaging is helpful in understanding the process of magnetic resonance imaging, in creating new pulse sequences and scan types, in optimizing the imaging hardware (e.g., coils), and in generating image data with known anatomical correspondence, e.g., for the development or validation of image segmentation or registration tools.

While the generation of the ViP models from medical image data has been described previously [1,2], their parametrization and (image-based) functionalization has not been systematically presented. This paper aims at (i) providing such an overview, (ii) discussing for the first time their application to virtual MR imaging, and (iii) illustrating how the different components combine. For a review of other existing computational anatomical phantoms, see [3]. More information on virtual MR imaging using realistic electromagnetic field distributions can be found in [4].

2   Materials and Methods

2.1   Image-Based Modeling - Model Generation

MRI data from currently ten healthy volunteers has been acquired, resampled at a uniform 0.5 mm resolution, and segmented using a mixture of automatic and (semi-)manual techniques [1,2]. More than 300 different tissues and organs have been distinguished. The models are chosen to provide optimal population coverage, with male and female models and an age range covering children, adults, and elderly. Some models were selected to ideally represent average Caucasian body height and weight, while an obese model helps to represent other population sectors. In addition neonate models are available, and segmented fetus image data has been combined with a female model to generate pregnant women models at different gestation stages.

High fidelity, smooth and water tight (closed) surface meshes with no gaps or self-intersections are extracted from segmented images. Surfaces are created by initially generating an optimized, adaptive tetrahedral mesh, then extracting interface and outer surface triangle-meshes, which are further processed (smoothing and simplification) while ascertaining that no intersections are introduced [2].

The Virtual Population model are an integrated part of the Sim4Life simulation platform for computational life sciences [8]. Sim4Life provides a range of physical and physiological simulators optimized for the modeling of interactions with/inside living tissues within the complexity of the human body are available.

2.2   Image-Based Modeling - Model Functionalization

In addition to using image data as a source of static information about the anatomical geometry, image data is also employed as part of the 'functionalization' of the Virtual Population models:

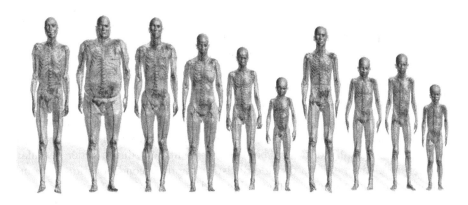

Fig. 1. The Virtual Population model range.

Dynamic Anatomy. The basic Virtual Population models provide static anatomical geometries. However, when processes are studied that occur on a similar time scale as organ motion due to breathing or heart-beat, it can become necessary to animate the anatomical models. For that purpose, breathing motion data has been extracted for part of the abdomen from 4D MRI and used to create a parameterized breathing motion model. The breathing model has been registered to the average adult male Virtual Population model and used to transiently deform it, thus mimicking breathing in a personalized way [6, 9].

Furthermore, near-interactive posture- and obesity level-parameterization has been developed for the Virtual Population models [7]. It simulates the tissues as biomechanical, hyperelastic materials, prescribing positions for rigid bones, assigning body-forces to selected tissues and allowing soft tissues to deform passively.

Material Properties. The Virtual Population models are synchronized with the ITIS Tissue Properties Database [5], a literature-based and on-line accessible resource of tissue properties information that includes suggested values (as well as data about variability) for density, dielectric properties, low frequency electrical conductivity, thermal properties, perfusion, acoustic properties, MRI related tissue properties, and for fluids rheological properties. However, occasionally material properties cannot be approximated as constant throughout a tissue. In such cases, image data has been used to extract property distributions in selected tissues that has then been associated with anatomical models. Examples include MRI liver perfusion maps for thermal modeling, computed tomography (CT) bone density maps for acoustic propagation modeling, or MRI diffusion tensor imaging (DTI) as source of low frequency conductivity anisotropy and inhomogeneity information.

Boundary Conditions. Simulations not only require geometry and material property information, but also suitable boundary conditions. In some cases, medical imaging can provide a valuable source for realistic boundary conditions. For example, 4D MRI velocimetry maps have been registered with the Virtual Population models to obtain realistic boundary conditions in blood fluid dynamics simulations.

Physiology. Fiber tracking in MRI diffusion image data has been used to place dynamic neurophysiology models that can be coupled to electromagnetic modeling inside anatomical phantoms. Vessel network segmentation and extraction from MRI angiography data can be used to facilitate reduced order vascular blood flow modeling, e.g., to provide realistic boundary conditions for 4D computational fluid dynamics modeling of blood flow at locations of interest.

2.3   Modeling Imaging

In the previous sections, the use of image data as source for anatomical modeling and model functionalization has been discussed. However, the reverse process, namely generating virtual image data from anatomical models, tissue properties, and occasionally physiological information, has also been studied. The Virtual Population has been used to simulate MR imaging by reproducing the electromagnetic (EM) and spin dynamics physics. MR imaging uses a static magnetic field, a radiofrequency (RF) EM field (typically from a bird-cage coil; used to control and record nuclear spin procession), and a gradient field (used to encode position information) to manipulate nuclear spins (Fig. 2). Both the dielectric properties, as well as parameters affecting spin dynamics, are tissue specific. Values for many different tissues can be found in the ITIS database [5].

RF-Coil Modeling. An RF-coil designer has been implemented within Sim4Life that can also place and tune the different capacitors, resistors and inductances required for coil resonance at the right mode. The *in situ* EM fields can then be computed using a finite-differences time-domain method solver and the Virtual Population models ([11], Fig. 3).

Gradient Coil Modeling. A gradient coil design tool can be used to create gradient coils that maximize field homogeneity, while minimizing power and inductance, for arbitrarily shaped coils. For an existing coil design, the induced low frequency fields within the Virtual Population models can be computed using a magneto-quasistatic EM solver (Fig. 3).

Scan Sequence and Spin Dynamics Modeling. Once the different EM fields, the anatomical tissue distribution, and its associated properties are known, the MR images resulting from a specific pulse sequence can be computed. For that purpose, Sim4Life simulates spin dynamics based on the Bloch equations, and reproduces image reconstruction from the simulated signal (Figs. 2 and 4). The presence of metallic implants can be considered by introducing corresponding dipole sources.

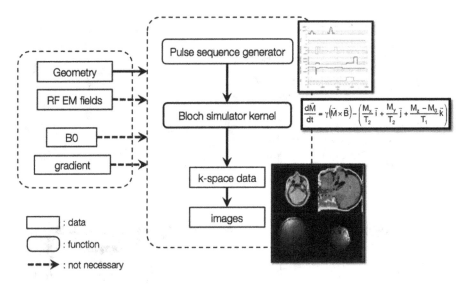

Fig. 2. Schematic representation of the data-flow and simulation modules involved in virtual MR image generation.

3 Results

3.1 Virtual Population Models

The Virtual Population models have found widespread application, as evident in more than 700 citations of the original paper [1]. Most applications have been related to dosimetry in the area of EM exposure (e.g., MRI related), quantifying energy deposition, but also induced effects such as heating or neurostimulation. Other applications have been related to device design, investigation of novel therapies, safety and efficacy assessment for regulatory purposes, and mechanistic studies. Investigated physics have included EM (ionizing and nonionizing), acoustics (e.g., ultrasound), flow, tissue growth and damage, biomechanics, and others.

3.2 Image-Based Model Functionalization

Applications of image-based model functionalization include the following examples:

Dynamic Anatomy. The MRI-based breathing animation of a Virtual Population model has been used to investigate the impact of breathing-related liver motion on focused ultrasound ablation of hepatic tumor and to devise superior targeting and focusing methodology [6,9].

Biomechanics-based morphing and posing has been used for diverse applications, including the assessment of MRI-safety of active implanted medical devices

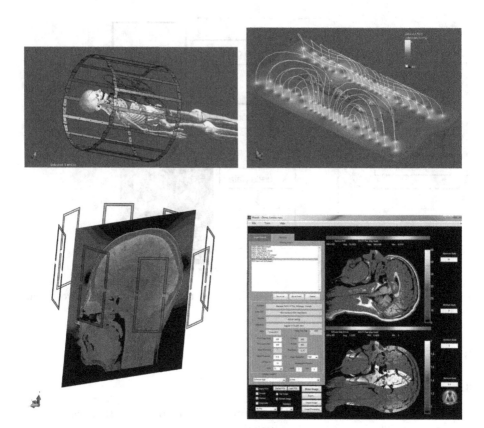

Fig. 3. MRI coils and induced fields: birdcage and surface coils (u.l.), gradient coil with induced magnetic field (u.r.), head coil and related D-field (b.l.), tool for receive coil array design and analysis (b.r.).

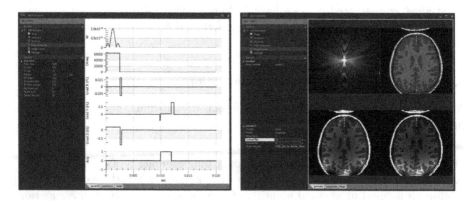

Fig. 4. Sequence definition (left) and simulated MR imaging (k-space and reconstructed; right).

(pace-makers, deep brain stimulators), where comprehensive population and situation coverage is required to assess that the RF-energy pick-up through implant leads, which act like antennas, does not result in inacceptable tissue heating near critical implant locations [12].

Material Properties. Model functionalization with image-derived tissue inhomogeneity information has been used, e.g., to:

- improve the quality of patient-specific treatment planning in hyperthermic oncology by consideration of MRI perfusion maps and related heat removal [13]
- investigate and compensate the degrading impact of skull-related aberration and defocusing in transcranial therapeutic ultrasound applications (ablation, reversible blood-brain-barrier disruption) by consideration of CT-derived speed-of-sound and absorption maps
- quantify the influence of highly inhomogeneous and anisotropic electrical conductivity in brain tissue on the penetration depth of transcranial electrical and magnetic stimulation [14].

Boundary Conditions. Image-based flow boundary conditions have been applied to simulate and validate realistic blood flow conditions, for the investigation of the magneto-hemodynamic (MHD) effect on ECG (electrocardiogram) measurements. When exposed to a strong magnetic field (e.g., inside an MRI machine), the MHD effect leads to a distortion of the ECG signal which can negatively affect heart-beat-synchronized triggering, but has been found to contain information about blood flow features that could serve as bio-marker [10].

Physiology. The image-based anatomical model functionalization with electro-physiological neuron models allows to study the mechanisms involved in deep brain stimulation [15] and to further understanding of unintended nerve stimulation by low frequency EM-field exposure. The latter has led to questioning a range of assumptions underlying current MRI safety guidelines [16].

3.3 Modeling Imaging

Virtual MR images of the Virtual Population models have been generated by combining the anatomical models, information about tissue properties, and coupled multi-scale modeling of the *in vivo* EM-fields generated by the MRI coils and the induced spin-dynamics. This permits to produce (under controlled conditions and with known base-anatomy) different image modalities with varying pulse sequences (e.g., T1- or T2-weighted, Fig. 6) and to investigate different imaging artefacts (e.g., related to field inhomogeneity, k-space undersampling, or the presence of metallic implants, Fig. 5). For example, the artefacts originating from the presence of different orthopedic screws and implants in different locations and orientations have been simulated.

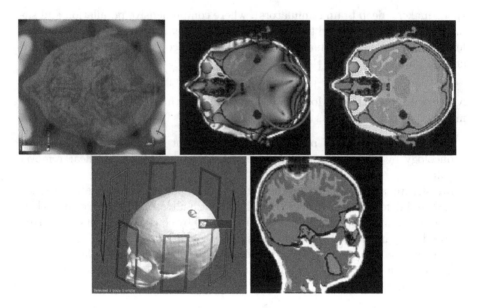

Fig. 5. Modeling of MRI artifacts. Top row: field inhomogeneity (left) related image artifact before (middle) and after correction (right). Bottom row: artifact (right) resulting from the presence of a metallic implant (left).

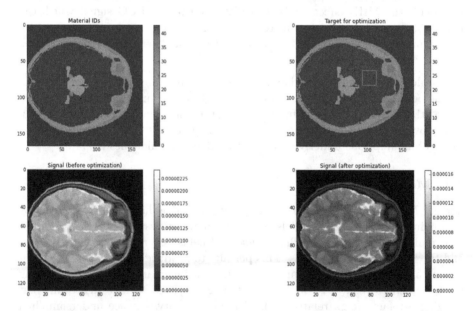

Fig. 6. Simulated image before and after optimizing contrast in a target volume (T1 vs. T2 contrast balancing).

4 Conclusion

The Virtual Population models are used in a wide range of computational life sciences applications, such as mechanistic research, clinical treatment planning, medical device design and optimization, and regulatory purposes (safety and efficacy assessment). The static anatomical models have been functionalized using a variety of image modalities, e.g. providing inhomogeneous tissue property distributions, model dynamics such as 4D breathing motion, realistic boundary conditions, and support in the integration of physiological models such as electrophysiological neuron models. These functionalized anatomical models have also been used for the reverse process of simulating magnetic resonance imaging using a Bloch equation solver and a collection of tools allowing to study the design of MR imaging hardware (RF and gradient coils) and pulse sequences. Thus, image data can be produced under controlled conditions and with known base-anatomy for different pulse sequences. Virtual imaging has been used to study different imaging artefacts.

References

1. Christ, A., Kainz, W., Hahn, E.G., Honegger, K., Zefferer, M., Neufeld, E., Rascher, W., Janka, R., Bautz, W., Chen, J., Kiefer, B., Schmitt, P., Hollenbach, H.-P., Shen, J., Oberle, M., Szczerba, D., Kam, A., Guag, J.W., Kuster, N.: The Virtual Family development of surface-based anatomical models of two adults and two children for dosimetric simulations. Phys. Med. Biol. **55**(2), N23 (2010)
2. Gosselin, M.-C., Neufeld, E., Moser, H., Huber, E., Farcito, S., Gerber, L., Jedensj, M., Hilber, I., Di Gennaro, F., Lloyd, B., Cherubini, E., Szczerba, D., Kainz, W., Kuster, N.: Development of a new generation of high-resolution anatomical models for medical device evaluation: the Virtual Population 3.0. Phys. Med. Biol. **59**(18), 5287 (2014)
3. Xu, X.G., Eckerman, K.F.: Handbook of Anatomical Models for Radiation Dosimetry. CRC Press, Boca Raton (2009)
4. Cao, Z., Sukhoon, O., Sica, C.T., McGarrity, J.M., Horan, T., Luo, W., Collins, C.M.: Bloch-based MRI system simulator considering realistic electromagnetic fields for calculation of signal, noise, and specific absorption rate. Magn. Reson. Med. **72**(1), 237–247 (2014)
5. Hasgall, P.A., Di Gennaro, F., Baumgartner, C., Neufeld, E., Gosselin, M.C., Payne, D., Klingenbck, A., Kuster, N.: IT'IS Database for thermal and electromagnetic parameters of biological tissues. Version 2.6, 13 January 2015
6. Kyriakou, A., Neufeld, E., Werner, B., Székely, G., Kuster, N.: Full-wave acoustic and thermal modeling of transcranial ultrasound propagation and investigation of skull-induced aberration correction techniques: a feasibility study. J. Ther. Ultrasound **3**(1), 1–18 (2015)
7. Lloyd, B., Cherubini, E., Chavannes, N., Kuster, N.: Realistic Physics-Based Posing of Anatomical Models for Safety Evaluations and Computational Life Science in Various Configurations, Latsis Symposium on Personalized Medicine, ETH Zurich, June 2016
8. Neufeld, E., Szczerba, D., Chavannes, N., Kuster, N.: A novel medical image database-based multi-physics simulation platform for computational life sciences. Interface Focus **3**(2), 20120058 (2013)

9. Baumgartner, C., Neufeld, E., Payne, D., Kuster, N.: A comprehensive database of physical tissue properties for computational simulations in realistic virtual anatomies. In: Proceedings of the 5th International Workshop on Computational Human Phantoms, pp. 67–68 (2015)

10. Kyriakou, A., Neufeld, E., Szczerba, D., Kainz, W., Luechinger, R., Kozerke, S., McGregor, R., Kuster, N.: Patient-specific simulations and measurements of the magneto-hemodynamic effect in human primary vessels. Physiol. Measur. **33**(2), 117 (2012)

11. Murbach, M., Cabot, E., Neufeld, E., Gosselin, M.-C., Christ, A., Pruessmann, K.P., Kuster, N.: Local SAR enhancements in anatomically correct children and adult models as a function of position within 1.5 t mr body coil. Prog. Biophys. Mol. Biol. **107**(3), 428–433 (2011)

12. Cabot, E., Lloyd, T., Christ, A., Kainz, W., Douglas, M., Stenzel, G., Wedan, S., Kuster, N.: Evaluation of the RF heating of a generic deep brain stimulator exposed in 1.5 t magnetic resonance scanners. Bioelectromagnetics **34**(2), 104–113 (2013)

13. Paulides, M.M., Stauffer, P.R., Neufeld, E., Maccarini, P.F., Kyriakou, A., Canters, R.A.M., Diederich, C.J., Bakker, J.F., Van Rhoon, G.C.: Simulation techniques in hyperthermia treatment planning. Int. J. Hyperth. **29**(4), 346–357 (2013)

14. Iacono, M.I., Neufeld, E., Akinnagbe, E., Bower, K., Wolf, J., Oikonomidis, I.V., Sharma, D., Lloyd, B., Wilm, B.J., Wyss, M., et al.: MIDA: a multimodal imaging-based detailed anatomical model of the human head and neck. PloS one **10**(4), e0124126 (2015)

15. Cassara, A., Neufeld, E., Guidon, M., Kainz, W., Kuster, N.: Large-scale multi neuronal simulation within anatomical models for transcranial alternative current stimulation investigation. In: Proceedings of the Joint Meeting of the Bioelectromagnetics Society (BEMS) and the European BioElectromagnetics Association (EBEA) (2016)

16. Neufeld, E., Oikonomidis, I.V., Iacono, M.I., Angelone, L.M., Kainz, W., Kuster, N.: Investigation of assumptions underlying current safety guidelines on em-induced nerve stimulation. Phys. Med. Biol. **61**(12), 4466 (2016)

Numerical Simulation of Ultrasonic Backscattering During Fracture Healing Using Numerical Models Based on Scanning Acoustic Microscopy Images

Vassiliki T. Potsika[1], Konstantinos N. Grivas[2], Theodoros Gortsas[2],
Vasilios C. Protopappas[1], Demosthenes Polyzos[2], and Dimitrios I. Fotiadis[1,3(✉)]

[1] Unit of Medical Technology and Intelligent Information Systems,
University of Ioannina, 45110 Ioannina, Greece
{vpotsika,vprotop,fotiadis}@cc.uoi.gr
[2] Department of Mechanical Engineering and Aeronautics,
University of Patras, 26500 Patras, Greece
{grivas,gortsas,polyzos}@mech.upatras.gr
[3] Department of Biomedical Research, Foundation for Research and Technology–Hellas,
Institute of Molecular Biology and Biotechnology, 45110 Ioannina, Greece

Abstract. Quantitative ultrasound has been used as a monitoring means of osteoporosis and fracture healing by several research groups worldwide applying experimental and computational techniques. However, fracture healing is a complex biological process and an interdisciplinary knowledge is required to fully comprehend the pathways of bone regeneration and gene expression as well as the structural and material changes occurring at different healing stages. Over the last decade, the incorporation of computational tools and the illustration of bone microstructure and material properties at different hierarchical levels using micro-computed tomography and scanning acoustic microscopy (SAM) have paved the way for the investigation of complex wave propagation phenomena which cannot be observed via traditional experimental procedures. In this study, we use the boundary element method to perform simulations of ultrasound propagation at successive bone healing stages. Bone healing is simulated as a three stage process and numerical models are established based on SAM images derived from week 3, week 6 and week 9 after the osteotomy. Callus is considered as a two-dimensional medium and its composite nature is integrated in the models via the combination of SAM images and an iterative effective medium approximation. We use a plane wave excitation at 1 MHz to investigate the interaction with cortical and callus tissues. The scattering amplitude variation is calculated in the backward and forward direction, as well. It was found that the scattering amplitude derived from appropriate directions and excitation frequencies could convey significant quantitative information for the evaluation of fracture healing.

Keywords: Scanning acoustic microscopy images · Fracture healing · Boundary element method · Ultrasonic backscattering

© Springer International Publishing AG 2016
S.A. Tsaftaris et al. (Eds.): SASHIMI 2016, LNCS 9968, pp. 55–64, 2016.
DOI: 10.1007/978-3-319-46630-9_6

1   Introduction

In recent years several non-destructive testing approaches and techniques have been proposed for the assessment of cortical and trabecular bone, especially in the cases of pathologies such as osteoporosis and fracture healing. As far as bone healing is concerned, the monitoring potential of low intensity quantitative ultrasound and its positive effect on treatment acceleration have been investigated extensively using experimental, numerical and theoretical methods. Axial transmission measurements of the first arriving signal (FAS) velocity have been mainly presented in the literature. The FAS velocity is strongly correlated with bone microstructure reflecting the evolution of fracture healing and osteoporosis. Specifically, it has been shown that the FAS velocity decreases as the porosity increases in osteoporotic bones, while it decreases during the first healing stages showing a constant increase at later healing stages.

The propagation of guided waves has also been studied as an advanced method for the investigation of deeper layers of cortical bone using ultrasound. The use of this method is significant when the wavelength is comparable to or smaller than the thickness of the cortical bone as the FAS wave propagates as a lateral (or head) wave conveying information for the upper cortical surface (periosteum). Also, it has been shown that bone anisotropy and geometry irregularity, as well as the material and geometrical changes of callus influence the propagation of guided modes, while the FAS velocity is not influenced by the irregularity and anisotropy of bone [1]. However, even if the study of guided waves provides valuable qualitative information, the results should be interpreted in combination with traditional FAS velocity measurements [2].

The study of scattering phenomena has also gained significant interest and several experimental and numerical methods have been presented [2–4]. Comparing to the transverse and axial transmission techniques, backscattering methods are not restricted to peripheral skeletal sites such as the heel or forearm and may provide easier access to central skeletal sites such as the hip and spine where many osteoporotic fractures occur [3]. Some studies have measured a parameter called broadband ultrasonic backscatter, which is the frequency averaged backscatter coefficient and has been shown to be sensitive to the density, mechanical properties, and microstructure of cancellous bone [4]. Other ultrasonic parameters of interest are the apparent integrated backscatter as well as the frequency slope of apparent backscatter, which are frequency dependent according to [3].

Measurements of ultrasonic backscattering have been mainly used for the evaluation of trabecular bone microstructure, while fewer studies have been presented for cortical bone. The ultrasound scattering phenomena induced by a composite object depend on a complex manner on its structure and mechanical properties [5]. From a microstructural point of view the two types of bone differ significantly. Cortical bone is more compact and composes the external surface of all bones with porosity from 5–10 %. On the other hand, trabecular bone is found in the inner parts of bones, it is less dense, softer and weaker with porosity from 50–95 %.

The rapid development of technological infrastructure and the evolution of imaging modalities such as micro-computed tomography and scanning acoustic microscopy (SAM) have opened new perspectives for the numerical study of backscattering parameters. Numerical and theoretical scattering models have been established to study the effect of frequency and microstructural characteristics on the backscatter coefficient. Specifically, the Faran cylinder model simulated trabeculae as solid cylinders in fluid and the dependence of the backscatter coefficient on frequency and thickness of the bone was examined [6]. In [5], three dimensional microstructural models were presented to investigate the ability of weak scattering statistical models to predict both the frequency-dependence and the magnitude of the backscatter coefficient. According to this study, the investigation of scattering by trabecular bone can be based on two approximations: (a) derive the pressure field by solving the propagation equation inside and outside the scatterers, and applying the proper boundary conditions at the interfaces, (b) assume bone microstructure as a random continuum, which permits a more flexible description of complex scattering geometry.

As far as cortical bone is concerned, fewer numerical studies have investigated the potential of the backscattering method to evaluate bone microstructure. The main ultrasonic parameters of interest are the backscattered amplitude integral and the attenuation slope of apparent backscatter. More recent studies [7–9] use the backscattering method to identify the occurrence of large pores called non-refilled basic multicellular unit. From a biological perspective, the size of Haversian canals increases due to a partial refilling in the course of tissue remodeling with ageing [7]. Thus, osteoporosis may provoke a complete lack of refilling and an accumulation of non-refilled basic multicellular unit in the cortex. It was shown in [8] that the scattering amplitudes and the calculated displacements in the backward direction can reveal differences due to changes in cortical porosity from 0–16 % as well as the occurrence of pores larger than the Haversian canals. High-frequency waves were applied in [9], to correlate the Haversian canal size and the occurrence of large pores with the backscatter characteristics. It was shown that the frequency dependence of cortical backscatter is strongly related to the size distribution of Haversian canals and the occurrence of large non-refilled basic multicellular unit can be detected revealing osteoporosis at an early stage.

In this study, we use SAM images to present realistic numerical models of long bones at different fracture healing stages to examine the monitoring potential of the backscattering method. To our knowledge this is the first numerical study of backscattering in bone healing based on imaging data. Two-dimensional geometries are established which incorporate the Gaussian-like curvature of callus tissue. The composite nature of callus is considered using the iterative effective medium approximation of [2], in which the material properties are derived from SAM data. Two series of simulations are performed to account for: (a) changes in both the material and geometrical features during bone healing (Series I), (b) changes only in the material properties keeping constant the callus geometrical characteristics at different postoperative weeks (Series II). We use a plane wave excitation at 1 MHz to investigate the interaction with cortical and callus tissues. The scattering amplitude is calculated in the backward and forward direction. It was found that the backscattering method could provide valuable information for the evaluation of the fracture healing process.

2   Materials and Methods

2.1   Model Geometry

In this section we present the developed two dimensional numerical models of long bones at different healing stages. The cortical bone was modeled as a 2D plate with length 40 mm and width 4 mm. The callus region was modeled by a Gaussian-like curvature mimicking the periosteal and endosteal region, as well. The 2D cortical model was assumed to be immersed in blood in order to account for the soft tissues surrounding the bone and callus. The fracture healing process was modeled assuming three successive stages for week 3, 6 and 9 after the osteotomy based on the SAM images of Fig. 1 [2]. Calibrated maps of the acoustic impedance Z were converted into maps of the elastic coefficient c_{11} using a calibration method and empirical relations between impedance and elastic coefficients, as described in [2, 10]. For comparison purposes, we have also considered a model of intact bone. Two sets of simulations were performed to account for: (a) changes in both the material and geometrical features of callus during fracture healing (Series I), (b) changes only in the material properties keeping constant the geometry of callus (Series II). In Fig. 2 the generalized model is presented and the parameter h_{callus} depicts the maximum distance of the upper callus surface from the cortical surface and was varying from 6 mm in week 3 to 5 mm in week 6 and to 3 mm

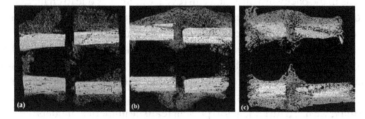

Fig. 1. Scanning acoustic microscopy images representing the: (a) third, (b) sixth and (c) ninth postoperative week [2].

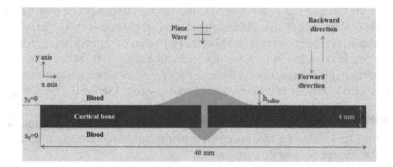

Fig. 2. Generalized computational model of a healing long bone including the callus periosteal and endosteal region. Series I: In week 3 h_{callus} was 6 mm, in week 6 h_{callus} was 5 mm and in week 9 h_{callus} was 3 mm. Series II: h_{callus} was set to 3 mm for all the healing stages.

in week 9 for Series I. On the other hand h_{callus} was constant for all the healing stages in Series II (hcallus was set to 3 mm). In this way, we intend to account for the shrinking of the callus size, increasing degree of mineralization and restoring of the intrinsic material properties which occur during the healing process.

2.2 Determination of Fracture Callus Material Properties Through the Itertive Effective Medium Approximation (IEMA)

The material properties of the callus were derived from SAM images representing successive healing stages based on [2]. The acoustic impedance images of longitudinal sections of osteotomies in the right tibia of female Merino sheep were obtained from a previous experimental study [10]. Each acoustic impedance map correspond to a specific healing stage after 3, 6 and 9 weeks of consolidation. From the imaging data, the original material properties of callus were used as the input to the IEMA procedure. Callus was considered as a composite medium consisting of a matrix with spherical inclusions to account for the porous nature of the newly formed osseous tissues. Concerning the numerical model of week 3, blood was assumed to compose the matrix of the medium and osseous tissue as the material of the spherical scatterers. The opposite assumption was made for the numerical models of weeks 6 and 9 as the presence of osseous tissue is dominant according to the SAM data. Specifically, in order to derive the effective material properties for each healing stage, the average scatterers' diameter and volume concentration were determined as: (a) 350 μm and 44.8 % in week 3, (b) 200 μm and 38.7 % in week 6, and (c) 120 μm and 22.7 % in week 9, respectively [2]. The effective material properties are presented in Table 1. It should be mentioned that the material properties of Table 1 were incorporated in the computational models of both Series I and Series II implying that the two sets of simulations differ only as far as the geometry of the callus is concerned.

Table 1. Callus effective material properties for Series I & II calculated using IEMA for the excitation frequency 1 MHz

Healing stage	Young's modulus (GPa)	λ (GPa)	μ (GPa)	Poisson's ratio	Density (Kg/m^3) -
Week 3	$1.9 * 10^{-6}$	3.8	$645.7 * 10^{-9}$	0.50	1201.0
Week 6	7.5	6.2	2.8	0.35	1867.0
Week 9	13.5	9.0	5.1	0.32	1880.8

The material properties of cortical bone were: Young's modulus $E_{bone} = 30.3$ GPa, density $\rho_{bone} = 2016$ kg/m^3 and Poisson's ratio $\nu_{bone} = 0.3$ [2]. The material properties of blood were: Young's modulus $E_{blood} = 3$ MPa, density $\rho_{blood} = 1055$ kg/m^3 and Poisson's ratio $\nu_{blood} = 0.49979$ [2].

2.3   Ultrasound Configuration

A 1 MHz-plane wave stimulation was used and its interaction with the numerical models was studied. A plane wave has a constant frequncy and its wavefronts are infinite parallel planes normal to the direction of propagation. Even if it is not possible in clinical practice to have a real plane wave, however, many waves can be considered as plane waves in a localized region of space.

2.4   Numerical Solution of the Scattering Problem Using the Boundary Element Method

The Boundary Element Method (BEM) was used for the solution of the 2D wave prop-agation problem (ISoBEM, BEM S&S, Greece [11]). The numerical method has been described in detail in our previous study [6] and this section summarizes the main equations used for the calculation of the scattering amplitude.

Specifically, the propagation of sound waves in an unbounded homogeneous acoustic medium is calculated as:

$$\partial_i^2 p(\mathbf{x}, t) = \frac{1}{c^2} \frac{\partial^2 p(\mathbf{x}, t)}{\partial t^2}, \tag{1}$$

where $i = 1,2$ for two dimensions, $p(x,t)$ is the acoustic pressure, c is the sound velocity, ∂_i denotes differentiation with respect to coordinate x_i, $\mathbf{x}$ is the position vector and t denotes the time.

Applying the Fourier transform or considering harmonic dependence in time, Eq. (1) obtains the form (Helmholtz equation):

$$\partial_i^2 P(\mathbf{x}, \omega) + k^2 P(\mathbf{x}, \omega) = 0, \tag{2}$$

where $P(x,\omega)$ denotes pressure in the frequency domain, ω is the frequency and $k = \omega/c$.

For a wave scattering problem involving an incident harmonic plane wave $P^{(i)}(\mathbf{x}) = P0e^{-ik(\hat{\mathbf{k}}\mathbf{x})}$ propagating in the $\hat{\mathbf{k}}$ direction, the pressure field $P(\mathbf{x},\omega)$ is calculated as the sum of the incident and the scattered wave $P^{(s)}(\mathbf{x},\omega)$ as:

$$P(\mathbf{x}, \omega) = P^{(i)}(\mathbf{x}, \omega) + P^{(s)}(\mathbf{x}, \omega), \tag{3}$$

The scattered field satisfies the far field radiation condition:

$$P^{(s)} = P0 \frac{e^{-ikR}}{ikR} g(\hat{\mathbf{x}}, \hat{\mathbf{k}}) \quad R \to \infty, \tag{4}$$

where $\hat{\mathbf{x}}$ is unit position vector and $g(\hat{\mathbf{x}}, \hat{\mathbf{k}})$ the scattering amplitude, which gives a measure of the scattering energy in the $\hat{\mathbf{x}}$ direction for an incident wave in the $\hat{\mathbf{k}}$ direction.

3 Results

This section presents the calculated scattering amplitudes for the two sets of simulations in the forward and backward direction, as well. The forward direction corresponds to the negative direction of the y axis and the backward direction to the positive values of y axis perpendicularly to the cortical cortex (Fig. 2). The results for intact bone are also included in order to examine whether the scattering amplitude values are restored as healing progresses and to what extent.

In Fig. 3, a decrease of the scattering amplitude in the forward direction is observed for Series I in week 3 followed by a gradual increase in weeks 6 and 9. Specifically, the scattering amplitude values were: (a) 0.21 for week 3, (b) 0.43 for week 6, (c) 0.55 for week 9 and (d) 0.62 for intact bone.

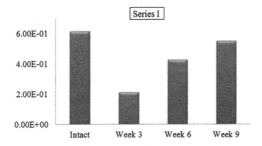

Fig. 3. Scattering amplitude values in the forward direction for different healing stages and the first set of simulations.

Similarly, Fig. 4 shows a decrease of the scattering amplitude calculations in the backward direction for Series II in week 3 and a gradual increase at later healing stages. The scattering amplitude values were: (a) 0.68 for week 3, (b) 1.04 for week 6, (c) 1.09 for week 9 and (d) 1.73 for intact bone. It can be observed that higher scattering amplitudes are calculated in the backward direction compared to the results in the forward direction for the first set of simulations.

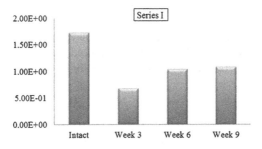

Fig. 4. Scattering amplitude values in the backward direction for different healing stages and the first set of simulations.

Then, in Fig. 5 we observe a decrease of the scattering amplitude in the forward direction for Series II in week 3 and a gradual increase at later healing stages which in agreement with the tendency observed in Series I (Fig. 3). The scattering amplitudes were: (a) 0.23 for week 3, (b) 0.44 for week 6, (c) 0.55 for week 9 and (d) 0.62 for intact bone. It should be mentioned that the values of intact bone and week 9 coincide with the corresponding values of Fig. 3 as the geometries are the same and h_{callus} varies only in weeks 3, 6 among Series I and Series II.

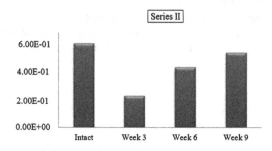

Fig. 5. Scattering amplitude values in the forward direction for different healing stages and the second set of simulations.

On the other hand, a different scattering amplitude tendency is presented in Fig. 6.

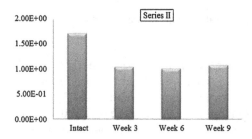

Fig. 6. Scattering amplitude values in the backward direction for different healing stages and the second set of simulations.

Specifically, the scattering amplitude decreases during the first two healing stages and increases only in week 9. The scattering amplitudes were: (a) 1.05 for week 3, (b) 1.02 for week 6, (c) 1.09 for week 9 and (d) 1.73 for intact bone.

4   Discussion

In this study, we presented 2D computational models of healing long bones aiming to investigate the evolution of the scattering amplitude during the bone healing process. The results are derived from calculations in the backward and forward direction as well corresponding to week 3, week 6, week 9 after the osteotomy. We consider the propagation of a 1 MHz plane wave and the interaction with osseous and callus tissue is examined. The Boundary Element Method was used for the solution of the 2D wave propagation problem. The convergence of the results was examining and the element size was set to 0.02 mm.

Comparing to our previous work [6], a more realistic geometry of callus was developed as the Gaussian-like curvature was incorporated. Also, the callus shrinkage was included via the parameter h_{callus} based on different healing stages from SAM images [9]. In *vitro* scanning acoustic microscopy is a microelastic imaging technique that provides large scale (cm range) structural and elastic properties at the tissue level with spatial resolution down to the μm-range [10]. Additionally, the porous nature of the callus was considered using the iterative effective medium approximation described in [2]. The accuracy of IEMA has been highlighted in [2] by comparing the outcome of the proposed theoretical method with experimental and theoretical findings in cancellous bone mimicking phantoms. The excitation frequency of 1 MHz is applied for the first time while a lower frequency (100 kHz) was used in [6]. According to [12], at diagnostic frequencies (around 500 kHz), the absorption is likely to be a larger component of attenuation than scattering. Additionally it was shown in [13] that for trabecular bone at frequencies ranging from 1 to 3.5 kHz, the ultrasound backscatter associated significantly with the tissue mechanical and structural parameters. To this end, the use of a 1 MHz-plane wave is considered as a convenient frequency for the study of scattering during fracture healing. However, further research is needed to examine the sensitivity and dependency of the selected frequency on the porous nature of the callus considering the pores' size at different healing stages.

Concerning the parameters of interest, the acoustic pressure in the backward direction was calculated in [6] as a quantitative indicator for the monitoring of fracture healing, while in this work we investigate the variation of the scattering amplitude in both the forward and the backward direction, as well. The scattering amplitude reflects the scattered energy far away from the examined geometry. Higher scattering amplitude values were calculated in the backward direction compared to the corresponding values in the forward direction indicating that scattering in most prominent in the backward direction which is in agreement with [12]. Also, the scattering amplitude was found to decrease at week 3 and increase in weeks 6, 9 due to the fact that the scattered intensity from soft tissues is generally considerably smaller than the reflected intensity from hard tissues. Finally, it was observed that the scattering amplitude in the backward direction is sensitive to the shrinkage of the callus at later healing stages and changes in structural features have a significant impact on the calculated parameters as well as the evolution of material properties. This is a significant advantage compared to traditional FAS velocity measurements as according to [1] when the first-arriving signal at the receiver corresponded to a nondispersive lateral wave, its propagation velocity was almost unaffected by the elastic symmetry and geometry of the bone and also could not characterize the callus tissue throughout its thickness.

However, further numerical and experimental research is needed to examine the effectiveness of the methodology and accuracy of the results. Our ongoing study investigates ultrasound scattering using both axial and transverse geometries of healing long bones.

5   Conclusions

The Boundary Element Method was applied to conduct ultrasonic backscattering simulations at different healing stages using scanning acoustic microscopy images. It was shown that the scattering amplitude derived in the forward and backward direction could potentially provide significant quantitative information for the competent monitoring of the fracture healing process.

References

1. Protopappas, V.C., Kourtis, I.C., Kourtis, L.C., Malizos, K.N., Massalas, C.V., Fotiadis, D.I.: Three dimensional finite element modeling of guided ultrasound wave propagation in intact and healing long bones. J. Accoust. Soc. Am. **121**(6), 3907–3921 (2007)
2. Potsika, V.T., Grivas, K.N., Protopappas, V.C., Vavva, M.G., Raum, K., Rohrbach, D., Polyzos, D., Fotiadis, D.I.: Application of an effective medium theory for modeling ultrasound wave propagation in healing long bones. Ultrasonics **54**(5), 1219–1230 (2014)
3. Hoffmeister, B.K., Holt, A.P., Kaste, S.C.: Effect of the cortex on ultrasonic backscatterer measurements of cancellous bone. Phys. Med. Biol. **56**(19), 6243–6255 (2011)
4. Hoffmeister, B.K., Wilson, A.R., Gilbert, M.J., Sellers, M.E.: A backscatter difference technique for ultrasonic bone assessment. J. Accoust. Soc. Am. **132**(6), 4069–4076 (2012)
5. Padilla, F., Peyrin, F., Laugier, P.: Prediction of frequency-dependent ultrasonic backscatter in cancellous bone using statistical weak scattering model. J. Accoust. Soc. Am. **29**(3), 1122–1129 (2002)
6. Potsika, V.T., Gortsas, T., Protopappas, V.C., Polyzos, D.K., Fotiadis, D.I.: Computational modeling of ultrasonic backscattering to evaluate fracture healing. In: 37th Annual International Conference of the IEEE EMBS (2015)
7. Bourgnon, A., Sitzer, A., Chabraborty, A., Rohde, K., Varga, P., Wendlandt, R., Raum, K.: Impact of microscale properties measured by 50-MHz acoustic microscopy on mesoscale elastic and ultimate mechanical cortical bone properties. In: Proceedings of IEEE International Ultrasonics Symposium, Chicago, IL, USA, pp. 636–638, 3–6 September 2014
8. Gortsas, T., Grivas, K., Polyzos, D., Potsika, V., Protopappas, V., Fotiadis, D., Raum, K.: The effect of cortical bone porosity on ultrasonic backscattering parameters. In: Proceedings of the IEEE 6th ESUCB, Corfu, Greece, 10–12 June 2015
9. Iori, G., Raum, K., Potsika, V., Gortsas, T., Fotiadis, D.: High-frequency cortical backscatter reveals cortical microstructure – a simulation study. In: Proceedings of the IEEE 6th ESUCB, Corfu, Greece, 10–12 June 2015
10. Preininger, B., Checa, S., Molnar, F.L., Fratzl, P., Duda, G.N., Raum, K.: Spatial-temporal mapping of bone structural and elastic properties in a sheep model following osteotomy. Ultrasound Med. Biol. **37**(3), 474–483 (2011)
11. http://www.bemsands.com
12. Wear, K.: Frequency dependence of ultrasonic backscatter from human trabecular bone: theory and experiment. J. Accoust. Soc. Am. **106**(6), 3659–3664 (1999)
13. Karjalainen, J.P., Töyräs, J., Riekkinen, O., Hakulinen, M., Jurvelin, J.S.: Ultrasound backscatter imaging provides frequency-dependent information on structure, composition and mechanical properties of human trabecular bone. Ultrasound Med. Biol. **35**(8), 1376–1384 (2007)

GBM Modeling with Proliferation and Migration Phenotypes: A Proposal of Initialization for Real Cases

Juan Ortiz-Pla$^{(\boxtimes)}$, Elies Fuster-Garcia, Javier Juan-Albarracin, and Juan Miguel Garcia-Gomez

Instituto Universitario de Aplicaciones de las Tecnologias de la Informacion y de las Comunicaciones, Universidad Politecnica de Valencia, Camino de Vera s/n, 46022 Valencia, Spain
juaorpl@etsii.upv.es

Abstract. Glioblastoma is the most aggressive tumor originated in the central nervous system. Modeling its evolution is of great interest for therapy planning and early response to treatment assessment. Using a continuous multi-scale growth model, which considers the angiogenic process, oxygen supply and different phenotype expressions, a new method is proposed for setting the initial values of the celular variables, based on a spatiotemporal characterization of their distribution in controlled synthetic simulations. The method is applied to a real case showing an improvement on the dynamic stability, compared to the usual method.

Keywords: Glioblastoma growth · Mathematical model · Phenotype expression · *in silico* oncology

1 Introduction

Glioblastoma (GBM), also known as grade IV astrocytoma, is a brain neoplasm involving glial cells. It represents around 12–15% of all intracranial tumors and 50–60% of all astrocytomas. The survival mean time is 14 months, and the standar treatment involves surgery, chemotherapy and radiotherapy [1]. They share a common morphology: presence of brain edema, irregular borders, and a tumor ring surrounding a necrotic center [2].

Most of the works about tumor growth, deal with gliomas instead of GBM [3–5]. However, because GBM is a high grade glioma, many aspects and considerations of modeling proposed by these works are still valid when focusing only in GBM. Also, many authors agree in the important role that phenotype expressions, characterized as different cellular populations, play in the tumor growth dynamics [3–7]. The 'go-or-grow' hypothesis is widely extended and accepted for modeling. It states that phenotype expressions can be simplified into two groups: enhanced proliferation when the environment is favorable, and enhanced mobility

© Springer International Publishing AG 2016
S.A. Tsaftaris et al. (Eds.): SASHIMI 2016, LNCS 9968, pp. 65–74, 2016.
DOI: 10.1007/978-3-319-46630-9_7

when the local availability of resources is low [8]. To model the local availability of resources in the tumor microenvironment, many studies have focused on modeling the angiogenesis cascade [3–5,9]. Although results are promising, the objective of these studies usually consists on replicating the branching and morphology of capillaries, rather than studying their effect on the growth dynamics. Recent articles of GBM growth include simplified versions of angiogenesis models to better characterize the supply of nutrients and its effect on phenotype change [6,7,10,11].

However, a common limitation to many of the mentioned works, is the lack of justification and methodology for the initialization of the variables of the model. This is due to the difficulty of establishing a relationship between the considered variables and the accessible clinical information for a patient. Even though anatomical images allow to segment the extension of the tumor, the information provided is typically a binary mask without quantifiable information about tumor cells or angiogenic variables. This problem becomes much more troublesome when different phenotype expressions, modeled as cellular populations, cohabit in the same segmented region.

In this work we use a continuous multi-scale GBM growth model, which considers the key physiological aspects of tumor progression: angiogenesis, oxygen supply and oxygen-mediated phenotype switch. Using this model we propose a methodology to initialize the values of the celular variables based on the characterization of their spatiotemporal distribution. We consider the hypothesis that, in a controlled homogeneous environment, after a certain time, the modeled physiological processes stabilize, and as a result, the spatial distributions of the different phenotypes across the tumor reach a stationary morphology. Our proposed method uses this knowledge in real cases, to assign an initial value to the variables for each point of the anatomical segmentation.

2   Materials and Methods

2.1   GBM Growth Model

We propose a set of spatiotemporal, coupled, non-linear partial derivative equations (PDE), which represent the most relevant features of the GBM's growth dynamics:

$$\frac{\partial g}{\partial t} = \nabla \cdot (D_g \nabla g) + \rho_g \, g \, (1 - T) + (\theta_{mg} \, H_{mg}) \, m - (\theta_{gm} \, H_{gm}) \, g \quad (1)$$

$$\frac{\partial m}{\partial t} = \nabla \cdot (D_m \nabla m) + \rho_m \, m \, (1 - T) + (\theta_{gm} \, H_{gm}) \, g$$
$$- (\theta_{mg} \, H_{mg}) \, m - (\theta_{mN} H_{mN}) m \quad (2)$$

$$\frac{\partial N}{\partial t} = (\theta_{mN} H_{mN}) m + (\theta_{vN} H_{vN}) v \quad (3)$$

$$\frac{\partial o}{\partial t} = (1 - o)\varphi \, v - o\left(\frac{\alpha_g g + \alpha_m m}{K_m + o}\right) \quad (4)$$

$$\frac{\partial a}{\partial t} = \nabla \cdot (D_a \nabla a) + \rho_{am} \, m - \gamma \, v \tag{5}$$

$$\frac{\partial v}{\partial t} = \nabla \cdot (\chi v \nabla a) + \rho_v \, v \, m \, (1 - N) - (\theta_{vN} H_{vN}) v \tag{6}$$

Where g is the density of proliferative cells, m is the density of invasive cells, N is the necrosis area of the tumor, o is the oxygen concentration, v is the density of vascularization and a is the concentration of angiogenic factors. T is the total tumor density, which is $T = g + m + N$. All variables are normalized by their maximum possible value, and as a result they all $\in [0, 1]$. A complete list and explanation of the parameters can be found in Table 1.

The basic assumptions of this model are:

- Cells diffuse through the extracellular matrix (ECM) with brownian movement. We assume that invasive cells m are more able to move than proliferative cells g, and thus we impose $D_m > D_g$.
- Cellular proliferation follows a logistic law. The total tumoral density T shall not grow over the maximum carrying capacity of the tissue K_{max}.
- Based on the modeling hypothesis 'go-or-grow' we consider two different phenotype expressions, separated into different cell populations: proliferative cells g and invasive cells m. The change from one population to another is mediated by the local availability of oxygen. We establish a hypoxia threshold O_{2hyp} and we define the functions H_{mg} and H_{gm} as step functions such as:

$$H_{mg} = \begin{cases} 1, & \text{if } o > O_{2hyp} \\ 0, & \text{otherwise} \end{cases} \tag{7}$$

$$H_{gm} = 1 - H_{mg} \tag{8}$$

- When hypoxia is too severe, cells die by necrosis. We set the severe hypoxia threshold to O_{2death} and, in the same way as before, we define the step functions H_{mN} and H_{vN} as:

$$H_{mN} = H_{vN} = \begin{cases} 1, & \text{if } o < O_{2death} \\ 0, & \text{otherwise} \end{cases} \tag{9}$$

- Oxygen consumption by cancer cells can be modeled in Eq. (4) using the Michaelis-Menten law for enzyme kinetics. This law corresponds to an asymptotic curve, implying that no matter how much oxygen available there might be, there is a maximum rate of consumption achievable.
- Oxygen supply from the capillaries to the ECM depends on the permeability of the capillary wall, but mainly on the difference of partial pressure between the vase and the exterior. We can consider the partial pressure of oxygen in the capillaries $[O_2]_a$, in Eq. (4), to be a constant parameter.
- Invasive cells m produce angiogenic factors a, which attract endothelial cells v by chemotaxis. As a consequence vascular density increases. To avoid introducing another non-linear term, we assume that the consumption of angiogenic factors by endothelial cells occurs at a constant rate γ. Chemotaxis is represented in Eq. (6) as a flux of v following the gradient of a.

To solve the equations we use an implicit finite difference scheme based on *Backwards-Time-Centered-Space* (BCTS) and an iterative predictor-corrector algorithm that allow us to initially decouple the whole system into two coupled subsystems to simplify the treatment of the non-linearities. The BCTS method has first order convergence in time and second order convergence in space. Is generally stable, so it is possible to use wide time-steps.

2.2   Parameters of the Model

A common limitation to all tumor growth models is the huge amount of free parameters needed when coupling different effects. It is not feasible to devise mathematical methods to optimize and identify the whole set of parameters, and therefore the usual approach consists on identifying most values from the existing literature. We consider a division of the parameters of the model into two groups: patient-independent and patient-dependent. The patient-dependent are the parameters which deal directly with the tumor cells and the physical properties of the GBM. That is its invasive capability, given by the diffusivity parameters, its proliferation rate, and the agility to switch from one phenotype to another. These characteristics may vary between patients. The patient-independent parameters on the other hand, deal with the rest of the physiological processes modeled, and is reasonable to assume that are quite less variable and more constant through patients (Table 1).

In order to evaluate the impact of variating the patient-dependent parameters, we conduct a parametric sweep with relative increments and decrements of 50 % and 20 % over the reference value. The effect of these variations on the outcome result is analyzed by measuring the temporal evolution of the tumor mass, the tumor area and the tumor density.

2.3   Reference Synthetic Case

This case consists on a free growth simulation of a tumor spheroid of 0.2 cm of radius for 20 days in a $15 \times 15 \, cm^2$ grid of homogeneous white matter. The spatial step was set to $\Delta x = 0.1 \, cm$ and the time-step to $\Delta t = 0.05 \, days$. The initial spheroid is composed only by proliferative cells with $g_0 = 1/3 \cdot K_{max}$ representing this way its young age and its growing phase. The initial oxygen concentration is set constant for the whole grid. Because the brain is an organ with a high oxygen consumption rate, we set the initial concentration to 60 % of its maximum partial pressure. The density of vascularization is also initialized as constant throughout the grid with $v_0 = 0.09 \cdot K_{max}$. Because initially there are no invasive cells m, the initial concentration for a is zero.

2.4   Characterization of the Temporal Evolution of Cell Distributions

To validate our hypothesis of stabilization of the physiological processes that leads to stationary distributions of cellular populations, we propose a methodology in which we compare the statistical distances between such distributions

Table 1. List of parameters of the model

Patient-dependent parameters

Parameter	Value	Description	Reference
D_g	$3.6 \cdot 10^{-8}$ cm^2/s	Diffusivity of g	[10]
D_m	$D_g/10$	Diffusivity of m	
ρ_g	1.8 $days^{-1}$	Proliferation rate of g	
ρ_m	$\rho_g/2$	Proliferation rate of m	
θ_{gm}	1 $days^{-1}$	Rate of change g to m	
θ_{mg}	$1/3$ $days^{-1}$	Rate of change m to g	[12]

Patient-independent parameters

Parameter	Value	Description	Reference
D_a	$1.0 \cdot 10^{-5}$ cm^2/s	Diffusivity of a	
ρ_{am}	$1.0 \cdot 10^{-9}$ mol/s	Production of a	
ρ_v	$\rho_g/10$	Proliferation rate of v	
θ_{mN}	1.2 $days^{-1}$	Rate of death of m	
θ_{vN}	$\theta_{mN}/10$	Rate of death of v	
O_{2hyp}	7 mmHg	Hypoxia threshold	[13]
O_{2death}	0.7 mmHg	Severe hypoxia threshold	[14]
$[O_2]_a$	60 mmHg	Arterial partial pressure of o	[15]
α_g	$1.0 \cdot 10^{-17}$ mol/cell $\cdot$ s	Rate of consumption of o by g	[16]
α_m	$\alpha_g/5$	Rate of consumption of o by m	[16]
γ	α_g	Rate of consumption of a by v	
φ	0.3	Vascular supply parameter	
χ	0.1	Chemotaxis mobility parameter	[9]
K_{max}	$1.0 \cdot 10^6$ cell/cm^2	Maximum carrying capacity of cells	[17]

at different stages of the evolution of GBM growth, using simulations based on the reference synthetic case.

We will use the Jensen-Shannon divergence (JS) to compare the similarities of the distributions of m and g in each time-step against the distribution of the last time-step. In order to do that we need to convert the curves to statistical distributions and align them at the point of their maximal cross-correlation, as we are only interested in comparing their morphology.

2.5   Initialization of g and m Cell Distributions for a Real Case

Our main objective in this study is to be able to initialize the variables of the model in a real case tumor based on information of magnetic resonance images (MRI). A correct estimation of the initial values of the variables is of the utmost importance for the success of the simulation and, therefore, for increasing the predictive capability of the model.

In MRI there is not a direct correspondence between the intensity of the voxel and tumor density. Some studies observed that the detection threshold for GBM in a T1-weighted image (T1) is much greater than that of a T2-weighted image [18]. Because active tumor segmentation masks are based mainly on T1, it is safe to assume that there is tumoral tissue outside the segmented area.

In simple models in which there is only one type of cellular population, the usual method of initialization is to consider the whole segmented ring to be saturated at the carrying capacity and smooth it with a gaussian filter. The same approach is used when two cellular populations are considered. However, to assume an homogenous distribution of both variables across the segmented ring, is too simple. Based on our hypothesis of the stabilization of the distributions over time in controlled homogeneous cases, we propose a methodology for real cases in which we assign a different density value to each point, depending on their relative position inside the active tumor. We will compare our methodology to the usual initialization method previously described.

Considering we have a distribution curve for g and m, we take into account the threshold of detection of GBM for T1 in order to define the active tumor region from these distribution curves. This threshold value is not given in the literature as it is not possible to estimate accurately, but we can consider it to be greater than 50 % of the maximum density based on the existing graphic representations in the literature [18]. We then normalize the distributions for the width of $(g + m)$ that should be detected by the mentioned threshold, resulting in $x = 0$ for the inner border and $x = 1$ for the outer border as can be seen in Fig. 1, with x being the relative spatial position.

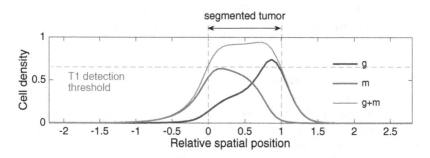

Fig. 1. Example of normalized distribution of g and m by the width given by the T1 detection threshold

In order to apply these distribution functions to a real case we differentiate between points belonging to the binary mask, points enclosed by the binary mask and points outside of the binary mask. In the first case we compute the geodesic distance of each point to the inner and outer boundary. We assume that the sum of those values is a good estimator of the width. Dividing the distance to the inner border by the estimated width, we obtain the relative position inside the segmentation. For the points enclosed by the mask we only need the geodesic distance to the inner boundary, and similarly, for the exterior points, only the distance to the outer boundary is needed. Those values are then used to get the corresponding density value from the distribution curves g and m.

To test the proposed method we used GBM data from the MICCAI BRATS Challenge 2013 training set. A detailed explanation of the method and parameters of acquisition of the data set can be found in [19].

3   Results

3.1   Variation of Parameters

Variation of Diffusivity (D_g). When varying the diffusivity of cells, a direct relationship is observed with the tumor mass and the tumor area: both variables increase when diffusivity increases, and decrease when diffusivity decreases. The density increases as the diffusivity decreases, which seems logical, but also increases when diffusivity increases. This may seem counterintuitive at first, however it can be explained by the fact that with higher mobility, tumor cells might be able to access better oxygenated areas and sustain a proliferative profile for a longer period of time.

Variation of Proliferation Rate (ρ). There is a direct relationship between the parameter and all the measured variables. It is noticeable that our model is very sensible to variations in this parameter: the relative variation of the outcome is greater than the relative variation of the parameter value.

Variation of Phenotype Change Rates (θ_{gm}, θ_{mg}). The variation of theses parameters has a minimum impact on the outcome of the simulations. Relative mass and area variations are consistently under 10 %, and density stays under 1 %.

3.2   Characterization of the Temporal Evolution of Cell Distributions

In Fig. 2a, we obtain a curve showing that the JS distance between each distribution and the last one, convergences to zero. That means that from a certain time-step onwards, the distribution of both cellular populations across the ring, reaches a constant shape. That shape is represented in Fig. 2b.

3.3   Initialization of a Real Case

Having demonstrated that our model reaches stationary distributions for g and m, we apply our initialization to a real tumor based on the segmentation of its

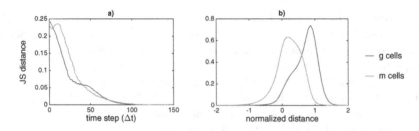

Fig. 2. (a) Convergence of the JS distance between distributions of g and m over time. (b) Stationary distribution of g and m for the reference case.

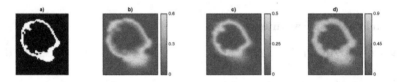

Fig. 3. (a) Segmentation mask. (b) Estimated density of g. (c) Estimated density of m. (d) Total estimated density $g + m$

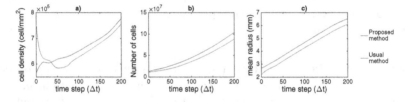

Fig. 4. Comparison between our proposed initialization method and the previous one. (a) Evolution of tumor density over time. (b) Number of cells over time. (c) Mean radius over time.

active tumor ring (Fig. 3a). The enclosed area inside corresponds to necrosis, and the peripheral edema is not represented. Figures 3b and c show the initial distribution of each phenotype according to our method, and Fig. 3d represents the total active tumor $g + m$.

Figure 4 compares the evolution of tumor density, number of cells and mean radius over time between our proposed method and the current one. Although both need some stabilization time at the beginning (Fig. 4a), it is much shorter for our methodology and the inertia of growth is better kept. The usual method needs to go through a transitory phase to reach the steady-state growth, and as a consequence it lags behind and initially loses the growth inertia.

4   Discussion

In this study we have proposed a new multi-scale GBM growth model which considers the angiogenic cascade, oxygen supply and its effect on the cellular population. The mathematical complexity is a problem, and as a consequence, a huge number of free parameters are needed. Most of these parameters could be assumed to be patient-independent which could be defined from the existing literature, and select just a small group to estimate for each patient. In this sense, our parametric study serves two purposes: first, we assess how the model responds to variations of the selected parameters, to identify those with the highest impact on the outcome. Then, with our sight set on evaluating real cases, we personalize the estimation of the most relevant parameters to each patient.

Our parametric sweep concluded that cellular diffusivity and proliferation rates are the most relevant of the patient-dependent parameters in terms of total mass, invaded area and density. Those results are consistent with the wave-front propagation speed of the Fisher-Kolmogorov equation ($v = 2\sqrt{\rho D}$). Due to the different formulation of our equations, our model is more sensible to ρ than to D, although both play a central role.

We have successfully demonstrated, using the JS divergence, that in an homogeneous controlled grid, after enough time-steps, our model yields a constant distribution of g and m along the tumor ring. Using this knowledge, we devised a method to successfully initialize a real tumor based on a binary segmentation and showed a dynamic improvement over the usual method. We consider this to be a good advance towards a more precise and more informed initialization of the variables in real cases, as we are able to assign density values to nodes beyond the binary mask. However, the current limitations of our method are: first the assumption of stationary growth state at the acquisition time, and second, it only has physiological sense for tumors with an enclosed necrotic center. There is need for more validation with longitudinal cases, comparing time points, and further characterization of the distributions, taking into account inhomogeneities that may be found on real brains.

5 Conclusion

We have demonstrated that our controlled reference simulation arrives, after certain time-steps, to a stationary growth state in which the distributions of g and m remain constant in shape across the tumor ring. Using this knowledge we have successfully initialized a real tumor from a binary segmentation mask. Our methodology for initializing the variables of the tumor is both informed and realistic, as it indicates the presence of cancer cells beyond the binary mask. It also shows an improvement in the dynamic performance of the model, compared to the usual method, as it takes less time-steps to stabilize and reach a stationary growth state.

Acknowledgments. This work was partially supported by Project TIN2013- 43457-R funded by the Ministerio de Economia y Competitividad of Spain, the GLIOMARK-ERS project funded by the INBIO joint action between UPV and IIS HUPLF, and the CURIAM-FDFT project funded by ITACA-UPV EMBLEMA action. E. Fuster-Garcia acknowledges the financial support from the UPV PAID-10–14 grant.

References

1. Harter, D.H., et al.: Glioblastoma multiforme: state of the art and future therapeutics. Surg. Neurol. Int. **5**(1), 64 (2014)
2. Kumar, V., et al.: Robbins and Cotran Pathologic Basis of Disease. Elsevier Saunders, Philadelphia (2005)
3. Tang, L., et al.: Computational modeling of 3D tumor growth and angiogenesis for chemotherapy evaluation. PLoS ONE **9**(1), e83962 (2014)
4. Swanson, K.R., et al.: Quantifying the role of angiogenesis in malignant progression of gliomas: in silico modeling integrates imaging and histology. Cancer Res. **71**(24), 7366–7375 (2011)
5. Cai, Y., et al.: Coupled modelling of tumour angiogenesis, tumour growth and blood perfusion. J. Theor. Biol. **279**(1), 90–101 (2011)
6. Martnez-Gonzlez, A., et al.: Hypoxic cell waves around necrotic cores in glioblastoma: a biomathematical model and its therapeutic implications. Bull. Math. Biol. **74**(12), 2875–2896 (2012)
7. Saut, O., et al.: A multilayer grow-or-go model for gbm: effects of invasive cells and anti-angiogenesis on growth. Bull. Math. Biol. **76**(9), 2306–2333 (2014)
8. Gerlee, P., et al.: The impact of phenotypic switching on glioblastoma growth and invasion. PLoS Comput. Biol. **8**(6), e1002556 (2012)
9. Manoussaki, D.: A mechanochemical model of angiogenesis and vasculogenesis. ESAIM. Math. Model. Numer. Anal. **37**(04), 581–599 (2003)
10. Marias, K., et al.: A proposed paradigm shift in initializing cancer predictive models with dce-mri based pk parameters: a feasibility study. Cancer Inf. **14**(Suppl. 4), 7 (2015)
11. Eikenberry, S.E., et al.: Virtual glioblastoma: growth, migration and treatment in a three-dimensional mathematical model. Cell Prolif. **42**(4), 511–528 (2009)
12. Jewell, U.R.: Induction of HIF-1a in response to hypoxia is instantaneous. FASEB J. **15**(7), 1312–1314 (2001)
13. Vaupel, P.: The role of hypoxia-induced factors in tumor progression. Oncologist **9**(Suppl. 5), 10–17 (2004)
14. Martin Brown, J., et al.: Exploiting tumour hypoxia in cancer treatment. Nat. Rev. Cancer **4**(6), 437–447 (2004)
15. McLellan, S.A., et al.: Oxygen delivery and haemoglobin. Continuing Educ. Anaesth. Crit. Care Pain **4**(4), 123–126 (2004)
16. Grimes, D.R., et al.: A method for estimating the oxygen consumption rate in multicellular tumour spheroids. J. Roy. Soc. Interface **11**(92), 20131124 (2014)
17. Rockne, R., et al.: Predicting the efficacy of radiotherapy in individual glioblastoma patients in vivo: a mathematical modeling approach. Phys. Med. Biol. **55**(12), 3271–3285 (2010)
18. Harpold, H.L.P., et al.: The evolution of mathematical modeling of glioma proliferation and invasion. J. Neuropathol. Exp. Neurol. **66**(1), 1–9 (2007)
19. Menze, B.H., et al.: The multimodal brain tumor image segmentation benchmark (BRATS). IEEE Trans. Med. Imaging **34**(10), 1993–2024 (2015)

PURE: Panoramic Ultrasound Reconstruction by Seamless Stitching of Volumes

Barbara Flach, Maxim Makhinya, and Orcun Goksel[✉]

Computer-Assisted Applications in Medicine, ETH Zürich, Zürich, Switzerland
{bflach,makhinya,ogoksel}@vision.ee.ethz.ch

Abstract. For training sonographers in navigating, acquiring, and inter-preting ultrasound images, virtual-reality based simulation offers a safe, flexible, and standardized environment. In data-based training simula-tions, images from a-priori acquired volumes are displayed to the trainee. To understand the relationship between organs, it is necessary to allow for free exploration of the entire anatomy, which is often not possible with the limited field-of-view (FOV) of a single ultrasound volume. Thus, large FOV ultrasound volumes are of paramount importance. Combining several volumes into one larger volume has also potential utility in many other applications, such as diagnostic and operative guidance. In this work, we propose a method for combining several ultrasound volumes with tracked positions into a single large volume by stitching them in a seamless fashion. For stitching, we determine an optimal cut interface such that each pixel value comes from a single image; preserving the inherent speckle texture and preventing any blurring and degradation from common mean/median binning approaches to combining volumes. The cut interface is found based on image content using graphical models optimized by graph-cut. We show that our method produces panoramic reconstructions with seamless transitions between individual 3D acqui-sitions. Regarding standard deviation in homogeneous regions we get 1–19% loss of ultrasound texture compared to small 3D volumes while mean value interpolation gives a loss of 15–68%. The histograms of our reconstruction match the original histograms of the small 3D volumes almost perfectly with a χ^2-distance of less than 0.01.

1 Introduction

Ultrasound is a safe and low-cost imaging modality. However, acquisition and interpretation of ultrasound images heavily rely on the experience and skill of the clinician. For training these skills, volunteers, cadavers, and phantoms all have associated ethical and realism issues. Virtual-reality based simulated training, on the other hand, offers a safe, flexible, and repeatable environment for the training of ultrasound imaging. Compared to *ray-tracing* based techniques, data-based ultrasound simulations provides relatively high image realism, where image slices are interpolated during simulation from a-priori acquired ultrasound volumes [1,4,8,11], which can also accommodate interactive tissue deformations [7].

© Springer International Publishing AG 2016
S.A. Tsaftaris et al. (Eds.): SASHIMI 2016, LNCS 9968, pp. 75–84, 2016.
DOI: 10.1007/978-3-319-46630-9_8

With 3D transducers, it is relatively easy to acquire volumetric ultrasound data. However, with the field-of-view (FOV) of a single 3D volume, it is not possible to freely explore within a large anatomical region (e.g., a third trimester fetus), which is an essential skill to be learned for diagnosing patients. The acquired simulation volume needs to ideally span, for example, the entire abdomen to provide a realistic scene for training. Large-FOV ultrasound volumes are also potentially beneficial for diagnostic applications. For instance, standardized, large-FOV ultrasound volumes of the breast can now be acquired using ABUS and ABVS platforms.

Gee et al. [6] proposed to use freehand 2D acquisition to reconstruct a 3D large-FOV volume. Despite the simplicity of acquisitions, the reconstructions, however, are often distorted and not up-to training standards due to the challenges in aligning several degrees of freedom for each frame without any out-of-plane information. In contrast, image volumes acquired using 3D transducers are inherently consistent. Accordingly, only continuity between such volumes needs to be ensured. This latter approach was followed in [3,12,14,16]. These works mainly investigate registration strategies to fine-tune the alignment of volumes, while combining the images using simple binning (e.g., averaging) and interpolation methods. Herein we focus on such combination strategy itself, for which we propose the seamless stitching of ultrasound volumes based on graph-cuts.

For aligning the volumes, we use tracked transducer positions. We first apply a pressure compensation step to eliminate any tissue deformation resulting from probe pressure during acquisition. Then, one needs to determine which intensity values to assign to voxels in the overlapping parts of acquired volumes. Simple approaches are setting the voxel intensity to mean or median value of any overlapping voxels (*binning*) [15]. As one can imaging and we show later, such simple methods lead to the loss of typical ultrasound speckle texture due to blurring and emphasizes the overlap boundaries as artifacts in the resulting volumes. One alternative approach could be to divide the overlapping region with a plane, where on each side the ultrasound content is taken from the corresponding input volume. Such *stitching* plane, however, becomes visible as an artifact in the reconstructed volumes, since the speckle pattern is interrupted and will not fit from both sides. We hereby propose a non-planar stitching *interface* (surface) based on image information. To find the interface that will yield a seamless transition between the volumes, we devise a graphical model based on image content from overlapping parts of volumes. We solve this using graph-cuts, resulting in a 2D cut manifold that divides the overlap into two regions where image content can be used from corresponding input volumes.

2   Methods

2.1   Position Tracking

For data acquisition we use a mechanically-swept transducer equipped with a 6-DOF electromagnetic tracking sensor, in order to get an initial position and orientation of the volumes. Sensor-to-image calibration is done with an N-wire phantom using the method of [10]. The probe position p_i is recorded at the time of each individual ultrasound volume acquisition i. Following each acquisition of probe position, another position r_i is also recorded after having lifted the probe normal to body surface until it is barely touching the skin. This latter position is used in the pressure correction step. Neighboring volumes are collected to have overlapping image regions and to leave minimal to no gap between them.

2.2   Pressure Correction

For stitching, the volumes have to reside a common coordinate frame and deformation state. For good skin contact during acquisitions, pressure is applied on the transducer, deforming anatomy differently for each volume. We thus chose to bring the volumes to a nominal (undeformed) state, before stitching them, using the model-based pressure correction procedure of [5]. For each image volume i, first, a box-shaped tetrahedral mesh covering the imaging field-of-view is generated centered on top at the nominal position r_i. A 3D probe model is then translated from r_i to p_i to simulate the indentation by compressing the FEM nodes falling inside this model onto the probe surface using displacement constraints. The inverse of this deformation field is then applied on the acquired volume i to "undeform" it to a nominal uncompressed state. We incorporate the inverse transformation into the scan-conversion process to avoid interpolation artifacts. The depth of the meshed volume is assumed to be sufficiently large for stresses caused by the surface compression to be negligible near the bottom surface, accordingly setting the nodes at the far end of the imaging volume fixed in all axes. A homogeneous tissue content with linear isotropic material is used. Note that we here use empirically-set boundary conditions to keep the level of complexity low. With more sophisticated methods like [13] the results may even improve. After the pressure correction above, the anatomical structures should better align, especially near the surface. Finally one needs to define the orientation of a Cartesian coordinate frame for the final stitched volume from combining several individual pressure-corrected volumes. We choose the orientation of the most central volume assuming this volume contains image content of great interest. To pick the most central volume, we first compute the center-of-mass c_i for all v volumes and then their centroid as $c = \sum_i \frac{c_i}{v}$. The global coordinate frame is then chosen as the coordinate frame of the volume closest to this centroid, i.e. $i = \arg\min_i |c_i - c|$. Before any stitching, all undeformed volumes are interpolated on a regular grid in this coordinate frame covering the bounding box of all available image data.

2.3   Image Stitching

Consider the *overlapping* volume that include image voxels with values from both of the two input volumes to be stitched as shown in Fig. 1. For the optimal transition interface (surface) for a seamless transition, we define a graphical model within the overlapping volume as a graph $G(N, E)$ where each node $n \in N$ represents an overlapping voxel connected by edges $e \in E$ to its six neighboring

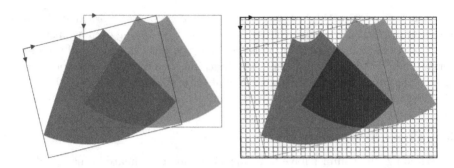

Fig. 1. Illustration of a graphical model in 2D showing two volumes. The green and blue areas represent voxels with image values from one or the other volume. The overlapping volume after interpolating both volumes on a regular grid in the common coordinate frame, is marked with green and blue stripes. The boundary voxels, connected to the source or the sink, are shown as thick lines. (Color figure online)

voxels in 3D. Each edge connecting two neighboring voxels $\mathbf{x}$ and $\mathbf{y}$ in overlapping volumes V_1 and V_2 is assigned a capacity (potential) based on a transition quality metric similarly to [9]. This edge potential P is based on neighbours image intensity as well as the image gradient between them as

$$P(\mathbf{x}, \mathbf{y}) = \frac{\|V_1(\mathbf{x}) - V_2(\mathbf{x})\| + \|V_1(\mathbf{y}) - V_2(\mathbf{y})\|}{\|\nabla^e_{V_1}(\mathbf{x})\| + \|\nabla^e_{V_1}(\mathbf{y})\| + \|\nabla^e_{V_2}(\mathbf{x})\| + \|\nabla^e_{V_2}(\mathbf{y})\| + \varepsilon}, \quad (1)$$

where $\nabla^e_{V_i}(.)$ is the gradient in image volume V_i along the graph edge e. To avoid division by zero, we add a small value $\varepsilon = 10^{-5}$ to the denominator. If the overlapping images match intensity-wise at both nodes x and y, then this is an ideal place for stitching and it is permitted by the vanishing nominator. In case images do not match, cuts along image edges are encouraged by the denominator. Since intensity changes are already anticipated at natural edges, even if mean intensities on either side do not match, such seams are not likely to be visible. A graph is constructed only for the overlapping voxels, with source s or sink t of the graph connected to all boundary voxels marked as thick blue and green lines in Fig. 1. Note that since this is an undirected graph, i.e. $P(\mathbf{x}, \mathbf{y}) = P(\mathbf{y}, \mathbf{x})$ for all neighboring voxels $\mathbf{x}$ and $\mathbf{y}$, the transition interface (solution) is independent of the order of input volumes (source and sink). Finally, the minimum cost cut of this graph is found using [2], giving a partition of G such that $\min \sum_{\mathbf{x} \in V_1, \mathbf{y} \in V_2 | e = (\mathbf{x}, \mathbf{y}) \in E} P(\mathbf{x}, \mathbf{y})$ with $s \in V_1$ and $t \in V_2$.

The solution labels for each voxel indicate whether its intensity is to be assigned from volume V_1 or volume V_2. We noticed that even with optimal cuts, there can still be artifacts along stitched interfaces where no suitable seams exists, e.g. due to a quite small overlap and view-dependent artifacts like shadows. We reduce these artifacts by blending the volumes across the seam using a sigmoid function with a small kernel. For stitching more than two volumes we start with the volume closest to the center-of-mass of all volumes and then iteratively merge in the volumes in order of descending proximity.

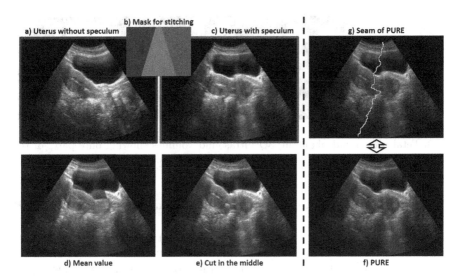

Fig. 2. A 2D stitching example showing the uterus (a) without and (c) with a speculum, using a PURE mask (b). The bottom row shows 3 images with the blue areas from (a) and the green areas from (c) and the middle yellow area been reconstructed using (d) mean value, (e) merging "bluntly" at a cutting line in the middle, and (f) using PURE. The cutting curve from graph-cut is depicted in (g). (Color figure online)

3   Results and Discussion

We first demonstrate a typical cut resulting from our method, Panoramic Ultrasound REconstruction (PURE), on a 2D sample in-vivo data in Fig. 2. This shows two B-mode images of the uterus, once prior to speculum placement and once afterward. These significantly deformed states present a challenging scenario to showcase our algorithm. This task also demonstrates a potential use of stitching for the seamless modification of ultrasound B-mode content, such as for artificially introducing tools, anatomical alterations, and even pathology. Images are considered spatially fully overlapping, where the blue (left) mask is taken from the image without speculum and the green right mask from the image with speculum. The middle yellow part is then reconstructed, using its borders with blue and green areas as the sink and the source. In comparison to results using mean value reconstruction and a simple transition exactly along the center line, PURE is seen in Fig. 2(f) to present a realistic image free from reconstruction artifacts, despite the relatively poor overlap of anatomy. In order to present the almost-invisible PURE stitching interface, we also depict the seam in Fig. 2(g).

For evaluation we applied our reconstruction technique on both the CIRS fetal ultrasound biometrics phantom (model 068) seen in Fig. 3 and the CIRS female pelvic ultrasound training phantom (model 404A) using an Ultrasonix SonixTouch machine with a convex 4D probe (4DC7-3/40). For both scans we

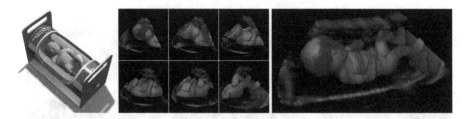

Fig. 3. Fetal ultrasound phantom, 3D ultrasound volumes showing only parts of the phantom, and 3D view of PURE covering the entire fetus.

recorded the positions tracked electromagnetically using an Ascension trakSTAR system.

For comparing reconstructions, Figs. 4(a) and (b) present PURE as well as alternative methods using mean and median value binning. With the latter methods, smoothing and deterioration of typical ultrasound speckle texture is apparent, especially in the blown-up insets of the fetus reconstructions. In addition to preserving speckle texture, view-dependent artifacts like shadows and reflections are also lost in the mean and median reconstructions, as marked by the arrows in the sagittal pelvic images. PURE is seen to accurately preserve these fundamental ultrasound artifacts, essential also for the training of image interpretation. For the pelvic phantom the boundaries of the small volumes are very obvious in mean and median result as pointed to by arrows in the top left image of Fig. 4(b). In the PURE result the single volumes are not apparent at all which means a really seamless transition.

To demonstrate the need for pressure correction, the right-most column of Figs. 4(a) and (b) show the stitching results without pressure correction. Elasticity parameters for pressure correction were set to a Young's modulus of 10 KPa and a Poisson's ratio of 0.45 in line with the phantom material composition. It is clearly visible that the surface of the non-corrected case is deteriorated by several probe footprints as pointed out by arrows in the top right image of Fig. 4(b). This hinders the alignment of the skin of a virtual or a physical model when integrating the stitched volume into a image-based ultrasound simulator. Note that the top part of the sagittal slice of the pelvic phantom shows a failure case marked by a red circle. Since bladder is a highly deformable organ, the corresponding volume is severely distorted and the pressure correction could not align the volumes sufficiently.

The phantoms contain regions with homogeneous echogenecity, which we used to assess the speckle appearance of the reconstructed volumes. We manually selected largest-possible 3D bounding boxes within homogeneous regions of the reconstructed phantom volumes, and applied intensity statistics to compare reconstructed volumes to original acquired images. This led to 7.6 K, 14.5 K and 41.3 K voxels, respectively, inside the abdomen of the fetus model, and inside and outside the uterus of the pelvic model. For each bounding box we characterize the texture for the original volumes V_i by computing the standard deviation σ_i.

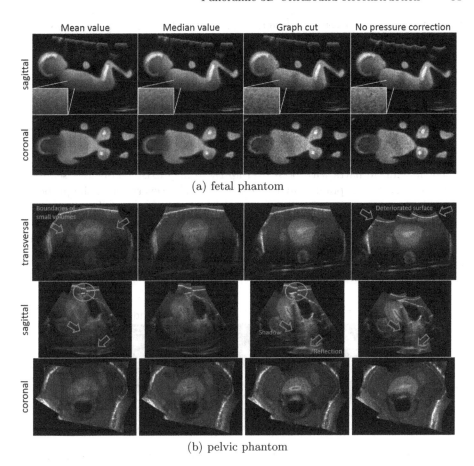

(a) fetal phantom

(b) pelvic phantom

Fig. 4. Comparison of large FOV reconstructions. Both phantom measurements has 6 volumes as input. The insets in the fetus phantom show the fine speckle pattern preserved by our method PURE. (a) fetal phantom. (b) pelvic phantom. (Color figure online)

We compared the standard deviation σ within the bounding box of the reconstructed volumes to the groundtruth standard deviation, set as the mean value of the standard deviations in the small volumes $\sigma_{GT} = \sum_i \frac{\sigma_i}{v}$. Normalizing σ to the ground-truth baseline, it is seen that the σ-error of the median approach is 2.6 to 12 times poorer than that of PURE (which is merely 1 % difference to our ground truth in fetus phantom). The large errors for the outside uterus part of pelvis phantom can be attributed to the more significant directional shadowing and enhancement artifacts in those regions. Additionally, the histograms of these homogeneous regions are compared by computing the χ^2 distance. The histograms of PURE match the histogram of the original images up to 100 % (χ^2 distance equal to zero) if all data is taken from one volume.

Table 1. Comparison of changes in ultrasound texture by combining several volumes

	σ				$(\sigma_{GT} - \sigma)/\sigma_{GT}$			χ^2		
	GT	Mean	Med	PURE	Mean	Med	PURE	Mean	Med	PURE
Fetus, corpus	13.3	11.3	11.7	13.2	15 %	12 %	1 %	0.12	0.11	0.01
Pelvis, in-utero	7.5	5.4	6.2	7.2	28 %	17 %	4 %	0.14	0.04	0.00
Pelvis, ex-utero	12.7	4.1	6.3	10.3	68 %	50 %	19 %	0.29	0.13	0.00

For few image parts with poor overlap there may exist no obvious seamless interface, e.g. the cut pointed by the arrow in Fig. 5. Nevertheless, the proposed sigmoidal blending (with a kernel of 3 voxels) is seen to successfully remove such "sharp" cuts locally. Note that, in contrast to mean-binning everywhere, such a small sigmoid kernel acting locally affects only a tiny part of the entire volume, preserving the overall quality of the volume. As can be seen from the results in Figs. 2, 4(a) and (b), the effect of such local blending is indiscernible.

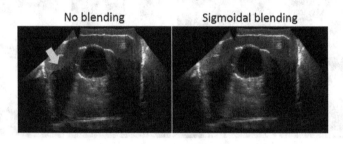

Fig. 5. Seamless stitching is improved by postprocessing by sigmoidal blending.

Finally we acquired in-vivo data of a volunteer's abdomen in the gynecological setting using a GE Voluson E8 machine with a convex 4D probe (RAB4-8-D). Positions were tracked electromagnetically using an Ascension trakSTAR system as for the phantom data. Figure 6 shows the promising results of stitching six volumes into a large FOV reconstruction. Organs and structures match very well and the seams are invisible compared to mean or median value interpolation while the texture is preserved. As for the pelvic phantom, the boundaries of the small volumes are again visible in mean and median results whereas they are not distinguishable in the PURE result.

Stitching two volumes, each of size $240 \times 210 \times 250$, needs 4 min with current implementation on an Intel i7-4770 K processor, where roughly 98 % of computation time is spent on the min-cut solution. In comparison, combining the volumes by mean-binning needs 4 s.

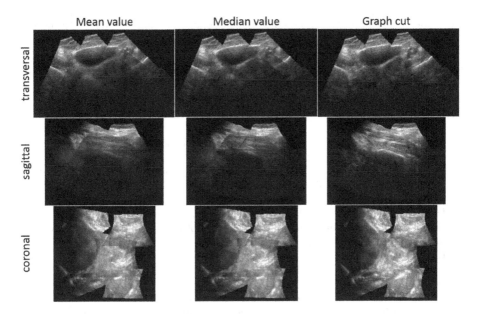

Fig. 6. Comparison of volumetric large FOV reconstructions of in-vivo data. The measurement has 6 volumes as input.

4   Conclusions

We have introduced a method for generating panoramic ultrasound volumes beneficial for training simulation and diagnostic purposes. Our method, called PURE, is based on stitching 3D volumes at optimal cut interfaces determined by graph-cut from image content. In contrast to conventional mean and median value reconstruction, PURE prevents the deterioration of typical ultrasound speckle texture in the overlapping regions. PURE necessitates more computation time compared to algebraic approaches such as median and mean, which is acceptable for simulation purposes where the large-FOV reconstruction is required offline only as a preprocessing step. A further application of our algorithm in simulation framework is to edit image content as demonstrated by the 2D stitching example in Fig. 2, where image parts are shown to be replaced by content from another image. This can simplify the generation of several pathological cases, which is a major bottle-neck of data-based ultrasound simulation. Similarly to algebraic reconstruction, PURE results may also suffer from stitching artifacts when organs are not aligned between given images, e.g. due to tracking errors and deformation. An image registration stage (e.g. [3,12,14,16]) prior to stitching will be investigated next for improving reconstruction results. This should improve the seamless transition especially in case of inaccurate tracking data. Note that a major motivation for stitching is simulated training, which does not require a fully unsupervised image reconstruction, but a clinician can easily check the quality of reconstructions. For diagnostic application the transition surface along with a confidence value, e.g. cutting cost from graph-cut, can be displayed to the clinician to prevent misleading diagnosis.

Acknowledgments. We thank Prof. Dr. med. Michael Bajka for his help in data acquisition and the Swiss CTI and NSF for funding.

References

1. Aiger, D., Cohen-Or, D.: Real-time ultrasound imaging simulation. Real-Time Imaging **4**(4), 263–274 (1998)
2. Boykov, Y., Kolmogorov, V.: An experimental comparison of min-cut/max-flow algorithms for energy minimization in vision. IEEE Trans. Pattern Anal. Mach. Intell. **26**(9), 1124–1137 (2004)
3. Dyer, E., Zeeshan Ijaz, U., Housden, R., Prager, R., Gee, A., Treece, G.: A clinical system for three-dimensional extended-field-of-view ultrasound. Br. J. Radiol. **85**(1018), e919–e924 (2012)
4. Ehricke, H.: SONOSim3D: a multimedia system for sonography simulation and education with an extensible case database. Eur. J. Ultrasound **7**(3), 225–300 (1998)
5. Flach, B., Makhinya, M., Goksel, O.: Model-based compensation of tissue deformation during data acquisition for interpolative ultrasound simulation. Proc. ISBI **2016**, 502–505 (2016)
6. Gee, A., Treece, G., Prager, R., Cash, C., Berman, L.: Rapid registration for wide field of view freehand three-dimensional ultrasound. IEEE Trans. Med. Imaging **22**(11), 1344–1357 (2003)
7. Goksel, O., Salcudean, S.E.: B-mode ultrasound image simulation in deformable 3-D medium. IEEE Trans. Med. Imaging **28**(11), 1657–1669 (2009)
8. Henry, D., Troccaz, J., Bosson, J., Pichot, O.: Ultrasound imaging simulation: application to the diagnosis of deep venous thromboses of lower limbs. Med. Image Comput. Comput. Assist. Interv. **1496**, 1032–1040 (1998)
9. Kwatra, V., Schödl, A., Essa, I., Turk, G., Bobick, A.: Graphcut textures: image and video synthesis using graph cuts. Proc. SIGGRAPH 2003 **22**(3), 277–286 (2003)
10. Lasso, A., Heffter, T., Rankin, A., Pinter, C., Ungi, T., Fichtinger, G.: PLUS: open-source toolkit for ultrasound-guided intervention systems. IEEE Trans. Biomed. Eng. **61**(10), 2527–2537 (2014)
11. Maul, H., Scharf, A., Baier, P., Wüstemann, M., Günter, H., Gebauer, G., Sohn, C.: Ultrasound simulators: experience with the SonoTrainer and comparative review of other training systems. Ultrasound Obstet. Gynecol. **24**(5), 581–585 (2004)
12. Ni, D., Chui, Y., Qu, Y., Yang, X., Qin, J., Wong, T.T., Ho, S., Heng, P.: Reconstructio of volumetric ultrasound panorama based on improved 3D SIFT. Comput. Med. Imaging Graph. **33**(7), 559–566 (2009)
13. Ozkan, E., Goksel, O.: Compliance boundary conditions for simulating deformations in a limited target region. Proc. EMBC **2015**, 929–932 (2015)
14. Poon, T., Rohling, R.: Three-dimensional extended field-of-view ultrasound. Ultrasound Med. Biol. **32**(3), 357–369 (2006)
15. Solberg, O., Lindseth, F., Torp, H., Blake, R., Nagelhus Hernes, T.: Freehand 3D ultrasound reconstruction algorithm - a review. Ultrasound Med. Biol. **33**(7), 991–1009 (2007)
16. Wachinger, C., Wein, W., Navab, N.: Three-dimensional ultrasound mosaicing. Med. Image Comput. Comput. Assist. Interv. **10**(Part II), 327–335 (2007)

Synthesis and Its Applications in Computational Medical Imaging

Pseudo-healthy Image Synthesis for White Matter Lesion Segmentation

Christopher Bowles[1(✉)], Chen Qin[1], Christian Ledig[1], Ricardo Guerrero[1],
Roger Gunn[2,7], Alexander Hammers[3], Eleni Sakka[4], David Alexander Dickie[4],
Maria Valdés Hernández[4], Natalie Royle[4,8], Joanna Wardlaw[4],
Hanneke Rhodius-Meester[5], Betty Tijms[5], Afina W. Lemstra[5],
Wiesje van der Flier[5], Frederik Barkhof[6], Philip Scheltens[5],
and Daniel Rueckert[1]

[1] Department of Computing, Imperial College London, London, UK
christopher.bowles10@imperial.ac.uk
[2] Imanova Ltd., London, UK
[3] PET Centre, Kings College London, London, UK
[4] Department of Neuroimaging Sciences, University of Edinburgh, Edinburgh, UK
[5] Alzheimer Center and Department of Neurology, VU University Medical Center,
Amsterdam Neuroscience, Amsterdam, The Netherlands
[6] Department of Radiology and Nuclear Medicine, VU University Medical Center,
Amsterdam Neuroscience, Amsterdam, The Netherlands
[7] Department of Medicine, Imperial College London, London, UK
[8] IXICO Technologies Ltd., London, UK

Abstract. White matter hyperintensities (WMH) seen on FLAIR images are established as a key indicator of Vascular Dementia (VD) and other pathologies. We propose a novel modality transformation technique to generate a subject-specific pathology-free synthetic FLAIR image from a T_1 -weighted image. WMH are then accurately segmented by comparing this synthesized FLAIR image to the actually acquired FLAIR image. We term this method *Pseudo-Healthy Image Synthesis* (PHI-Syn). The method is evaluated on data from 42 stroke patients where we compare its performance to two commonly used methods from the Lesion Segmentation Toolbox. We show that the proposed method achieves superior performance for a number of metrics. Finally, we show that the features extracted from the WMH segmentations can be used to predict a Fazekas lesion score that supports the identification of VD in a dataset of 468 dementia patients. In this application the automatically calculated features perform comparably to clinically derived Fazekas scores.

1 Introduction

White matter hyperintensities (WMH) are commonly found in brain fluid attenuated inversion recovery (FLAIR) magnetic resonance imaging (MRI). Their aetiology is diverse but they are known to be associated with an increased risk of stroke, dementia and death [1]. WMH are usually clearly visible as hyperintense regions in FLAIR images, and potentially appear as hypointense regions in T_1 -weighted images (Fig. 1).

© Springer International Publishing AG 2016
S.A. Tsaftaris et al. (Eds.): SASHIMI 2016, LNCS 9968, pp. 87–96, 2016.
DOI: 10.1007/978-3-319-46630-9_9

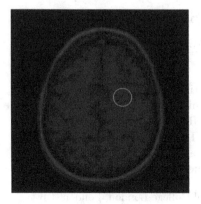 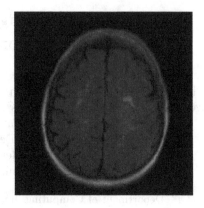

Fig. 1. An example pair of T_1-weighted (left) and FLAIR (right) images. The FLAIR image exhibits clear WMH. The corresponding locations in the T_1-weighted image show little change, apart from the circled region which is slightly hypointense.

The accurate annotation of WMH from FLAIR images is a laborious task that requires a high level of expertise and is subject to both inter- and intra-rater variability. To enable effective image analysis in large scale studies or the reproducible quantification of lesion load in the clinic without expert knowledge (e.g. in the context of a comprehensive decision support system) an accurate and fully automatic method for lesion segmentation is desirable.

In this paper, we present a novel method of segmenting WMH from FLAIR images using modality transformation. Modality transformation is the task of generating a synthetic image with the appearance characteristics of a specific imaging modality (or protocol) by using information from images acquired from one or more other modalities. The accurate generation of these images can be critical in the context of, for example, non-linear multi-modality registration [2] where the problem can be reduced to a mono-modality problem when one modality is synthesised from the other. Additionally, many segmentation or classification algorithms require an input image from a certain modality. The ability to synthesise these modalities from another modality could substantially expand the applicability of these algorithms [3].

This paper investigates the principle of synthesising an image with healthy appearance in order to identify pathology in a real scan. Similar to previous work [4,5], we aim to produce a "pseudo-healthy" version of a particular modality without any signs of pathology. The synthetic image is then compared with the potentially pathological real image and the differences are identified.

Existing modality transformation algorithms can be divided into model and data driven approaches. In the former, intrinsic physical properties of the tissue being imaged are estimated from the available modalities [6]. Once known, a new modality can be synthesised by simulating the image acquisition protocol. However, accurate estimation of these tissue properties requires particular acquisition protocols, which are not routinely carried out. The more commonly used algorithms therefore rely on a data driven approach where the synthesised image is derived directly from the intensities of the source image(s). Most state of the art algorithms employ a patch based, dictionary learning approach [2,3,5]. A dictionary of source-target patch pairs is stored with synthesis being performed by using the target patch with the corresponding source patch which most closely matches a given patch in source image. Approaches using a restricted nearest neighbour search [5], compressed sensing [3] and sparse coding [2] are among those proposed for searching and combining patches from the dictionary. Recently, deep learning approaches have also received attention [7] with good results. Another data driven approach, to which our proposed method is more closely related, uses local joint histograms to find the target image intensity with which a given source image intensity most commonly co-occurs [8].

The problem when employing these existing methods for the synthesis of pseudo-healthy images is that WMH are often synthesised. This is because the relationship between WMH intensities in T_1 -weighted and FLAIR images can be similar to that of gray matter (GM) [9]. Existing methods will learn this WMH-GM similarity and synthesise WMH as hyperintense. Whilst this ability has been exploited for better T_1 -weighted image segmentations [10], it is not desirable for the production of pseudo-healthy images.

In this paper we present a novel modality transformation method, which can be used effectively to generate pseudo-healthy images. The proposed approach exploits only information from small neighbourhoods around a given voxel to predict a synthetic intensity, and will therefore not be influenced by the WMH-GM relationship described above, which would be learnt in other regions of the brain. We employ this method to address the problem of WMH segmentation with results that compare favourably with two established reference methods from the Lesion Segmentation Toolbox (LST). Finally, we demonstrate the clinical potential of the proposed automatic lesion segmentation method when applied to the identification of VD in a clinical dataset, and show performance comparable to identification using manually assessed Fazeka scores, a clinical measure of WMH.

2   Method

In the following, we describe the two essential components of the proposed PHI-Syn method. A pseudo-healthy FLAIR image is first synthesised from a patient's T_1 -weighted image. The estimated FLAIR image is then compared to the real FLAIR image of the patient and abnormally hyperintense regions are identified.

2.1   Image Synthesis

To synthesise a subject's FLAIR image that does not exhibit WMH (if present in the T1 weighted image), we propose a method that relies on voxel-wise kernel regression to learn local relationships between intensities in T_1 -weighted and FLAIR image pairs of healthy subjects. The regression model is then used to synthesise pseudo-healthy FLAIR images from T_1-weighted images. There are three factors that enable the synthesis of a pseudo-healthy image: (a) the pathology is in general not prominent in T_1-weighted images; (b) the model is trained on image pairs of healthy subjects without WMH and does therefore not learn how to synthesise pathology; (c) the method uses only information from small local regions from the training data to synthesise each voxel, meaning intensity relationships learnt from other regions of the brain will not be applied.

Preprocessing. As voxel directly between scans it is important that all images of a respective modality are on the same intensity scale. We employ the following steps to ensure that the distributions of intensities within tissue classes are the same across all images of that modality.

Each T_1-weighted image is bias field corrected [11], skull stripped [12] and anatomically segmented [13]. GM and white matter (WM) masks are generated from these segmentations and a transformation from native to MNI space using free form deformations (FFD) [14] is computed.

Intensity normalisation is a key step that is particularly challenging in the presence of pathology, as it needs to be ensured that varying levels of pathology have no impact on intensity mappings. To do this we use the method employed in [15] using the previously computed WM and GM masks. This approach establishes a robust fixed point as the mean of the average intensities of the WM and GM which is then set to a common value. This method has the advantage of only using information from regions in which we are highly confident the tissue type is either healthy WM or GM and is therefore unaffected by WMH.

FLAIR images are also bias corrected and masked using the brain mask derived from the T_1-weighted image, rigidly transformed into the native space of the FLAIR image. The GM and WM masks are also transformed into FLAIR space and used for intensity normalisation.

Synthesis Training. The training set consists of pairs of T_1-weighted and FLAIR images, $\mathbf{T}^{\text{train}}$ and $\mathbf{F}^{\text{train}}$ respectively. All images are aligned to MNI space and re-sampled on a $1\,\text{mm}^3$ voxel lattice using linear interpolation. The T_1-weighted image intensities are rescaled to the range $[0; m]$, where m is the number of points the model will be evaluated at. The value of m will ultimately control the size and training time of the model, with a larger value leading to more accurate results. A kernel regression model with bandwidth h is generated at each voxel $\mathbf{x}$ relating the T_1-weighted and FLAIR intensities in an s-by-s-by-s patch around $\mathbf{x}$. The result of evaluating the model at each k in the range $[1, m]$ is stored in vector $\mathbf{M_x}$ (1) using the regression model outlined below.

$$\mathbf{M_x}(k) = R(n_{\mathbf{x}}^{\text{T}}, n_{\mathbf{x}}^{\text{F}}, k), \ n_{\mathbf{x}}^{\text{T}} = N(\mathbf{x}; \mathbf{T}^{\text{train}}, s), \ n_{\mathbf{x}}^{\text{F}} = N(\mathbf{x}; \mathbf{F}^{\text{train}}, s), \quad (1)$$

$$R(\mathbf{a}, \mathbf{b}, k) = \frac{\sum_i (K((k - a_i)/h) b_i)}{\sum_i K((k - a_i)/h)}, \ K(p) = \frac{1}{\sqrt{2\pi}} e^{-\frac{1}{2}p^2}, \quad (2)$$

where $N(\mathbf{x}; \mathbf{T}, s)$ and $N(\mathbf{x}; \mathbf{F}, s)$ return a vector containing the voxels in a patch around voxel $\mathbf{x}$ of size s-by-s-by-s from each image in $\mathbf{T}$ and $\mathbf{F}$ respectively.

Synthesis Testing. To estimate the synthetic FLAIR image, the intensities of the T_1-weighted image, $\mathbf{T}$, are rescaled to be between 0 and m and transformed into the native space of the FLAIR image along with mapping $\mathbf{M}$. The synthetic image $\mathbf{S}$ at voxel $\mathbf{x}$ is then calculated,

$$\mathbf{S_x} = \mathbf{M_{x''}}(\lceil \mathbf{T_{x'}} \rceil), \mathbf{x'} = L_{FT}(\mathbf{x}), \ \mathbf{x''} = L_{FM}(\mathbf{x}), \ L : \mathbb{R}^3 \to \mathbb{R}^3, \qquad (3)$$

where L_{FT} denotes the rigid transformation between FLAIR and T_1-weighted image spaces and L_{FM} the FFD transformation between FLAIR and MNI spaces.

2.2 Lesion Segmentation

We identify lesions by detecting regions which are hyperintense in the FLAIR image relative to the synthetic image. A consequence of using kernel regression is a tendency for synthesised image intensities to be closer to the mean intensity in the respective regions, resulting in reduced image contrast. The method used for intensity normalisation determines two values corresponding to the mean intensities of healthy GM and WM. To correct tissue contrast we scale the synthetic image such that these two values match those of the acquired FLAIR images.

The confidence Σ in the intensity-normalised synthesised images is computed by calculating the standard deviation of the errors achieved on the training images in MNI space. This yields a spatial variance map, which is used to assign a relative confidence to the synthesised intensities at each voxel. A z-score corresponding to the likelihood of the intensity of a voxel $\mathbf{x}$ falling outside of what is expected is then computed, $\mathbf{Z_x^S} = (\mathbf{F_x} - \mathbf{S_x})/\Sigma_{\mathbf{x'}}$ where $\mathbf{x'} = L_{FM}(\mathbf{x})$, which is turned into a p-value, $\mathbf{P_x^S}$. Another set of p-values $\mathbf{P^F}$ are computed to reflect areas of hyperintensity in the FLAIR image. An individual image based z-score will be affected by the volume of hyperintense regions in the image. Therefore, the mean and standard deviation required to compute $\mathbf{P^F}$ are estimated from intensity histograms of the normalised training images.

We combine the previously computed anatomical segmentations to create a binary mask $\mathbf{B}$ to constrain the search for WMH to areas of the brain where they are expected to be present. This mask includes the WM and a number of cortical and deep GM structures which are close to areas where WMH is commonly found. The final WMH likelihood $\mathbf{L}$ at voxel $\mathbf{x}$ was thus computed by the multiplication of the three likelihood maps at $\mathbf{x}$, $\mathbf{L_x} = \mathbf{P_x^F P_x^S B_x}$.

There are two main types of WMH. Small punctate lesions such as those visible in Fig. 2, and larger, lower intensity regions, such as those seen in Fig. 3. To account for both types, a low threshold t_l is first used to binarize $\mathbf{L}$ and only large ($>200\,\mathrm{mm}^3$) areas are kept. A higher threshold t_h is then used and the initial segmentation taken to be the union of these two segmentations.

A refinement step is then carried out in which segmentations are repeatedly grown into neighbouring voxels with an intensity which lies above the lowest intensity in the original segmentation. A 5 mm limit is imposed to prevent the growth of incorrect "lesions". Finally, small ($<20\,\mathrm{mm}^3$) segmentations are removed as these are often visually indistinguishable from noise.

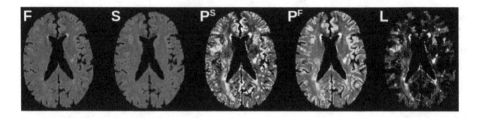

Fig. 2. The intermediate steps for segmentation. Left to right: FLAIR image, synthetic image, likelihood map $\mathbf{P}^S$, likelihood map $\mathbf{P}^F$, likelihood map $\mathbf{L}$. Note how the brightest areas in the $\mathbf{L}$ correspond to the WMH in the FLAIR image.

3   Experiments and Results

Experiments were carried out to evaluate PHI-Syn against two widely used segmentation methods, and to investigate its applicability in a clinical setting.

3.1   Data

In the first experiment, we used a stroke dataset of 42 patients (mean age 64.9 years (SD 10)) from a study of mild stroke [16], obtained as described in [17]. Images were acquired with an in plane resolution of 0.94-by-0.94 mm and slice thickness 4 mm. Reference WMH segmentations were obtained semi-automatically. In a second experiment we used a dementia dataset of 468 subjects from VUMC, Amsterdam, which were provided for the PredictND study[1]. This clinical dataset contains MRI scans of varying resolutions and field strengths along with clinical scores for patients with a diagnosis of either subjective memory complaints (110), Alzheimer's Disease (204), Frontotemporal Dementia (88), Lewy Body Dementia (47) and Vascular Dementia (19). Clinical Fazekas scores were visually assessed. Of the 468 subjects, 173 had a Fazekas score of 0, 205 (score 1), 61 (2) and 29 (3). Images were acquired at 3T (295), 1.5T (91) and 1T (82).

For both experiments, the synthesis model was trained on 31 subjects selected from the dementia dataset as the visually least pathological. However, a consequence of training on subjects from an elderly dataset is that most subjects have a small degree of periventricular WMH due to their age. These were, undesirably, reproduced in the synthetic images. An additional post-processing step on the synthetic images was added to address this: Voxels located up to 15 mm from the ventricular wall were capped at a maximum intensity value equal to the average between the mean FLAIR intensities of GM and WM. A special case must then be made for the region around posterior prolongations of the ventricles where non-pathological low level hyperintense streaks are often seen. A squaring of the probabilities in these regions was sufficient to ensure that true lesions would still be segmented, whilst the probabilities corresponding to low

---

[1] http://www.predictnd.eu/.

level hyperintensities would be suppressed. This additional step would not be required if a set of pathology free subjects were available for a particular application. Free parameters for synthesis were chosen empirically for all experiments as: $m = 100$, $s = 7$, $h = 5$ as they balanced model size and computational speed with visually appealing synthesised images.

3.2 Evaluation Against Reference Segmentations

In this experiment we employ the stroke dataset to compare the proposed method against two standard methods from the Lesion Segmentation Toolbox v.2.0.12[2] - the Lesion Growth Algorithm (LST-LGA) [18] and the Lesion Prediction Algorithm (LST-LPA). The former requires a T_1-weighted image as well as a FLAIR image. White matter, grey matter and CSF segmentations are obtained from the T_1-weighted image and used to create a lesion belief map from the FLAIR image. This is first thresholded at a value κ and the resulting segmentations are grown along hyperintense voxels. LST-LPA is a supervised method for which a logistic regression model was trained on 53 Multiple Sclerosis patients with severe white matter lesion loads. Both methods output a lesion probability map, which the documentation suggests should be thresholded at 0.5. For LST-LGA, a κ of 0.3 is the default but it is strongly suggested that this is optimised. For each method, we provide results for both the suggested parameters and parameters selected through a grid search which maximised Dice Similarity Coefficient (DSC). These were found to be: LST-LGA*, $\kappa = 0.07$, threshold $= 0.10$. LST-LPA*, threshold $= 0.10$. PHI-Syn*, $t_l = 0.76$, $t_h = 0.85$.

Segmentations were compared across a set of quantitative measures used previously in the ISLES 2015 segmentation challenge[3]: Average Symmetric Surface Distance (ASSD, mm), DSC, Hausdorff Distance (HD, mm), Precision and Recall. A further metric, Load Correlation (LC) defined as the correlation between automatic and reference segmentation volumes over all subjects was also used with results shown in Table 1.

Table 1. Comparisons of segmentation results. * indicates results for optimised parameters. [1,2,3,4,5] indicate improvement on LST-LGA, LST-LPA, LST-LGA*, LST-LPA* and PHI-Syn* respectively using a Wilcoxon signed rank test at a 5 % significance level.

Method	ASSD	DSC	HD	Precision	Recall	LC
LST-LGA	7.84	0.294	50.4	0.619[3]	0.225	0.790
LST-LPA	3.68[1,3]	0.477[1,3]	37.3[1]	0.683[1,3,4,5]	0.417[1]	0.779
LST-LGA*	5.89[1]	0.367[1]	40.3[1]	0.467	0.359[1]	0.760
LST-LPA*	2.58[1,2,3]	0.599[1,2,3]	33.2[1,2,3]	0.593[3]	0.713[1,2,3]	0.711
PHI-Syn*	2.39[1,2,3]	0.603[1,2,3]	30.1[1,2,3,4]	0.610[3]	0.669[1,2,3]	0.849

---

[2] http://www.statistical-modelling.de/lst.
[3] http://www.isles-challenge.org.

3.3 Relation to Clinical Scores

The Fazekas score is a commonly used four point clinical score derived from FLAIR images relating to the presence and degree of WMH [19]. It has particular use in the diagnosis of VD as it relates to the most significant pathological changes in the patient's brain.

In this experiment we predicted synthetic Fazekas scores from the segmentations given by PHI-Syn and compared them to clinical Fazekas scores. The experiment was carried out using 1000 runs of 10-fold cross validation. Three features were extracted from the PHI-Syn segmentations: volume of lesions as a percentage of WM, volume of lesions greater than 15 mm from the ventricles as a percentage of WM, and volume of the largest lesion. At each fold, the training set was balanced by oversampling under-represented Fazekas scores classes. A set of support vector machine (SVM) classifiers using an error-correcting output code schema for multi-class classification (classifier A) were trained on the training set to predict a synthetic Fazekas score. A further binary SVM (classifier B) was trained on data balanced with respect to disease to predict a diagnosis of VD or not-VD from the clinical Fazekas scores. Synthetic Fazekas scores were then calculated for subjects in the test set using classifier A and diagnoses were predicted from both the true and synthetic Fazekas scores using classifier B.

The balanced accuracy for predicting a synthetic Fazekas score using classifier A was 61.5 %, with only 4 %/0.25 % being predicted a score of more than 1/2 points from their respective true clinical score. The balanced accuracy for predicting a diagnosis was 83.3 % from the true Fazekas scores and 83.9 % from the synthetic Fazekas scores with standard deviations of 1.2 % and 3.3 % respectively.

4   Discussion

The conducted experiments show that PHI-Syn achieves the highest or statistically joint highest scores in ASSD, DSC, HD, Recall and LC. Figure 3 shows three sample segmentations. Visual examination confirms superior ability of PHI-Syn, as compared to LST-LPA*, to locate smaller lesions distant from the ventricles (A and C). A lower HD score supports this observation. Instances in which PHI-Syn tends to be outperformed by LST-LPA* include cases of large areas of low intensity (B). Objective measurements and visual inspection both suggest PHI-Syn performs well in the majority of situations. A limitation of this experiment is that only WMH are included in the reference segmentation, and other hyperintense appearing pathologies such as stroke lesions, are not. All methods tested will identify all hyperintensities and as such the results of these experiments can only be used to compare methods relative to each other, and should not be used as an indicator of expected performance on another dataset.

The balanced accuracy of predicted diagnoses from the synthetic Fazekas scores is comparable to those predicted when using the clinically assessed Fazekas scores, however the data is highly imbalanced and as such the balanced accuracy can be unstable and susceptible to noise. Future work involves using more VD

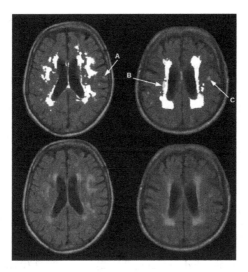

Fig. 3. A sample of two FLAIR images (bottom) and segmentations (top). Reference (blue), LST-LPA* (green) and PHI-Syn (red) segmentations are shown. Colours are additively mixed where segmentations overlap. e.g. purple indicates overlap between PHI-Syn and the reference, cyan: LST-LPA* and reference, yellow: LST-LPA* and PHI-Syn, white: all methods. Arrows draw attention to regions of particular interest. (Color figure online)

cases to further investigate using synthetic over true Fazekas scores. However, these initial results suggest that a synthesised score is a valuable marker in cases where a clinical Fazekas score is not available.

We have shown that effective synthesis of pseudo-healthy images can be carried out using voxel-wise kernel regression, and that these images can be used to reliably identify WMH. We have also shown that the resulting segmentations can predict a Fazekas score which discriminates between vascular and non-vascular cases of dementia comparably to labour-intensive clinical scores.

References

1. Debette, S., Markus, H.S.: The clinical importance of white matter hyperintensities on brain magnetic resonance imaging: systematic review and meta-analysis. BMJ **341**, c3666 (2010)
2. Cao, T., Zach, C., Modla, S., Powell, D., Czymmek, K., Niethammer, M.: Registration for correlative microscopy using image analogies. In: Dawant, B.M., Christensen, G.E., Fitzpatrick, J.M., Rueckert, D. (eds.) WBIR 2012. LNCS, vol. 7359, pp. 296–306. Springer, Heidelberg (2012)
3. Roy, S., Carass, A., Prince, J.: A compressed sensing approach for MR tissue contrast synthesis. In: Székely, G., Hahn, H.K. (eds.) IPMI 2011. LNCS, vol. 6801, pp. 371–383. Springer, Heidelberg (2011). doi:10.1007/978-3-642-22092-0_31

4. Tsunoda, Y., Moribe, M., Orii, H., Kawano, H., Maeda, H.: Pseudo-normal image synthesis from chest radiograph database for lung nodule detection. Adv. Intell. Syst. Comput. **268**, 147–155 (2014)
5. Ye, D.H., Zikic, D., Glocker, B., Criminisi, A., Konukoglu, E.: Modality propagation: coherent synthesis of subject-specific scans with data-driven regularization. In: Mori, K., Sakuma, I., Sato, Y., Barillot, C., Navab, N. (eds.) MICCAI 2013, Part I. LNCS, vol. 8149, pp. 606–613. Springer, Heidelberg (2013)
6. Fischl, B., Salat, D.H., van der Kouwe, A.J.W., Makris, N., Ségonne, F., Quinn, B.T., Dale, A.M.: Sequence-independent segmentation of magnetic resonance images. Neuroimage **23**, S69–S84 (2004)
7. Nguyen, H., Zhou, K., Vemulapalli, R.: Cross-domain synthesis of medical images using efficient location-sensitive deep network. In: Navab, N., Hornegger, J., Wells, W.M., Frangi, A.F. (eds.) MICCAI 2015. LNCS, vol. 9349, pp. 677–684. Springer, Heidelberg (2015). doi:10.1007/978-3-319-24553-9_83
8. Kroon, D.-J., Slump, C.H.: MRI modalitiy transformation in demon registration. ISBI **2009**, 963–966 (2009)
9. Roy, S., Carass, A., Prince, J.: Magnetic resonance image example based contrast synthesis. IEEE Trans. Med. Imaging **32**(12), 2348–2363 (2013)
10. Roy, S., Carass, A., Shiee, N., Pham, D.L.: MR contrast synthesis for lesion segmentation. ISBI **2010**, 932–935 (2010)
11. Tustison, N.J., Avants, B.B., Cook, P.A., Zheng, Y., Egan, A., Yushkevich, P.A., Gee, J.C.: N4ITK: improved N3 bias correction. IEEE Trans. Med. Imaging **29**(6), 1310–1320 (2010)
12. Heckemann, R.A., Ledig, C., Gray, K.R., Aljabar, P., Rueckert, D., Hajnal, J.V., Hammers, A.: Brain extraction using label propagation, group agreement: pincram. PloS ONE **10**(7), e0129211 (2015)
13. Ledig, C., Heckemann, R.A., Hammers, A., Lopez, J.C., Newcombe, V.F., Makropoulos, A., Lötjönen, J., Menon, D.K., Rueckert, D.: Robust whole-brain segmentation: application to traumatic brain injury. Med. Image Anal. **21**(1), 40–58 (2015)
14. Rueckert, D., Sonoda, L.I., Hayes, C., Hill, D.L., Leach, M.O., Hawkes, D.J.: Non-rigid registration using free-form deformations: application to breast MR images. IEEE Trans. Med. Imaging **18**(8), 712–721 (1999)
15. Huppertz, H.J., Wagner, J., Weber, B., House, P., Urbach, H.: Automated quantitative FLAIR analysis in hippocampal sclerosis. Epilepsy Res. **97**(1), 146–156 (2011)
16. Heye, A.K., Thrippleton, M.J., Chappell, F.M., Hernández, M., Armitage, P.A., Makin, S.D., Maniega, S.M., Sakka, E., Flatman, P.W., Dennis, M.S., Wardlaw, J.M.: Blood pressure, sodium: association with MRI markers in cerebral small vessel disease. J. Cereb. Blood Flow Metab. **36**(1), 264–274 (2016)
17. Hernández, M.D.C.V., Armitage, P.A., Thrippleton, M.J., Chappell, F., Sandeman, E., Maniega, S.M., Shuler, K., Wardlaw, J.M.: Rationale, design and methodology of the image analysis protocol for studies of patients with cerebral small vessel disease and mild stroke. Brain Behav. **5**(12), e00415 (2015)
18. Schmidt, P., Gaser, C., Arsic, M., Buck, D., Förschler, A., Berthele, A., Hoshi, M., Ilg, R., Schmid, V.J., Zimmer, C., Hemmer, B.: An automated tool for detection of FLAIR-hyperintense white-matter lesions in multiple sclerosis. Neuroimage **59**(4), 3774–3783 (2012)
19. Fazekas, F., Chawluk, J.B., Alavi, A., Hurtig, H.I., Zimmerman, R.A.: MR signal abnormalities at 1.5 T in Alzheimer's dementia and normal aging. Am. J. Neuroradiol. **8**(3), 421–426 (1987)

Registration of Pathological Images

Xiao Yang[1]([⊠]), Xu Han[1], Eunbyung Park[1], Stephen Aylward[3],
Roland Kwitt[4], and Marc Niethammer[1,2]

[1] UNC Chapel Hill, Chapel Hill, USA
xy@cs.unc.edu
[2] Biomedical Research Imaging Center, Chapel Hill, USA
[3] Kitware, Inc., Carrboro, USA
[4] Department of Computer Science, University of Salzburg, Salzburg, Austria

Abstract. This paper proposes an approach to improve atlas-to-image registration accuracy with large pathologies. Instead of directly registering an atlas to a pathological image, the method learns a mapping from the pathological image to a quasi-normal image, for which more accurate registration is possible. Specifically, the method uses a deep variational convolutional encoder-decoder network to learn the mapping. Furthermore, the method estimates local mapping uncertainty through network inference statistics and uses those estimates to down-weight the image registration similarity measure in areas of high uncertainty. The performance of the method is quantified using synthetic brain tumor images and images from the brain tumor segmentation challenge (BRATS 2015).

1 Introduction

Atlas-to-image registration provides spatial information to map anatomical locations from an atlas to a patient. This procedure is crucial for atlas-based segmentation which is used in lesion detection and treatment planning for traumatic brain injury, tumor and stroke cases [7]. However, large brain pathologies often produce appearance changes which may result in large misregistrations, if appearance-mismatch is falsely accounted for by image deformation. This is especially acute for deformable image registration methods, which are needed to capture subtle deformations and, for example, mass effects of tumors.

Several approaches have been proposed for atlas-to-image registration[1] with large pathologies. The most straight-forward method is *cost function masking*, where the lesion area is not considered during image similarity computation [1]. However, this method could be problematic if the lesion area contains important brain structure information. Other methods include joint segmentation and registration that mitigates missing correspondences [3], explicit tumor growth modeling [5], geometric metamorphosis that separates the deformation of healthy

---

[1] Such approaches, as well as our proposed approach, are of course also applicable to general image-to-image registration. We use atlas-to-image registration as our motivating application here.

© Springer International Publishing AG 2016
S.A. Tsaftaris et al. (Eds.): SASHIMI 2016, LNCS 9968, pp. 97–107, 2016.
DOI: 10.1007/978-3-319-46630-9_10

brain areas from lesion changes [14], and registration methods accounting for deformation and intensity changes [21].

While effective, these methods require either explicit lesion segmentation, knowledge of lesion location, or the modeling of tumor growth. Two alternatives exist: (1) using a robust cost-function [17] or a mutual saliency map [15] to mitigate the effect of outliers or, instead, (2) learning desired mappings between image types from large-scale image databases. We follow this second approach. A learned mapping then allows synthesizing one image type from another. Image synthesis has been extensively explored to synthesize MR imaging sequences [8], to facilitate multi-modality registration [2,19] and to segment lesions [18]. Our goal is to synthesize quasi-normal images from images with lesions to simplify atlas-to-lesion-image registration. Using image synthesis rather than a robust cost-function or a mutual saliency map allows reconstructing *structural* information to guide registration even in highly pathological areas.

Liu et al. [10] proposed a low-rank-plus-sparse (LRS) technique to synthesize quasi-normal brain images from pathological images and to simultaneously estimate a quasi-normal atlas. This approach decomposes images into normal (low-rank) and lesion (sparse) parts. The low-rank part then constitutes the synthesized quasi-normal images, effectively removing lesion effects. By *learning* from data, no prior lesion information is required. However, the LRS decomposition itself requires good image alignment, hence decomposition and registration have to be interleaved to obtain good results.

Contributions. Our contributions to improve atlas-to-image registration can be summarized as follows: *First*, similar to [10], we propose a method to directly map a pathology image to a synthesized *quasi-normal* image to simplify the registration problem. No registration is needed in this process. *Second*, we use a deep variational encoder-decoder network to learn this mapping and train it using stochastic gradient variational Bayes [9]. *Third*, since the normal appearance of pathological tissue is unknown per se, we propose loss-function masking and pathology-like "structured noise" to train our model. These strategies ignore mappings between image regions without known correspondence, and artificially create areas with known correspondence which can be used for training, respectively. *Fourth*, based on the variational formulation, we estimate the reconstruction uncertainty of the predicted quasi-normal image and use it to adjust/improve the image similarity measure so that it focuses more on matching areas of low uncertainty. *Fifth*, we validate our approach on synthetic tumor[2] images and data from the BRATS 2015 challenge. Our framework requires no prior knowledge of lesion location (at test time; lesion segmentations are required during training only) and provides comparable or, in many cases, better registration accuracy than the LRS method and cost function masking.

Organization. Section 2 discusses variational Bayes for autoencoders, as well as its denoising criterion. Section 3 introduces our methods to remove brain lesions

---

[2] In this paper we use brain tumors as example pathologies; however, our approach is applicable to other pathologies.

from images and to compute uncertainty estimates for the prediction of quasi-normal images. Section 4 presents experimental results (for 2D synthetic and real data), discusses extensions to 3D, and possible improvements.

2   Denoising Variational Autoencoding

The problem of mapping a pathology image to a quasi-normal image is similar to the objective of a denoising autoencoder, which aims to transform a noisy image into a noise-free image. Next, we introduce variational inference for autoencoders, followed by an explanation of inference for a denoising autoencoder.

Given a clean brain image x and the latent variable z, we want to find the posterior distribution $p(z|x)$. Since $p(z|x)$ is intractable, we approximate it with a tractable distribution $q_\phi(z|x)$, where ϕ is the parameter of the variational approximation. For a variational autoencoder, the posterior distribution is $p_\theta(z|x) \propto p_\theta(x|z)p(z)$, where the prior $p(z)$ is usually an isotropic Gaussian, and θ are the parameters of the observation model $p_\theta(x|z)$. When mapping these parameters to an autoencoder, z corresponds to the hidden layer, $q_\phi(z|x)$ refers to the *encoding* operation and $p_\theta(x|z)$ refers to *decoding*. Thus, ϕ and θ correspond to the weights in the encoder and decoder.

To approximate the true posterior with the variational posterior, we minimize the Kullback-Leibler (KL) divergence between these two distributions.

$$
\begin{aligned}
D_{\mathrm{KL}}(q_\phi(z|x)\|p_\theta(z|x)) &= \mathbb{E}_{q_\phi(z|x)}\left[\log\frac{q_\phi(z|x)}{p_\theta(z|x)}\right] \\
&= \log p_\theta(x) - \mathbb{E}_{q_\phi(z|x)}\left[\log\frac{p_\theta(z,x)}{q_\phi(z|x)}\right].
\end{aligned}
\tag{1}
$$

Since the data x is independent of the latent variable z, $\log p_\theta(x)$ in Eq. (1) is constant. Thus, minimizing the KL-divergence is equivalent to maximizing the term $\mathbb{E}_{q_\phi(z|x)}(\log p_\theta(z, x) - \log q_\phi(z|x))$. Since the KL-divergence is non-negative, we have $\mathbb{E}_{q_\phi(z|x)}[\log p_\theta(z, x) - \log q_\phi(z|x)] \leq \log p_\theta(x)$, and we call this term the variational lower bound of the data likelihood $\mathcal{L}_{\mathrm{VAE}}$, i.e.,

$$
\begin{aligned}
\mathcal{L}_{\mathrm{VAE}} &= \mathbb{E}_{q_\phi(z|x)}\left[\log\frac{p_\theta(z,x)}{q_\phi(z|x)}\right] \\
&= -D_{\mathrm{KL}}(q_\phi(z|x)\|p_\theta(z)) + \mathbb{E}_{q_\phi(z|x)}[\log p_\theta(x|z)],
\end{aligned}
\tag{2}
$$

where the first term can be regarded as the regularizer, matching the variational posterior to the prior of the latent variable, and the second term is the expected network output likelihood w.r.t. the variational posterior $q_\phi(z|x)$. During training, the optimization algorithm maximizes this variational lower bound.

Our goal is a denoising autoencoder for pathology-removal. In other words, we regard lesions as a special structured noise. Removing lesion appearance is then equivalent to removing noise in the denoising autoencoder theory. To do this, we introduce the input noise (lesion) corruption distribution as $p(\widetilde{x}|x)$.

The variational posterior distribution is then $\widetilde{q}_\phi(z|x) = \int q_\phi(z|\widetilde{x})p(\widetilde{x}|x)d\widetilde{x}$. If the original variational posterior distribution is a Gaussian, this new posterior can be regarded as a mixture of Gaussians, which has better representation power. As shown in [6], the variational lower bound for a denoising autoencoder is

$$\mathcal{L}_{\text{DVAE}} = \mathbb{E}_{\widetilde{q}_\phi(z|x)}\left[\log\frac{p_\theta(z,x)}{q_\phi(z|\widetilde{x})}\right] \geq \mathcal{L}_{\text{VAE}} = \mathbb{E}_{\widetilde{q}_\phi(z|x)}\left[\log\frac{p_\theta(z,x)}{\widetilde{q}_\phi(z|x)}\right]. \quad (3)$$

This means that the denoising variational lower bound is higher than the original one, leading to a smaller KL-divergence between the true and the approximated posterior. In the following section, we discuss our implementation of the encoder-decoder network and how to maximize the denoising variational lower bound.

3   Network Model and Registration with Uncertainty

Figure 1 shows the structure of our denoising variational encoder-decoder network. The input is a brain image **x** with intensities normalized to $[0, 1]$. The encoder network consists of convolution followed by max-pooling layers (`ConvPool`), and the decoder has max-unpooling layers followed by convolution (`UnpoolConv`). We choose max-unpooling instead of upsampling as the unpooling operation, because upsampling ignores the pooling location for each pooling patch, which results in severe image degradation. The encoder and decoder are connected by fully connected layers (`FC`) and the re-parameterization layer (`Reparam`) [9]. This layer takes the parameters for the variational posterior as input, which in our case is the mean μ and standard deviation Σ of the Gaussian distribution, and generates a sampled value from the variational posterior. This enables us to compute the gradient of the regularizer $-D_{\text{KL}}(q_\phi(z|x)||p_\theta(z))$ for ϕ using the variational parameters instead of the sampled value, which is not differentiable for ϕ. Below we discuss specific techniques implemented for our task.

Training Normal Brain Appearance Using Pathology Images. A model of normal brain appearance would ideally be learned from a large number of healthy brain images with a consistent imaging protocol. Our goal, instead, is to learn a mapping from a pathological image to a quasi-normal image, i.e., train a denoising autoencoder for the lesion 'noise', and maximize the denoising variational lower bound. This poses two challenges: *first*, in general, we do not know what the normal appearance in a pathological area should be; *second*, pathological images may exhibit spatial deformations not seen in a normal subject population (such as the mass effect for brain tumors). To mitigate these problems, we learn the brain appearance from the *normal areas of the pathological brain images* only. This can be accomplished by (1) introducing lesion-like structured noise (i.e., circles filled with the mean intensity of the normal brain area for brain tumor cases) via the `QuasiLesion` layer in Fig. 1, and (2) *loss function masking*, i.e., ignoring lesion-areas during learning. Suppose we have the lesion segmentation for the training data. For loss-function masking, we first change the

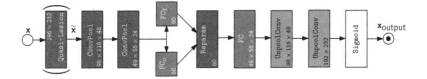

Fig. 1. Network structure (numbers indicate the data size).

input with structured noise $\widetilde{x}$ to $\widetilde{x}_{\mathrm{normal}}$ using the following rule: if $\widetilde{x} \in$ Normal, then $\widetilde{x}_{\mathrm{normal}} = \widetilde{x}$; otherwise, (i.e., $\widetilde{x} \in$ Lesion) $\widetilde{x}_{\mathrm{normal}} = a + \mathcal{N}(0, \sigma)$. This prevents the network from using tumor-appearance. Experiments show only small differences for different settings of a and σ. However, performance suffers when σ is too high, and setting $a = 0$ increases the mean intensity error for the whole image. In our model, we set a to the mean intensity value of the normal area and $\sigma = 0.03$. Second, we set our network output likelihood for x_{output} to

$$\log p_\theta(x_{\mathrm{output}}|z)_{\mathrm{normal}} = \begin{cases} |x_{\mathrm{output}} - x|, & x_{\mathrm{output}} \in \text{Normal} \\ 0, & x_{\mathrm{output}} \in \text{Lesion.} \end{cases} \quad (4)$$

Hence, we disregard any errors in the lesion area during backpropagation. We refer to this two-step strategy as *loss-function masking*.

The overall training procedure for our network is: (1) sample one corrupted input $\widetilde{x}$ from $p(\widetilde{x}|x)$, (2) mask out the lesion area to get $\widetilde{x}_{\mathrm{normal}}$, (3) sample one z from $q_\phi(z|\widetilde{x}_{\mathrm{normal}})$ and obtain a reconstructed image x_{output} from the network, (4) calculate the denoising lower bound $\mathcal{L}_{\mathrm{DVAE}}$ with the change in Eq. (4) and (5) perform stochastic gradient descent backpropagation to update the network.

Reconstruction Uncertainty for Atlas Registration. During testing, due to the small amount of data available and the possibly large appearance differences among training cases, it is useful to utilize the uncertainty of the reconstructed image to guide registration. In our case, we sample z from the approximated posterior $q_\phi(z|x)$ to generate multiple reconstruction images x_{output} with different z. Then, we choose the mean of the sampled images $\mu_{x_{\mathrm{output}}}$ as the reconstruction result, and the (local) standard deviation $\sigma_{x_{\mathrm{output}}}$ as uncertainty measure. We define areas of high uncertainty as those areas with large variance, and, for registration, our method down-weights the contribution of those areas to the image similarity measure. We simply use $w(x_{\mathrm{output}}) = \exp(-\sigma_{x_{\mathrm{output}}}^2 \times 2000)$ as a local weight for the image similarity measure in our experiments[3]. This function ensures that the weight drops to near 0 for a large standard deviation. Note that this is different from cost function/pathology masking. Cost function masking uses a simple binary mask, which is equivalent to setting the weight of the lesion area to zero. Our uncertainty-based weighting, on the other hand, *downweights* ambiguous areas in the reconstruction process which may not be

---

[3] Other, potentially better choices are of course possible.

highly reliable for registration. Our uncertainty weight is in $[0, 1]$. Hence, structural information is rarely discarded completely as in cost-function masking. Our experimental results in Sect. 4 show that this is indeed desirable.

4   Experiments and Discussion

We evaluate our model in two experiments: one using 2D synthetic images, and one with real BRATS tumor images. The image intensity range is $[0, 1]$. We implement the network with Torch and use the *rmsprop* [20] optimization algorithm; we set the learning rate to 0.0001, the momentum decay to 0.1 and the update decay to 0.01. Further, we use a batch size of 16, and for a training dataset with 500 images of size 196×232, training 1000 epochs takes about 10 h on a 2012 Nvidia Titan GPU. For data augmentation, we apply random shifting up to 10 pixels in both directions for a training image and add zero-mean Gaussian noise with standard deviation of 0.01. During testing, we sample 100 images for each test case, and calculate their mean and standard deviation. All images for training and testing are extracted from the same slice of their original 3D images, which are pre-aligned to a 3D ICBM T1 atlas [4] using affine registration and judged to be limited to having in-plane deformations. We use `NiftyReg` [13] (with standard settings) together with normalized cross correlation (NCC) to register the 2D ICBM atlas slice to the reconstructed result. Note that we modified `NiftyReg` to integrate image uncertainty into the cost function. We used a large number of B-spline control points (19×23 for a 196×232 image). This ensures that displacements large enough to capture the mass effect observed in the BRATS data can be expressed. B-spline registration approaches similar to `NiftyReg` have successfully been used for registrations of various difficulty [16]; and given sufficient degrees of freedom poor registration performance is likely due to an unsuitable similarity measure, which should be investigated in future work. To capture even larger deformations, `NiftyReg` could easily be replaced by a fluid-based registration approach. The focus here is to *synthesize* quasi-normal images and to exploit them and their associated reconstruction uncertainty for registration. For our images, 1 pixel corresponds to 1mm × 1mm.

For comparison, we use the LRS method, which is an alternative approach to image synthesis for tumor images. We select the parameters maximizing $2 \times NCC_{tumor} + NCC_{normal}$ for the training data. Due to high computational cost of current LRS approaches [10], we use 50 training images for each case. Furthermore, to demonstrate that using synthesized images in fact improves registration accuracy, we also compare our method against using the reconstruction uncertainty map in combination with the original tumor image for registration.

Synthetic Tumor Experiment. We use 436 brain images from the OASIS [11] cross-sectional dataset as base images. This chosen dataset is a mix of 43 % Alzheimer's and 57 % control subjects. We create a synthetic tumor dataset by registering random OASIS images to random BRATS 2015 T1c images (to account for the mass effect of tumors) with tumor area masking, followed by pasting the BRATS' tumor regions into the OASIS images. We generate 500 training

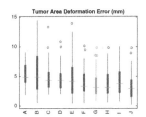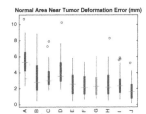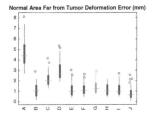

Fig. 2. *Mean deformation error* of all synthetic tumor test cases for various models. Our model is highlighted in red. Masking tumor area = MT. Add structured noise = ASN. Use uncertainty for registration = UR. *(A):* affine registration; *(B):* register to tumor image; *(C):* low-rank-sparse (LRS) with registration; *(D):* LRS w/o registration; *(E):* MT, no ASN, no UR; *(F):* MT, ASN, no UR; *(G):* MT, ASN, UR; *(H):* network trained with clean images, ASN; *(I):* Use uncertainty on tumor image directly; *(J):* cost function masking. (Color figure online)

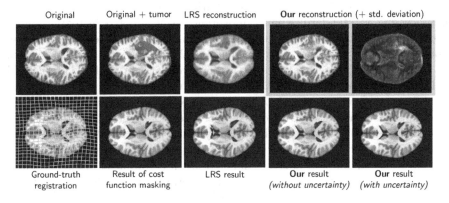

Fig. 3. Exemplary synthetic tumor test case reconstruction and checkerboard comparison with ground truth registration. Best viewed zoomed-in.

and 50 testing images using separate OASIS and BRATS images. Figure 2 shows boxplots of mean deformation errors of different areas per test case, with respect to the ground truth deformation obtained by registering the atlas to the normal image (i.e., without added tumor). The highlighted boxplot is the network model trained with tumor images, added quasi-tumor (i.e., structured noise) and using uncertainty weighting for the registration. We evaluate the deformation error for three areas: (1) the tumor areas, (2) normal areas within 10 mm from the tumor boundary (*near tumor*) and (3) normal areas more than 10 mm away from the boundary (*far from tumor*). By evaluating all three areas we can assess how well the mass effect is captured. This is generally only meaningful for our synthetic experiment. Landmarks (outside the tumor area) are more suitable for real data. For the tumor areas, our method (MT+ASN+UR) outperforms most other methods. For the normal areas, the registration difference between our method and directly registering to the original tumor image is very small, especially compared with the LRS method which tends to remove fine details. Compared to using the tumor image directly for registration, our model decreases the 99.7 % upper limit of the mean of the tumor area deformation error from 14.43 mm to 7.83 mm, the mean error from 5.62 mm to 3.60 mm, and the standard deviation from 3.49 mm to 2.16 mm. The significantly decreased deformation error only causes a small increase of mean deformation error for the normal area, from 1.36 mm to 1.49 mm. The only method performing better than our model for this *synthetic* test is cost function masking, which *requires* tumor segmentation. Figure 3 shows one example test case. Notice that the LRS method erroneously reconstructs the upper lateral ventricle, resulting in a wrong deformation.

BRATS Experiment. We also evaluate our network using the BRATS 2015 training dataset [12], which contains 274 images. This is a very challenging dataset due to moderate sample size and high variations in image appearance and acquisition. We use cross-validation, and partition the dataset into 4 sets of 244 training images and 30 testing images, resulting in a total of 120 test cases. For preprocessing, we standardize image appearance using adaptive histogram equalization. For evaluation, we manually label, on average, 10 landmarks per case around the tumor area and at major anatomical structures for the test images. We report the target registration error for the landmarks in Table 1. Our method still outperforms most methods, including LRS without registration. Although, the difference of our model and LRS+registration is not statistically significant, the figures in combination with our synthetic results suggest that our method is overall preferable. Note also that LRS requires image registrations for *each* decomposition iteration and introduces blurring to the brain's normal area (see Fig. 4), while our method does not suffer from these problems. Moreover, it is interesting to see that cost function masking performs worse than our method. This could be explained by the observation that in cases where the tumor is very large, cost function masking hides too much of the brain structure, making registration inaccurate. Figure 4 shows one exemplary BRATS test case. Because the tumor covers the majority of the white matter in the left hemisphere, cost function masking removes too much information from the registration. As a result, the left lateral ventricle is misregistered. Combining our network reconstructed image and uncertainty information, our registration result is much better.

Modeling Quasi-tumor Appearance. One interesting problem is the choice of quasi-tumor appearance. In our work we use the mean normal brain area intensity as the appearance, while other choices, such as using simulated[4] tumor appearance or random noise, are also sensible. To show the effect of quasi-tumor appearance choice on the registration result, we conduct additional experiments using 4 textures to create quasi-tumors: (1) real tumors of the BRATS dataset, (2) mean intensity (our approach), (3) random constant intensities and (4) random noise. Registration performance for all 4 methods is similar, with (2) having lower registration error in normal areas (e.g. median of 1.07/2.78 mm compared to 1.28/2.84 mm using (1) for synthetic/BRATS data). A possible reason why

---

[4] Real tumor appearance is not known in such areas.

Table 1. Statistics for landmark errors over the BRATS test cases. The best results in each category are marked in **bold**.

	Mean error [mm]					Max. error [mm]				
Data Percentile	99.7 %	75 %	50 %	25 %	0.3 %	99.7 %	75 %	50 %	25 %	0.3 %
Affine (baseline)	11.29	6.90	5.06	3.72	2.28	19.25	12.61	9.83	7.04	3.52
Use tumor image directly	6.32	4.20	3.29	2.77	**1.54**	20.48	12.47	7.52	5.22	**1.95**
Cost function masking	6.12	4.22	3.12	2.65	1.89	21.00	11.75	6.98	4.97	2.65
LRS+registration	5.26	3.77	3.06	2.74	1.88	12.04	8.20	6.30	5.45	3.54
LRS, no registration	6.15	4.30	3.25	2.79	2.12	14.62	9.61	6.83	5.72	4.05
Tumor image+uncertainty	5.52	3.79	3.08	2.65	1.81	13.91	8.76	6.24	**4.95**	2.63
Our model (no uncertainty)	5.08	3.63	**2.98**	2.64	1.66	12.79	8.12	6.21	4.96	2.82
Our model (with uncertainty)	**4.74**	**3.52**	3.02	**2.61**	1.83	**11.77**	**7.99**	**5.93**	5.08	2.48

using tumor appearance is not superior is the limited training data available (∼200 images). For a larger dataset with more tumor appearance examples to learn from, using tumor appearance could potentially be a better choice.

Discussion. One interesting finding in our work is that while a high-quality lesion area reconstruction is desirable, it is not necessary to improve atlas registration. Lesion reconstruction may be affected by many factors (limited data, large image appearance variance, etc.), but the atlas registration result depends on the quasi-normal reconstruction of the lesion *and* the faithful reconstruction of the normal tissue. For example, in some cases the LRS method achieves visually pleasing results in the lesion area. However, at the same time it smoothes out the normal area losing important details for image registration. Our method on the other hand preserves details in the normal areas more consistently and hence results in overall better registration accuracy. Moreover, for tightly controlled data (e.g., a synthetic dataset) our method generates better reconstructions for the lesion area. Thus, future experiments using more controlled data (e.g. BRATS 2012 synthetic images) would be interesting. Besides, synthesizing a quasi-normal image generates useful structural information that can help guide the registration, and reconstruction uncertainty can be used to focus the registration on regions of high confidence.

Another interesting question is how to extend our approach to 3D images. In initial experiments, we implemented a 2.5D network which reconstructs 14 slices at once. Training the network on 500 2.5D training cases takes 3 days, which, while not fast, is feasible. One possible approach is to learn mappings for 3D patches using patch location as additional feature, which would enable us to train on a much larger dataset (patches) at a reasonable computational cost.

Finally, designing a more "lesion-like" noise model and exploring the impact of training data size on the predictions are interesting directions to explore.

Support. This research is supported by NIH R42 NS081792-03A1, NIH R41 NS086295-01 and NSF ECCS-1148870.

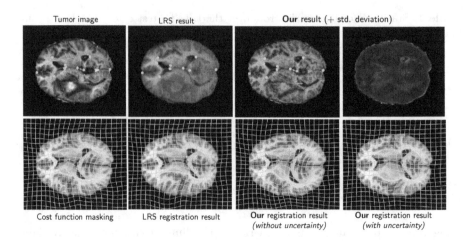

Fig. 4. Exemplary BRATS test case with landmarks for test image (*top row*) and warped atlas (*bottom row*).

References

1. Brett, M., Leff, A.P., Rorden, C., Ashburner, J.: Spatial normalization of brain images with focal lesions using cost function masking. Neuroimage **14**(2), 486–500 (2001)
2. Cao, T., Zach, C., Modla, S., Powell, D., Czymmek, K., Niethammer, M.: Multimodal registration for correlative microscopy using image analogies. MedIA **18**(6), 914–926 (2014)
3. Chitphakdithai, N., Duncan, J.S.: Non-rigid registration with missing correspondences in preoperative and postresection brain images. In: Jiang, T., Navab, N., Pluim, J.P.W., Viergever, M.A. (eds.) MICCAI 2010, Part I. LNCS, vol. 6361, pp. 367–374. Springer, Heidelberg (2010)
4. Fonov, V., Evans, A.C., Botteron, K., Almli, C.R., McKinstry, R.C., Collins, D.L.: Unbiased average age-appropriate atlases for pediatric studies. Neuroimage **54**(1), 313–327 (2011)
5. Gooya, A., Pohl, K.M., Bilello, M., Cirillo, L., Biros, G., Melhem, E.R., Davatzikos, C.: GLISTR: glioma image segmentation and registration. TMI **31**(10), 1941–1954 (2012)
6. Im, D.J., Ahn, S., Memisevic, R., Bengio, Y.: Denoising criterion for variational auto-encoding framework. CoRR abs/1511.06406 (2015)
7. Irimia, A., Wang, B., Aylward, S.R., Prastawa, M.W., Pace, D.F., Gerig, G., Hovda, D.A., Kikinis, R., Vespa, P.M., Horn, J.D.V.: Neuroimaging of structural pathology and connectomics in traumatic brain injury: toward personalized outcome prediction. Neuroimage Clin. **1**(1), 1–17 (2012)
8. Jog, A., Roy, S., Carass, A., Prince, J.L.: Magnetic resonance image synthesis through patch regression. In: ISBI, pp. 350–353 (2013)
9. Kingma, D.P., Welling, M.: Auto-encoding variational Bayes. CoRR abs/1312.6114 (2013)
10. Liu, X., Niethammer, M., Kwitt, R., Singh, N., McCormick, M., Aylward, S.: Low-rank atlas image analyses in the presence of pathologies. TMI **34**(12), 2583–2591 (2015)

11. Marcus, D.S., Wang, T.H., Parker, J., Csernansky, J.G., Morris, J.C., Buckner, R.L.: Open access series of imaging studies (OASIS): cross-sectional MRI data in young, middle aged, nondemented, and demented older adults. J. Cogn. Neurosci. **19**(9), 1498–1507 (2007)
12. Menze, B.H., Reyes, M., Leemput, K.V.: The multimodal brain tumor image segmentation benchmark (BRATS). TMI **34**(10), 1993–2024 (2015)
13. Modat, M., Ridgway, G.R., Taylor, Z.A., Lehmann, M., Barnes, J., Hawkes, D.J., Fox, N.C., Ourselin, S.: Fast free-form deformation using graphics processing units. Comput. Methods Prog. Biomed. **98**(3), 278–284 (2010)
14. Niethammer, M., Hart, G.L., Pace, D.F., Vespa, P.M., Irimia, A., Van Horn, J.D., Aylward, S.R.: Geometric metamorphosis. In: Fichtinger, G., Martel, A., Peters, T. (eds.) MICCAI 2011, Part II. LNCS, vol. 6892, pp. 639–646. Springer, Heidelberg (2011)
15. Ou, Y., Sotiras, A., Paragios, N., Davatzikos, C.: DRAMMS: deformable registration via attribute matching and mutual-saliency weighting. MedIA **15**(4), 622–639 (2011)
16. Ou, Y., Akbari, H., Bilello, M., Da, X., Davatzikos, C.: Comparative evaluation of registration algorithms in different brain databases with varying difficulty: results and insights. TMI **33**(10), 2039–2065 (2014)
17. Reuter, M., Rosas, D.H., Fischl, B.: Highly accurate inverse consistent registration: a robust approach. Neuroimage **53**(4), 1181–1196 (2010)
18. Roy, S., Carass, A., Shiee, N., Pham, D.L., Prince, J.L.: MR contrast synthesis for lesion segmentation. In: ISBI, pp. 932–935 (2010)
19. Roy, S., Carass, A., Jog, A., Prince, J.L., Lee, J.: MR to CT registration of brains using image synthesis. SPIE Med. Imaging **9034**, 903419 (2014)
20. Tieleman, T., Hinton, G.: Lecture 6.5-RMSprop, COURSERA: neural networks for machine learning (2012)
21. Wang, B., Prastawa, M., Awate, S., Irimia, A., Chambers, M., Vespa, P., Horn, J.V., Gerig, G.: Segmentation of serial MRI of TBI patients using personalized atlas construction and topological change estimation. In: ISBI, pp. 1152–1155 (2012)

Generation of Realistic 4D Synthetic CSPAMM Tagged MR Sequences for Benchmarking Cardiac Motion Tracking Algorithms

Yitian Zhou[1,3]([✉]), Mathieu De Craene[1], Oudom Somphone[1],
Maxime Sermesant[2], and Olivier Bernard[3]

[1] Philips Research Medisys, Suresnes, France
yitian.zhou@philips.com
[2] Inria, Asclepios Research Project, Sophia Antipolis, France
[3] CREATIS, CNRS UMR5220, Inserm U1044, INSA-Lyon,
Université Lyon 1, Villeurbanne, France

Abstract. This paper introduces a novel pipeline for synthesizing realistic 3D+t CSPAMM cardiac tagged magnetic resonance (MR) images. The proposed framework is based on the combination of an electro-mechanical model for generating cardiac deformation fields and a template tagging recording for assigning realistic voxel intensities. We developed a spatio-temporal alignment strategy for mapping voxel positions in the simulation space to the template recording space. As a preliminary result, we generated a synthetic dataset of a normal heart, and further compared the performance of two state-of-the-art cardiac motion tracking algorithms using this synthetic data. In this study, we aim at showing the capability of the proposed pipeline to simulate realistic cardiac tagged MR images, and its extension to more synthetic cases especially pathological ones are currently left to future work.

Keywords: Synthetic image · 3D cardiac tagged MR · CSPAMM · Benchmarking

1 Introduction

The diagnosis and follow up of cardiac diseases require a precise assessment of the cardiac morphology and function. Cardiac magnetic resonance imaging modalities, such as Cine or tagged MR, have shown to be able to provide accurate evaluation of global and regional cardiac functions. However, the analysis of cardiac deformation still largely relies on manually tracing the contours in Cine images, which is a time-consuming process. Although tagged MR is considered as the gold standard for quantifying local myocardial deformations, its use in clinical practice is somewhat held back by the lack of reliable automatic post-processing tools.

Recently, fast automatic or semi-automatic quantification algorithms in 3D were proposed for processing tagged MR [1]. Obviously, the introduction of

© Springer International Publishing AG 2016
S.A. Tsaftaris et al. (Eds.): SASHIMI 2016, LNCS 9968, pp. 108–117, 2016.
DOI: 10.1007/978-3-319-46630-9_11

these new algorithms requires a solid validation process. One of the common approaches is to use synthetic sequences with known ground truth. In such cases, the exact motion and/or deformation of the myocardium is known and serves as reference to assess the accuracy of semi/fully automatic algortihms. The usefulness of such tool is strongly linked to the degree of realism of the generated sequence.

Several groups already worked on the *in silico* generation of synthetic cardiac tagged MR sequences. Crum *et al.* [2] and Waks *et al.* [3] were among the first to simulate tagged MR images. Both of them simulated the tagging pattern by applying a sinusoidal modulation function in the spatial domain. Crum *et al.* [2] simulated the left ventricle (LV) in short axis slices. They modeled the corresponding anatomy using a simple ring shape. Using a motion directly computed from a real Cine sequence, the authors then proposed to warp the initial simulated image at end-diastole to the rest of the sequence. Later in [4], Crum *et al.* improved the generation of tag intensity profiles by using a frequency-domain model. Similarly, Waks *et al.* [3] used a prolate sphere to define the LV geometry and a 13-parameter kinematic motion model. The model parameters were determined by a least-squares fit to the displacements of the implanted markers tracked from a Cine sequence of a dog heart. Sermesant *et al.* [5] segmented myocardium from a real tagged MR image and further added tag lines to the binary mask. Finally, this image was warped by cardiac deformations generated by an electro-mechanical (E/M) model. Clarysse *et al.* [6] warped a real short-axis tagged MR image at end-diastole by a simple kinematic mode-based heart motion model. The use of real images ensures the realism of myocardium/background intensities. However, the motion model is too simplistic to represent the complexity of true heart motion and the integration of pathological case is not straightforward.

Figure 1 shows typical simulated images obtained from the work described in [2,3,5]. From these images one can see that in all cases only the intensity inside the myocardium is simulated. The absence of any intensity or motion artifact in the background considerably reduces the realism of the synthetized images. Moreover, these methods make appear highly contrasted borders between the myocardium and the background which is not realistic. Finally, it is worth pointing out that all the proposed tagged MR simulators generate synthetic data in 2D, nothing having been proposed for 3D yet.

In this study, we propose a pipeline for generating realistic 3D+t tagged MR images. The proposed pipeline is inspired by the work presented in [7] and [8] where realistic ultrasound/cine MR images were simulated. In particular, we propose to combine a template tagging sequence acquired from a volunteer (in order to derive realistic pixel intensity mapping) and an electro-mechanical (E/M) model [9] (in order to apply realistic cardiac motion and deformation). The template sequence we used come from 3D CSPAMM acquisitions [12] and it consists of three sequences with orthogonal tagging directions.

Our contributions in this paper are two-fold: (1) the reference displacement field involved in the simulation was generated by the E/M model. It is therefore

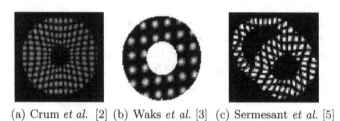

(a) Crum *et al.* [2] (b) Waks *et al.* [3] (c) Sermesant *et al.* [5]

Fig. 1. Synthetic 2D short-axis tagged MR images presented in [2,3,5].

unbiased to any motion estimation algorithm. Another interest of using the E/M model is the possibility to generate a wide range of synthetic deformation fields, from normal to different pathological cases; and (2) we made full use of the real tagging sequence in order to simulate realistic intensity information for the myocardium and the surrounding structures. A background with artifacts, or subject to a different motion field than the myocardium, represents a difficult challenge for any tracking algorithm. It is therefore important to have such challenges properly represented in the validation data.

2   Methodology

Figure 2 shows the pipeline of the proposed method. We first segment and track the heart in the template sequence (named as the image space hereinafter). Next, we use the E/M model to generate myocardial deformations (named as the simulation space hereinafter) corresponding to the heart geometry in the template sequence. In this way, the obtained image and simulation spaces are naturally aligned at the first frame. Further, as it will be described later in Sect. 2.3, we defined a set of spatio-temporal transformations which allows making a direct correspondence between a point in the simulated space and its equivalent in the image space. As a result, one is able to assign for each voxel of the simulated sequence a corresponding intensity value sampled from the real image sequence. In the following, we will describe the proposed pipeline in more details.

2.1   Segmenting and Tracking the LV in the Template Sequence

The left ventricle (LV) needs to be segmented and tracked for two reasons: (1) the E/M model requires a heart geometry at end-diastole as input; and (2) the heart motion needs to be tracked in order to build the spatio-temporal alignment that serves to assigning voxel intensities later.

Since with the template tagged MR sequence used, tissue and blood are both tagged and cannot be distinguished at the first frame, we chose to perform the segmentation at the last frame. A bandpass filter introduced in [1] was applied to untag the last frame image of the template sequence. We then segmented the LV manually as is described in [1]. This yields a surface mesh encompassing

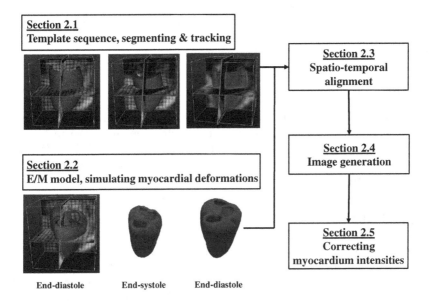

Fig. 2. The proposed pipeline for simulating tagged MR sequences. The three tagged MR sequences with line tagging patterns were multiplied for better visualization.

both the endo- and epi- cardium. In order to have a dense representation of the LV myocardium, we further resampled the surface into a volumetric mesh by methods described in [1].

Finally, this mesh was tracked backward in time in order to obtain the LV segmented shapes for each frame in the sequence [1]. In the sequel, $\mathcal{M}_t$ denotes the LV volumetric mesh generated from the template sequence at time t.

2.2 Simulating Heart Deformations by the E/M Model

To launch the E/M model [9] for simulating myocardial deformations, a biventricle heart geometry (tetrahedral mesh) with defined LV/RV electrical (activation) and mechanical (fibers, contractilities) properties is required. Instead of redefining all those informations on the segmented LV mesh, we opted for mapping a template heart geometry to the image space through a Thin Plate Spline (TPS)-based transformation.

To achieve this goal, the LV AHA segments were defined manually for both the tracked LV mesh $\mathcal{M}_0$ (Sect. 2.1) and the template geometry. The centers of these 17 AHA segments were then taken as control points to build the TPS transformation from the template geometry to $\mathcal{M}_0$. This transformation was then applied to both the mesh nodes and the fiber orientation vectors, leading to a well-defined biventricle geometry corresponding to the first frame of the template sequence.

We then simulated myocardial deformations by the E/M model taking the transformed heart geometry as input. The output of the simulation was a sequence of tetrahedral meshes denoted as $\mathcal{S}_t$.

2.3   Spatio-Temporal Alignment

The simulated heart motion is completely independent of the template sequence's. Since we intend to sample image intensities from the real acquisition, a spatio-temporal alignment of the template sequence and the E/M model is required. This enables us to sample intensities from the template image and further assign them to voxels located in the simulation space.

Temporal Alignment. We propose to match each time point in the simulation space to a continuous timing in the real space by linearly stretch/shrinking the time axis. Both the template sequence and the E/M simulation consist of one cardiac cycle, but with different numbers of frames (denoted as $\mathcal{N}_{img}$ and $\mathcal{N}_{simu}$, respectively). Besides, the end-systolic frame indexes (denoted as n_{img}^{es} and n_{simu}^{es} respectively) vary. As a result, we opted for aligning the systolic and diastolic time intervals respectively.

We aim to map a discrete time point t_{simu} of the simulation space to a continuous timing t_{img} in the real image space. We used linear mappings defined as follows:

$$\phi(t) = \begin{cases} \dfrac{n_{img}^{es}}{n_{simu}^{es}} t, & \text{if } t \leq n_{simu}^{es} \\[2ex] \dfrac{\mathcal{N}_{img}-1-n_{img}^{es}}{\mathcal{N}_{simu}-1-n_{simu}^{es}}(t - n_{simu}^{es}) + n_{img}^{es}, & \text{otherwise} \end{cases} \tag{1}$$

Then the non-integer timing value in the image space corresponding to the discrete time instant in the simulation is computed by $t_{img} = \phi(t_{simu})$.

Spatial Alignment. Once the simulation and the real recording are temporally aligned, we need to compute the correspondences between the spatial locations at these two time points.

In this section, we describe how to map a spatial position $\mathbf{x}_{simu}$ (at time t_{simu} in the simulation space) to its corresponding position $\mathbf{x}_{img}$ (at time t_{img} in the real image space). This can be achieved by chaining two TPS transformations.

First, in the simulation space, it is easy to compute a TPS transformation from the simulation meshes $\mathcal{S}_{t_{simu}}$ to $\mathcal{S}_0$ (Sect. 2.2). We denote this TPS as $\mathcal{T}_{\mathcal{S}_{t_{simu}} \to \mathcal{S}_0}$. In the meantime, in the real recording sequence, we match time 0 and time t_{img} using the two meshes $\mathcal{M}_0$ and $\mathcal{M}_{t_{img}}$ (Sect. 2.2). A second TPS transformation is computed and denoted as $\mathcal{T}_{\mathcal{M}_0 \to \mathcal{M}_{t_{img}}}$.

Thanks to these transformations, a point $\mathbf{x}_{simu}$ in the simulated sequence can then be located in the template image space through the following expression:

$$\mathbf{x}_{img} = \mathcal{T}_{\mathcal{M}_0 \to \mathcal{M}_{t_{img}}} \circ \mathcal{T}_{\mathcal{S}_{t_{simu}} \to \mathcal{S}_0}(\mathbf{x}_{simu}) \tag{2}$$

where $\mathcal{M}_{t_{img}}$ (i.e. the tracking mesh at t_{img}) was computed by a linear interpolation between $\mathcal{M}_{\lfloor t_{img} \rfloor}$ and $\mathcal{M}_{\lceil t_{img} \rceil}$ ($\lfloor \rfloor$ and $\lceil \rceil$ are respectively the floor and ceiling operators).

2.4   Image Generation

Our goal is to assign realistic image intensities for voxels located in the simulation space. In this section, we will describe how to assign voxel intensities using the spatio-temporal alignment technique we introduced previously in Sect. 2.3.

First of all, we need to define the voxel positions. Since the simulation and image spaces are naturally aligned at the first frame as is described in Sect. 2.2, we chose to follow the image information (origin, spacing, size and axis orientations) of the template recording used. This further defines the voxel positions.

Next, using the temporal alignment, we associated each time frame t_{simu} in the simulation space to a continuous time t_{img} in the template sequence. A new image $\mathcal{I}(t_{img})$ was created by linearly interpolating images of the two closest time frames $\lfloor t_{img} \rfloor$ and $\lceil t_{img} \rceil$.

Finally, using the spatial alignment, each voxel position of frame t_{simu} in the simulation space was mapped to a spatial location at time t_{img} in the template space. Spatially interpolating $\mathcal{I}(t_{img})$ at that position yields the intensity value to be assigned.

2.5   Correcting the Intensities of Myocardium

By far, the cardiac motion represented in the simulated images corresponds actually to the TPS transformation $\mathcal{T}_{\mathcal{S}_{t_{simu}} \to \mathcal{S}_0}$ described in Sect. 2.3. This transformation is computed from the simulation meshes $\mathcal{S}_{t_{simu}}$ and $\mathcal{S}_0$ but slightly differs with the true displacements represented in the simulations, due mainly to the use of spatial regularization when computing the TPS. As a result, it is necessary to further correct the intensities of the myocardium so that the motion corresponds exactly to that simulated by the E/M model.

We chose not to modify the image at the first frame, and further propagate the corresponding myocardial intensities to all the other time instants through the transformation contained in the simulation sequence $\mathcal{S}_t$.

For each myocardial voxel $\mathbf{x}^t$ at time t, we first find the tetrahedron cell of the simulation mesh $\mathcal{S}_t$ that contains $\mathbf{x}^t$, and further compute the barycentric coordinates of $\mathbf{x}^t$ in that local tetrahedron cell. Since all the tetrahedrons are indexed, we can find the tetrahedron with the same index at the first frame. By combining the positions of this tetrahedron at time 0 and the previously evaluated barycentric coordinates of $\mathbf{x}^t$, we can compute the voxel's corresponding position at the first frame, denoted as $\mathbf{x}^0$. Finally, since the simulation and image spaces are naturally aligned at the first frame, we computed the voxel intensity by linearly interpolating intensities at position $\mathbf{x}^0$.

After refining all the myocardial voxels' intensities by this way, the myocardial motion underlying the synthetic images corresponds to the E/M model, making it reasonable to compare displacement field tracked by cardiac motion tracking algorithms against the E/M model generated ground truth.

3 Result

3.1 Simulation of a Normal Heart

A healthy volunteer dataset from [11] was used as the template sequence. The tagged MR images for a normal heart were simulated and shown in Fig. 3. Three sequences with orthogonal line tagging directions were generated with line tag spacing 7 mm. Each sequence consists of 17 slices. The inter-slice thickness is 7.71 mm, and the in-plane pixel resolution is 0.96 mm × 0.96 mm.

Compared to the previous work of several groups as shown in Fig. 1, the images simulated by the proposed method show more realistic surrounding tissue intensities instead of a whole-black background. Moreover, the appearance of the myocardium is less binary-like. To faciliate the use of our simulated images for benchmarking, we put this synthetic dataset (both the images and the ground truth meshes) at http://bit.ly/1nnEIMl which is publicly available to the research community.

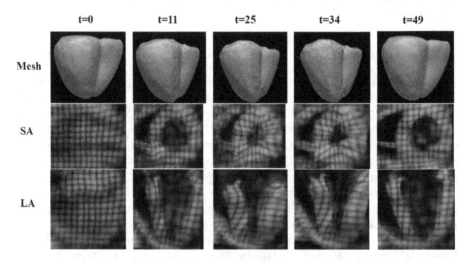

Fig. 3. Synthetic tagged MR images for a normal heart using the proposed pipeline. The intensities of the three line tagging sequences were multiplied for better visualization.

3.2 Evaluation of State-of-the-Art Algorithms

In this section, we show the interest of using the simulated synthetic dataset for evaluating the performance of two recent cardiac motion tracking algorithms:

HarpAR [1] and Sparse Demons (with default parameters) [10]. They were compared using the synthetized tagging sequence described in Sect. 3.1.

The LV of the first simulation mesh was tracked over the cardiac cycle by both methods. The tracking results were compared against the ground truth (i.e. the E/M simulations). Since the motion error reaches its maximum at end-systole, we compare the two methods at that time point. In Fig. 4, we can observe that HarpAR gave smaller median and variance of the tracking errors. This result is further confirmed by two statistical tests. The Levene's test returned a p-value below 0.05, rejecting the hypothesis that their variances are equal. Also, we applied the Wilcoxon signed-rank test to see if their median values are equal. The returned p-value is below 0.05, rejecting the hypothesis that their median values are equal. The results from the statistic tests are coherent with what we observe in Fig. 4. Note that here our aim is to show the possibility of using the simulated dataset for benchmarking different algorithms, rather than determining which one is superior to the other, especially given that a thorough parameter tuning task remains to be done for SparseDemons.

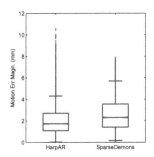

Fig. 4. Comparison of HarpAR [1] and Sparse Demons [10] with respect to end-systolic tracking errors using the synthesized 3D+t tagged MR sequence (each data point represents the motion error of certain mesh node).

4   Discussion

The proposed pipeline has several limitations. First, since the myocardial intensities are corrected *a posteriori* as described in Sect. 2.5, the transitions between the myocardium and the remaining parts are not smooth enough as revealed by a careful visual inspection of the output image. This is due to the fact that the warping fields applied to the myocardium and the surrounding tissues are different: the myocardial motion corresponds to the E/M simulations while the warping applied to other parts comes from the TPS transformation. Although the two kinds of warping fields are close, it does result in intensity inconsistencies that can be perceived by human eyes as shown in Fig. 3. This somehow reduces the degree of the realism of the simulated images and it should be specially dealt with in the future.

Second, as described in Sect. 2.5, the intensities of the myocardium are all assigned from the first frame, meaning that no tag fading over the cardiac cycle is simulated. Obviously, tag fading has always been one of the key issues in tagged MR. However, in CSPAMM acquisitions, tag fading effects are much less apparent after the subtraction of two SPAMM acquisitions of inverse tagging preparation patterns [12]. Indeed, in the kind of CSPAMM images we aim to simulate, tag fading is rather limited, as can be seen in [13]. The absence of tag fading in the myocardium seems to decrease the realism of the simulation, but far from a significant level. Nonetheless, we expect to integrate additional considerations about tag fading into the pipeline which remains parts of future work as well.

A final aspect to be improved is the MR simulator. The proposed simulation pipeline is principally based on warping image intensities. A physical MR simulator taking tissue-specific properties (T1, T2 and proton density) as inputs should be more reasonable and might yield better results. In the future, we wish to integrate a MR simulator based on solving Bloch equations, which we think would perform better than simply warping the image intensities.

5   Conclusion

In this paper, we proposed a novel pipeline for synthesizing realistic 3D+t cardiac tagged MR images. We combined an electro-mechanical model and a template tagged MR sequence of a healthy volunteer for achieving this goal. The E/M model was used for simulating heart motions and the template sequence is used for picking up realistic image intensities. A spatio-temporal alignment technique was applied to help mapping the simulation and image spaces. One major advantage brought by the E/M model is that the heart deformation results solely from the model and is thus unbiased to any motion tracking algorithms.

As a preliminary result, we generated a synthetic dataset of a normal heart despite that the E/M model used is quite flexible and can generate a range of heart deformations corresponding to both normal and pathological cases. In the future, we intend to extend the simulation to different levels of pathological extents. The current work merely aims to show the feasibility of combining the E/M model and a template sequence for simulating CSPAMM images that represent a relatively good level of realism. Moreover, we show in this paper the interest of using our simulated dataset for comparing the performance of two recent cardiac motion tracking algorithms (HarpAR and Sparse Demons). This comparison can be easily extended to more algorithms and can be done more thoroughly while including more measurements such as myocardial strains. All these are currently left to future work.

References

1. Zhou, Y., Bernard, O., Saloux, E., Manrique, A., Allain, P., Makram-Ebeid, S., De Craene, M.: 3D harmonic phase tracking with anatomical regularization. Med. Image Anal. **26**(1), 70–81 (2015)
2. Crum, W., Berry, E., Ridgway, J., Sivananthan, U., Tan, L., Smith, M.: Simulation of two-dimensional tagged MRI. J. Magn. Reson. Imaging **7**(2), 416–424 (1997)
3. Waks, E., Prince, J., Douglas, A.: Cardiac motion simulator for tagged MRI. In: Proceedings of the Workshop on Mathematical Methods in Biomedical Image Analysis, pp. 182–191. IEEE (1996)
4. Crum, W., Berry, E., Ridgway, J., Sivananthan, U., Tan, L., Smith, M.: Frequency-domain simulation of MR tagging. J. Magn. Reson. Imaging **8**(5), 1040–1050 (1998)
5. Sermesant, M., Moireau, P., Camara, O., Sainte-Marie, J., Andriantsimiavona, R., Cimrman, R., Hill, D., Chapelle, D., Razavi, R.: Cardiac function estimation from MRI using a heart model and data assimilation: advances and difficulties. Med. Image Anal. **10**(4), 642–656 (2006)
6. Clarysse, P., Tafazzoli, J., Delachartre, P., Croisille, P.: Simulation based evaluation of cardiac motion estimation methods in tagged-MR image sequences. J. Cardiovasc. Magn. Reson. **13**(1), 1–1 (2011)
7. Alessandrini, M., De Craene, M., Bernard, O., Giffard-Roisin, S., Allain, P., Weese, J., Saloux, E., Delingette, H., Sermesant, M., D'hooge, J.: A pipeline for the generation of realistic 3D synthetic echocardiographic sequences: methodology and open-access database. IEEE Trans. Med. Imaging **34**(7), 1436–1451 (2015)
8. Prakosa, A., Sermesant, M., Delingette, H., Marchesseau, S., Saloux, E., Allain, P., Villain, N., Ayache, N.: Generation of synthetic but visually realistic time series of cardiac images combining a biophysical model and clinical images. IEEE Trans. Med. Imaging **32**(1), 99–109 (2013)
9. Marchesseau, S., Delingette, H., Sermesant, M., Ayache, N.: Fast parameter calibration of a cardiac electromechanical model from medical images based on the unscented transform. Biomech. Model. Mechanobiol. **12**(4), 815–831 (2013)
10. Somphone, O., De Craene, M., Ardon, R., Mory, B., Allain, P., Gao, H., D'hooge, J., Marchesseau, S., Sermesant, M. Delingette, H., et al.: Fast myocardial motion and strain estimation in 3D cardiac ultrasound with sparse demons. In: IEEE 10th International Symposium on Biomedical Imaging (ISBI), pp. 1182–1185. IEEE (2013)
11. Tobon-Gomez, C., De Craene, M., Mcleod, K., Tautz, L., Shi, W., Hennemuth, A., Prakosa, A., Wang, H., Carr-White, G., Kapetanakis, S., et al.: Benchmarking framework for myocardial tracking and deformation algorithms: an open access database. Med. Image Anal. **17**(6), 632–648 (2013)
12. Fischer, S., McKinnon, G., Maier, S., Boesiger, P.: Improved myocardial tagging contrast. Magn. Reson. Med. **30**(2), 191–200 (1993)
13. Rutz, A., Ryf, S., Plein, S., Boesiger, P., Kozerke, S.: Accelerated whole-heart 3D CSPAMM for myocardial motion quantification. Magn. Reson. Med. **59**(4), 755–763 (2008)

Geometry Regularized Joint Dictionary Learning for Cross-Modality Image Synthesis in Magnetic Resonance Imaging

Yawen Huang[1(✉)], Leandro Beltrachini[1], Ling Shao[2],
and Alejandro F. Frangi[1]

[1] Centre for Computational Imaging and Simulation Technologies
in Biomedicine, University of Sheffield, Sheffield, UK
Yhuang36@sheffield.ac.uk
[2] Department of Computer Science and Digital Technologies,
Northumbria University, Newcastle upon Tyne, UK

Abstract. Multi-sequence MRI protocols are used in comprehensive examinations of various pathologies in both clinical diagnosis and medical research. Various MRI techniques provide complementary information about living tissue. However, a comprehensive examination covering all modalities is rarely achieved due to considerations of cost, patient comfort, and scanner time availability. This may lead to incomplete records owing to image artifacts or corrupted or lost data. In this paper, we explore the problem of synthesizing images for one MRI modality from an image of another MRI modality of the same subject using a novel geometry regularized joint dictionary learning framework for non-local patch reconstruction. Firstly, we learn a cross-modality joint dictionary from a multi-modality image database. Training image pairs are first co-registered. A cross-modality dictionary pair is then jointly learned by minimizing the cross-modality divergence via a Maximum Mean Discrepancy term in the objective function of the learning scheme. This guarantees that the distribution of both image modalities is taken jointly into account when building the resulting sparse representation. In addition, in order to preserve intrinsic geometrical structure of the synthesized image patches, we further introduced a graph Laplacian regularization term into the objective function. Finally, we present a patch-based non-local reconstruction scheme, providing further fidelity of the synthesized images. Experimental results demonstrate that our method achieves significant performance gains over previously published techniques.

1 Introduction

Magnetic Resonance Imaging (MRI) is a versatile and noninvasive imaging technique extensively used in neuroimaging studies. MRI comes in many different flavors (viz. MRI sequences, or henceforth also referred as MRI modalities[1]), each providing diverse and complementary image contrast mechanisms unraveling structural and

---

[1] Here, we use the word modality in the sense of a specific kind of MRI sequence. Note that the proposed technique would equally be applicable when the protocol involves different imaging modalities in a more classical sense (e.g. MRI, CT, US, SPECT, and PET).

© Springer International Publishing AG 2016
S.A. Tsaftaris et al. (Eds.): SASHIMI 2016, LNCS 9968, pp. 118–126, 2016.
DOI: 10.1007/978-3-319-46630-9_12

functional information about brain tissue. Multi-modality MRI are nowadays very common in many pharmaceutical clinical trials, in research studies of neurosciences, or in population imaging cohorts targeted to understand neurodegeneration and cognitive decline. The acquisitions of a full battery of all these MR images can face constraints associated with their cost, limited availability of scanning time, patient comfort or safety considerations. Moreover, in large scale studies it is not uncommon to face incomplete datasets due to the presence of imaging artifacts, acquisition errors or corrupted data. While many such studies use imputation techniques to compensate for these latter issues, this is usually only at the level of the derived imaging biomarkers and not of the data itself. Finally, in longitudinal imaging studies where image data is collected over several years, evolution of imaging technology may lead to the appearance of new MRI sequences that are added to an existing imaging protocol at some point in time but for which are not available as part of the imaging battery acquired at earlier time points. In these and other applications, it would be desirable to have a methodology that is able to synthesize the unavailable data from the available MRI studies. The assumption here is that the synthesis ability comes from the cross-modality correspondences of sparse codes obtained during training, and can be used to encoding missing MRI. The degree to which this hypothesis is valid will have to be scrutinized in each application but is worth exploring.

To cope with this problem, several methods were proposed through either transforming MRI intensities or reconstructing tissue contrasts to obtain the missing MRI data. Histogram matching is the most common approach within this group. Although this technique is widely used in neuroimaging, it has been pointed out its inefficacy for multi-modality image synthesis due to the lack of specificity for certain ratios of tissue types [1]. On the other hand, techniques based on sparse representations have been presented, which separately learn two corresponding dictionaries from co-registered image pairs and synthesize a desired MRI modality data from the patches of the available MRI modality [1]. These approaches, however, boil down to an example-based synthesis strategy, which does not fully exploit the available training data to its fullest. In contrast, here, we establish fundamental connections with transfer learning (a.k.a. domain adaptation) used in many fields, e.g. [2, 3]. Such methods can successfully solve the above problem by learning a paired dictionary from both modalities while assuming each co-registered image pair with a nearly identical distribution [1]. However, this assumption cannot be fully satisfied in practice since cross-modality data may have very different feature distributions in different spaces.

In this paper, we propose a novel geometry regularized joint dictionary learning method for synthesizing any unavailable MRI from available MRI data. This paper offers the following three contributions: (1) We address cross-modality MRI synthesis by jointly learning a cross-modality dictionary that penalizes differences in the statistical distribution of the sparse codes in both domains rather than directly imposing the same code to both domains as done before. This is achieved by incorporating a new term in the computation of the joint sparse codes using the Maximum Mean Discrepancy measure; (2) We exploit the geometrical information underlying the input data and incorporate this new term into the cross-modality joint dictionary learning optimization; (3) A non-local reconstruction framework that provides a more expressive and compact patch representation is adopted to synthesize the corresponding patch from a different MRI protocol. To the best of our knowledge, this is the first time that joint dictionary learning is computed by minimizing the discrepancy between the statistical distributions of the codes of the involved MRI modalities while preserving the intrinsic geometrical structure of the image. In the remainder of this paper, we first define the cross-modality synthesis problem, and then introduce our proposed method in Sect. 2. The experimental results are demonstrated in Sect. 3. Finally, we discuss the results and conclude the paper in Sect. 4.

2 Method

In this section, we propose cross-modality image synthesis via geometry regularized joint dictionary learning for effectively minimizing the cross-modality discrepancy. This consists in an extension of the conventional dictionary learning by jointly learning from the data of two modalities at the same time while minimizing the sparse codes divergence between the different modalities.

2.1 Problem Definition

Let $L^{M_K} = \{I_i^{M_k}\}_{i-1}^m$ be a library of m subjects imaged with k modalities each ($k = 1$ or 2), with I_i being the training image of the i-th sample. Each pair of images in both libraries, i.e. $\{I_i^{M_1}, I_i^{M2}\}$ is assumed co-registered. Further, images are treated as the combination of many patches and denoted as $X^{M_k} = \{x_i^{M_k}\}_{i-1}^n \in \mathbb{R}^{s \times n}$ where s is the size of a vectorized patch, and n represents the number of training patches for both modalities. We denote the test image in the same way by a matrix $Y = \{y_l\}_{l=1}^c \in \mathbb{R}^{s \times c}$, where c is the number of patches in the test image. All of the elements in Y are considered with either modality M_1 or modality M_2. A summary of the notation used throughout this paper is presented in Table 1.

Table 1. Summary of notations and their meanings as used in this paper

Notation	Description	Notation	Description
L_1, L_2, L_t	Training library of modality 1 or 2, testing library	M, G	MMD matrix, graph Laplacian matrix
X^{M_1}, X^{M_2}, Y	Training matrix of modality 1 or 2, testing matrix	Φ, W, N	Diagonal degree/weight matrix, nearest-neighbor graph
D^{M_1}, D^{M_2}	Dictionary matrix of modality 1 or 2	λ, β, γ	Sparsity, balance parameter of MMD/graph Laplacian
$\alpha^{M_1}, \alpha^{M2}$	Sparse codes matrix of modality 1 or 2 in training set	Ω, μ	Similar patch set/weight matrix in testing domain
$\alpha^t, \hat{\alpha}^t, \alpha^u,$	(Optimal) sparse codes matrix in testing/unified space	C, h	Normalization constant, scalar parameter

Problem: Given X^{M_1} and X^{M_2}, our goal is to learn a pair of dictionaries $\{D^{M_1}, D^{M_2}\}$ and the unified sparse codes α^u minimizing the cross-modality discrepancy of α^{M_1} and α^{M_2}, where α^{M_k} is the sparse codes matrix of X^{M_k}

2.2 Dictionary Learning

Let $X = \{x_i\}_{i-1}^n \in \mathbb{R}^{s \times n}$ be a training data matrix with n input items sampled in the s-dimensional space, $D = \{d_i\}_{i-1}^K \in \mathbb{R}^{s \times K}$ be a projection dictionary with K atoms, where $K > s$ to make the dictionary overcomplete. Learning D from a sparse representation of X can be formulated as:

$$\min_{D,\alpha} \left\| X - D\alpha \right\|_F^2 + \lambda \left\| \alpha \right\|_0, \tag{1}$$

where $\alpha = \{\alpha_i\}_{i-1}^n \in \mathbb{R}^{K \times n}$ is a set of n K-dimensional sparse codes of X, $\|\cdot\|_F$ is the Frobenius norm, $\|\cdot\|_0$ is l_0-norm, which fixes the number of non-zero elements of α, and λ denotes a regularization parameter to trade off the sparsity and the reconstruction error. As shown in [4], the minimization problem as stated in (1) is an NP-hard problem under the l_0-norm constraint. An alternative solution is to relax the l_0-norm constraint with the l_1-norm constraint to obtain a near-optimum result [5].

2.3 Geometry Regularized Joint Dictionary Learning

Following the dictionary learning procedure described in Sect. 2.2, instead of transferring the estimated sparse codes from the first domain to the other [1, 6], we can learn the dictionaries of both domains independently:

$$\min_{D^{M_1}, \alpha^{M_1}} \left\| X^{M_1} - D^{M_1} \alpha^{M_1} \right\|_F^2 + \lambda_1 \left\| \alpha^{M_1} \right\|_1,$$
$$\min_{D^{M_2}, \alpha^{M_2}} \left\| X^{M_2} - D^{M_2} \alpha^{M_2} \right\|_F^2 + \lambda_2 \left\| \alpha^{M_2} \right\|_1. \tag{2}$$

However, such a strategy is time-consuming and results in two sets of independent sparse codes that do not necessarily satisfy the assumption of high-correlation between both modalities to reconstruct M_2-like images from M_1-like ones. To solve a similar problem, Yang et al. [6] proposed an image super-resolution approach that uses coupled dictionary learning. Their method maps image pairs (e.g. low and high resolution or, here, two different modalities) into a common space, which enforces the sparse codes of paired data possess the same values. Instead of directly imposing the same sparse codes across each pair, our work allows the codes to be different for each modality, and fosters the most similar distributions across them. This is done by measuring the distribution divergence for the co-registered image pairs over the empirical Maximum Mean Discrepancy (MMD), which is then minimized and incorporated into the dictionary learning problem.

Maximum Mean Discrepancy Regularization: We seek that the probability distributions of the codes associated to cross-modality patch pairs is identical when computing the optimal sparse representation. To this effect, the MMD [7] is used. The MMD is a nonparametric statistic utilized to assess whether two samples are drawn from the same distribution. In our case, the two samples correspond to the sparse codes of the training set for the two modalities involved. The MMD is calculated as the largest difference in the expected mean value of the K-dimensional codes for both modalities. To compute the MMD, we follow [7–9] to estimate the largest difference in expectations over functions in the unit ball of a reproducing kernel Hilbert space:

$$\text{MMD} = \left\| \frac{1}{n} \sum_{i-1}^{n} \alpha_i - \frac{1}{n} \sum_{j=n+1}^{2n} \alpha_j \right\|_{H}^{2} = Tr\left(\alpha^u M \alpha^{u^T} \right), \tag{3}$$

where α^u represents the unified sparse codes, α^{u^T} is the transposed matrix of α^u, and M denotes the MMD matrix defined as:

$$M_{i,j} = \begin{cases} 1/n^2, & x_i, x_j \in X^{M_1} \ or \ x_i, x_j \in X^{M_2} \ . \\ -1/n^2, & otherwise \end{cases} \tag{4}$$

Graph Laplacian Regularization: During dictionary learning, high-level patch semantics are captured in each dictionary atom. However, this process fails to introduce any prior knowledge on the geometrical structure within patches. Instead, by introducing a graph Laplacian (GL) term [10], we can preserve the local manifold structure of the sparse graph and better capture the intrinsic geometrical properties of the entire data space. Given $\{X^{M_1}, X^{M_2}\} \in \mathbb{R}^{s \times 2n}$, a q-nearest neighbor graph $\mathcal{G}$ with $2n$ vertices can be constructed. The weight matrix of $\mathcal{G}$ is $W \in \mathbb{R}^{2n \times 2n}$, defined as the matrix with elements $W_{i,j} = 1$ if and only if for any two data points x_i, x_j, x_i, x_i is among the q-nearest neighbors of x_j or *vice versa* ($w_{i,j} = 0$, otherwise). Let $\phi = diag(\phi_1, \cdots, \phi_{2n})$ be the diagonal degree matrix with elements $\phi_i = \sum_{j=1}^{2n} W_{i,j}$. The GL term, incorporated into the sparse representation as a regularization criterion [10], imposes that the obtained sparse codes vary smoothly along the geodesics of the manifold that is captured by the graph. The GL matrix is then defined as $G = \phi - W$. In order to preserve the geometrical structure in $\mathcal{G}$, we map $\mathcal{G}$ to the unified coefficients α^u by:

$$\frac{1}{2} \sum_{i,j=1}^{2n} \| \alpha_i - \alpha_j \|_2^2 W_{i,j} = \sum_{i=1}^{2n} \alpha_i \alpha_i^T \phi_{ii} - \sum_{i,j=1}^{2n} \alpha_j \alpha_i^T W_{ii} = \text{Tr}\left(\alpha^u G \alpha^{u^T} \right). \tag{5}$$

Objective Function: To maximize the correlation between patch pairs in both modalities, we map them into a common higher-dimensional space that meets two complementary objectives to those of Eq. (2), viz. the MMD and GL terms. Therefore, our geometry regularized joint dictionary learning objective function becomes:

$$\min_{D^{M_1},\alpha^{M_1},\alpha^u} \frac{1}{2}\left\|X^{M_1} - D^{M_1}\alpha^u\right\|_F^2 + \frac{1}{2}\lambda_2\left\|X^{M_2} - D^{M_2}\alpha^u\right\|_F^2$$
$$+ \text{Tr}\left(\alpha^u(\gamma M + \delta G)\alpha^{u^T}\right) + \lambda\|\alpha^u\|_1. \tag{6}$$

where γ and δ are the regularization parameters for trading off the effect of the MMD and GL terms, respectively.

2.4 Image Synthesis via Nonlocal Reconstruction

Once the cross-modality dictionary pairs have been computed by solving Eq. 6, we seek to reconstruct a test image $Y \in \mathbb{R}^{s \times c}$ by, first, sparsely representing Y with respect to $D^{M_1} \in \mathbb{R}^{s \times K}$ by solving Eq. (1) with l_1-norm as:

$$\alpha^t = arg \min_{\alpha^t}\|Y - D^{M_1}\alpha^t\|_F^2 + \lambda\|\alpha^t\|_1, \tag{7}$$

where $\alpha^t \in \mathbb{R}^{K \times c}$ denotes the sparse codes of Y. The estimated coefficients can be directly used (or "transferred") to synthesize the image $\hat{Y}$ of our target modality M_2 by a linear combination of elements in the dictionary D^{M_2}, namely, $\hat{Y} = D^{M_2}\alpha^t$.

To achieve richer synthesis ability, in this paper, we improve the sparse representation performance through an optimized nonlocal reconstruction model. To faithfully synthesize the desired image, we enforce the sparse coefficients α^t as close as possible to the target codes. That is, by groups of similar patches being encoded onto subsets of the dictionary that are similar, the estimated sparse codes vary smoothly as the patches themselves vary. This makes the whole reconstruction scheme more robust to the influence of patch noise and more accurate. To this end, we adopt the representative non-local means [11] in the sparse representation model by modifying Eq. (7) as

$$\hat{\alpha}^t = arg \min_{\beta^t}\|Y - D^{M_1}\beta^t\|_F^2 + \lambda\|\beta^t\|_1, \tag{8}$$

where $\beta^t = \sum\sum_{p \in \Omega_i} \mu_{i,p}\alpha_{i,p}^t$, and α_i^t indicates the sparse codes of y_i. For each y_i, we express its similar patch set as Ω_i, and define p as a random element within Ω_i. Also, we define $\mu_{i,p}$ as the weight for computing the level of similarity between y_i and y_q, where $\mu_{i,p} = \frac{1}{C}\exp\left\{-\frac{\|y_i - y_{i,p}\|_2^2}{h^2}\right\}$, with C being the normalization constant and h being a scalar (note that $\mu_{i,p}$ satisfies $0 \leq \mu_{i,p} \leq 1$ and $\sum_{p \in \Omega_i} \mu_{i,p} = 1$). Then, we can update the synthesized image via $\tilde{Y} = D^{M_2}\hat{\alpha}^t$.

3   Experiments

In this section, we show extensive experiments for the MRI cross-modality synthesis problem to verify the effectiveness of our proposed method.

Experiment Setup: We evaluated our method in two different scenarios. Firstly, we used the IXI dataset [12] for synthesizing the T_2-w image considering the proton density (PD) acquisition from the same subject. We randomly selected 12 subjects from IXI containing both T2-w and corresponding PD-w images. We trained the dictionaries from 5 subjects including both modalities, and the other 7 subjects were used for testing. In the second experiment, we considered the generation of magnetization-prepared rapid gradient-echo (MPRAGE) images based on spoiled gradient recalled (SPGR) acquisitions, allowing us to compare our method with an existing approach [1]. In each experiment, for each co-registered image pair in the training set, we randomly selected 100,000 patch pairs of $5 \times 5 \times 5$ voxels size to train our dictionaries. We also took the factor of dictionary size and sparsity into consideration, and fixed the dictionary size as 1024 and $\lambda = 0.15$ based on our experiments trading off cost and synthesis quality. For other parameters, we used the following settings according to our extensive experiments: $q = 5$, $\gamma = 10^5$, $\delta = 1$, and the searching window for nonlocal reconstruction equals 10. Finally, we adopted Root Mean Square Error (RMSE), Peak Signal to Noise Ratio (PSNR) in decibels (dB), Structural Similarity Index (SSIM) and voxelwise relative error (RE) as evaluation metrics.

Compared Methods: To show the performance of our approach, we compared our results of the following state-of-the-art methods: (a) Joint Dictionary Learning (JDL); (b) MRI example-based contrast synthesis (MIMECS) [1]; (c) Geometry Regularized Joint Dictionary Learning (GRiDLE) with only MMD term; (d) The proposed GRiDLE. Note that JDL is a special case of GRiDLE with $\gamma = \delta = 0$, and GRiDLE with only MMD term is another special case with $\delta = 0$.

Experimental Results: Table 2 shows the error measures of the synthesized T_2 images using JDL, GRiDLE ($\delta = 0$) and GRiDLE. We did not compare our GRiDLE with MIMECS in this case, because there is no available dictionary within this algorithm to generate arbitrary results. We can see that the proposed method outperforms the other two, obtaining the lowest RMSEs and the highest PSNRs and SSIMs for all 7 subjects. In the second example we compared the performance of the proposed method with that of the state-of-the-art MIMECS. The clear advantage of our approach over the MIMECS and JDL is shown in Fig. 1, which can be seen in overall tissue contrast, as well as in the lowest voxelwise RE. Table 3 compares the average error measures of all the methods for MPRAGE synthesizing from SPGR images. As shown, the proposed method achieves the best results.

Table 2. Error measures of the synthetic images using JDL, GRiDLE, and GRiDLE.

	RMSE			PSNR (dB)			SSIM		
	JDL	GRiDLE $(\delta = 0)$	GRiDLE	JDL	GRiDLE $(\delta = 0)$	GRiDLE	JDL	GRiDLE $(\delta = 0)$	GRiDLE
Sub .1	9.43	8.53	**8.29**	36.72	39.93	**41.73**	0.9025	0.9069	**0.9075**
Sub .2	9.42	8.53	**8.27**	37.15	39.92	**42.05**	0.9021	0.9054	**0.9062**
Sub .3	10.42	9.73	**9.49**	39.35	38.23	**40.35**	0.8997	0.9018	**0.9029**
Sub .4	10.53	9.26	**9.01**	36.17	37.61	**41.34**	0.8669	0.8999	**0.9016**
Sub .5	12.03	11.07	**10.94**	34.12	36.01	**39.17**	0.8990	0.8962	**0.8970**
Sub .6	10.21	9.30	**9.06**	36.73	38.66	**41.02**	0.9002	0.9049	**0.9062**
Sub .7	10.98	9.87	**9.63**	36.18	38.18	**41.01**	0.8964	0.9028	**0.9034**
Avg.	10.43	9.47	**9.24**	36.63	38.36	**40.95**	0.8953	0.9026	**0.9035**

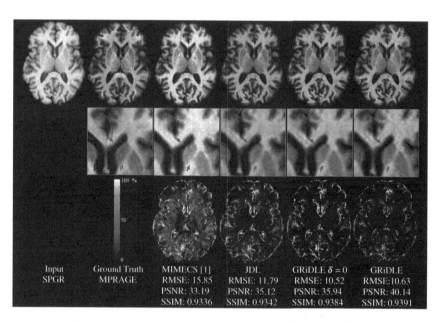

Fig. 1. Comparison of the synthesized results with ground truth.

Table 3. Comparison of methods used for synthesizing MPRAGE based on SPGR.

	MIMECS [1]	JDL	GRiDLE $(\delta = 0)$	GRiDLE
RMSE	14.55	12.58	11.03	**10.89**
PSNR (dB)	32.76	34.51	35.52	**39.35**
SSIM	0.9303	0.9368	0.9403	**0.9500**

4   Conclusion

In this paper, we proposed a novel geometry regularized joint dictionary learning (GRiDLE) approach for MRI cross-modality synthesis. The distribution divergence is effectively reduced by including the MMD term for both modalities and a mapping function in the sparse domain. The learned dictionary pair can not only minimize the distance between each coupled coefficients but also preserve the geometrical structure in the data while spanning both spaces for stable mapping of image details. Extensive experiments have demonstrated that GRiDLE can achieve superior performance over the state-of-the-art methods. Future work will focus on the simultaneous generation of multimodality images.

References

1. Roy, S., Carass, A., Prince, J.L.: Magnetic resonance image example-based contrast synthesis. IEEE TMI **32**(12), 2348–2363 (2013)
2. Shao, L., Zhu, F., Li, X.: Transfer learning for visual categorization: a survey. IEEE TNNLS **26**(5), 1019–1034 (2015)
3. Pan, S.J., Yang, Q.: A survey on transfer learning. IEEE TKDE **26**(5), 1345–1359 (2010)
4. Davis, G., Mallat, S., Avellaneda, M.: Adaptive greedy approximations. Constr. Approx. **13**(1), 57–98 (1997)
5. Chen, S.S., Donoho, L.D., Saunders, A.M.: Atomic decomposition by basis pursuit. SIAM Rev. **43**(1), 129–159 (2001)
6. Yang, J., Wright, J., Huang, T.S., Ma, Y.: Image super-resolution via sparse representation. IEEE TIP **19**(11), 2861–2873 (2010)
7. Gretton, A., Borgwardt, K., Rasch, M.J., Scholkopf, B., Smola, A.J.: A kernel two-sample test. JMLR **13**, 723–773 (2012)
8. Long, M., Wang, J., Ding, G., Shen, D., Yang, Q.: Transfer learning with graph co-regularization. IEEE TKDE **26**(7), 1805–1818 (2014)
9. Steinwart, I.: On the influence of the kernel on the consistency of support vector machines. JMLR **2**, 67–93 (2002)
10. Zheng, M., Bu, J., Chen, C., Wang, C., Zhang, L., Qiu, G., Cai, D.: Graph regularized sparse coding for image representation. IEEE TIP **20**(5), 1327–1336 (2011)
11. Buades, A., Coll, B., Morel, J.M.: Image denoising methods. A new nonlocal principle. SIAM Rev. **52**(1), 113–147 (2010)
12. Rowland, A.L., Burns, M., Hartkens, T., Hajnal, J. V., Rueckert, D., Hill, D.L.G.: Information eXtraction from Images (IXI). In: DiDaMIC, pp. 55–6 (2004)

Whole Image Synthesis Using a Deep Encoder-Decoder Network

Vasileios Sevetlidis[1,2(✉)], Mario Valerio Giuffrida[1,2],
and Sotirios A. Tsaftaris[1,2]

[1] PRIAn, IMT School Advanced Studies Lucca, Lucca, Italy
{vasileios.sevetlidis,valerio.giuffrida}@imtlucca.it
[2] School of Engineering, University of Edinburgh, Edinburgh, UK
s.tsaftaris@ed.ac.uk

Abstract. The synthesis of medical images is an intensity transformation of a given modality in a way that represents an acquisition with a different modality (in the context of MRI this represents the synthesis of images originating from different MR sequences). Most methods follow a patch-based approach, which is computationally inefficient during synthesis and requires some sort of 'fusion' to synthesize a whole image from patch-level results. In this paper, we present a whole image synthesis approach that relies on deep neural networks. Our architecture resembles those of encoder-decoder networks, which aims to synthesize a source MRI modality to an other target MRI modality. The proposed method is computationally fast, it doesn't require extensive amounts of memory, and produces comparable results to recent patch-based approaches.

Keywords: Image synthesis · MRI · Stacked neural network · Autoencoder

1 Introduction

Image synthesis has attracted a lot of attention lately due to exciting potential applications in medical imaging, since synthesized images for example may be used to impute missing images (in a large database, e.g., as in [22]), to derive images lacking a particular pathology, which is not present in the input modality (for detection purposes, e.g., [29]), to increase the resolution of input data (e.g., [14]), to perform attenuation correction (e.g., [3]), and others.

Early works in image synthesis followed a physics driven approach [6,26], using the physical models of the acquisition, they applied directly the transformation on images. Polynomial mixture models like in [7] or non parametric approaches like joint histogram [15] optimized a transformation map from a single image into an other modality. The idea of using raw data directly within the synthesis started with [20], which utilized non-local pair-wise interactions in a super-resolution context. This idea, together with the pioneering work in image

---

V. Sevetlidis and M.V. Giuffrida—Equal contribution.

© Springer International Publishing AG 2016
S.A. Tsaftaris et al. (Eds.): SASHIMI 2016, LNCS 9968, pp. 127–137, 2016.
DOI: 10.1007/978-3-319-46630-9_13

analogies [8], spawned several works in data driven synthesis. Typically this happens in a supervised fashion[1], where pairs of images (or volumes) corresponding to the same subject but of different modality are being used. Modality can refer to different physical imaging schemes such as CT, MRI, US, PET but also within an MRI context to distinguish images acquired by different sequences for example T_1 vs. T_2. Typically, these approaches break the available training data in patches and construct a database linking patches among each other. During inference, the query image is used to find similar in appearance patches in the database and the synthesized modality is generated by fusing the matched patches. For example, similar to label propagation [2,19,28], the authors in [11,29] approached the problem of synthesis with nearest neighbors patch-matching. Similarly, the work in [4] used a generative model of image synthesis using a probabilistic framework. These methods are simple but they require a lot of memory and computational time during inference. Also, the process of how individual patch results are fused together into a final image may have undesired effects. Blending the patches by using simple averaging leads to smoothing, and approaches which they use only the central pixel of the patches, only they may lead to noisy and locally discontinuous outcomes.

One approach which at least reduces the computational cost at run-time during inference, is treating the image synthesis as a regression [23]. A mapping is learned to relate features around a local neighborhood from the input modality to a pixel in the target modality, for example with the use of a neural network [23]. Another example is in [14], where they learn the joint probability between high resolution and low resolution patches, for the purpose of super resolution. Similarly, coupled sparse representation [21], and random forest approaches [1,12] use patches from the source images for regression analysis, in order to perform the synthesis of a target modality. These approaches are usually less computationally intensive, because they usually store only the mapping function. Also, depending on the approach, inference can be simple, but still they operate at the patch or pixel level.

In this paper, motivated by the above shortcomings, we introduce a new deep learning approach which we term *Deep Encoder-Decoder Image Synthesizer* (DEDIS). Compared to patch-based methods, DEDIS retains low computational/memory requirements, and it is capable of predicting the *whole* image directly, and hence it provides homogeneous and sharp synthetic images. This multi-output regression is achieved based on a deep encoder network which draws inspiration from Stacked Denoising Autoencoders [16]. Essentially, DEDIS (with its architecture shown in Fig. 1), given an input source image, provides as an output a synthesized modality of the same size as the input. Our training input consists of input-output pairs of imaging data. To prevent over-fitting, which can occur when networks are deep, we use dataset augmentation and bottleneck middle layers, which they compress and find useful representations [25]. To initialize the network with reasonable weights (filters), ensuring better convergence,

---

[1] There is also the recent exciting unsupervised work by [24], however for ease of introducing the reader to the topic this is not discussed here.

we rely on layer-wise pre-training with Restricted Boltzmann Machine (RBM), because it has been shown in the literature the relationship between RBM and Autoencoders [13]. The fine tuning of the complete network is obtained via back-propagation such that the filters are being updated, in order the reconstructed (synthesized) modality to match the desired output.

To evaluate our method we used the SISS brain multimodal MR dataset from the ISLES 2015 workshop [17] and we compared with a classical patch-based approach [29]. Overall, our findings show that the proposed method is capable of preserving anatomical details. and the quantitative analysis, which has been measured with classical measures according to the literature, showed similar performance amongst the two. DEDIS can synthesize a full volume in ~0.63 s.

The rest of the paper is organized as follows. In Sect. 2, the proposed DEDIS architecture is described alongside its pre-training and inference steps. Section 3 presents experimental results, while Sect. 4 offers conclusions.

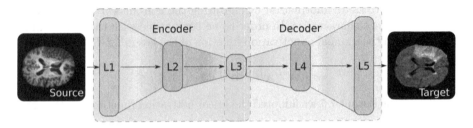

Fig. 1. The proposed DEDIS network, which is able to synthesize a source image into the target modality. Pre-training is performed using Restricted Boltzmann Machines. The GB-RBM and the BB-RBM are being used greedily to initialize the weights between *L1*, *L2*, and *L3*, using the source modality images. The same protocol is followed for *L5*, *L4*, and *L3*, but instead with the use of the target modality.

2   Deep Encoder-Decoder Image Synthesizer (DEDIS)

Our image synthesis approach relies essentially on finding a mapping between an input image I_S and a desired I_T, which they correspond to the source and target modalities. Assuming that the sizes are identical, this is a multi-input multi-output regression problem. To find this mapping we rely on a Deep Neural Network architecture. We present sequentially its description, the pre-training of the layer weights, the fine-tuning of the network parameters, and finally we describe inference at test time.

2.1   The DEDIS Architecture

The architecture we devised is inspired by *Stacked Autoencoders* [16] and it is shown in Fig. 1. It can be easily trained in supervised fashion to learn the non-linear mapping, which relates two modalities.

Our goal is to find the relationship which associates the representations of two different modalities. Thus, we added an intermediate layer between the encoding/decoding layers, in order to observe this latent relationship. Specifically, the input layer $L1$ receives a full slice of a 2D image $\mathbf{I_S}$ from the source modality's volume acquisition. Then, $L2$ and $L3$ aim to "encode" the input. Observe that, as depicted in Fig. 1, they have lower dimensions. This is deliberate, as by adding this bottleneck improves regularization and reduces over-fitting [25]. The subsequent layers $L4$ and $L5$ essentially "decode" the information coming from previous layers, providing at the output the desired target modality.

The entire set of parameters in our network is $\Theta = \{\mathbf{W}^{(l)}, \mathbf{b}^{(l)}\}$, for all $1 \leq l \leq 4$, where l denotes the number of the layer, $\mathbf{W}^{(l)}$ is the weight matrix that connects two consecutive layers l and $l+1$, and $\mathbf{b}^{(l)}$ denotes the bias term. These parameters are being optimized using the back-propagation algorithm [27].

Particularly, we use back-propagation to optimize the whole network with pre-trained weights, as described below, in order to improve the correspondence between the source and target modality. Moreover, the back-propagation will allow the layer to share information by capturing the non-linearity that the pre-training could not characterize. In order to be compatible with the pre-training phase, we used the sigmoid as activation function of the layers $L2$-$L4$ (cf. Eq. (1)) namely,

$$\mathbf{a}^{l+1} = \sigma\left(\mathbf{W}^{(l)}\mathbf{a}^{(l)} + \mathbf{b}^{(l)}\right), \qquad 1 \leq l \leq 3, \tag{1}$$

whereas for the output $L5$ we adopted the linear activation function (cf. Eq. (2)),

$$\hat{\mathbf{I}}_{\mathbf{T}} = \mathbf{W}^{(4)}\mathbf{a}^{(4)} + \mathbf{b}^{(4)}. \tag{2}$$

Note that $\mathbf{a}^{(1)} \equiv \mathbf{I_S}$, specifically it is a slice of the source modality. These functions are differentiable and their derivative is known and easy to compute. The back-propagation error optimizes the parameters in Θ by minimizing the following cost function

$$J(\mathbf{I_S}, \mathbf{I_T}; \Theta) = \frac{1}{2}\|\hat{\mathbf{I}}_{\mathbf{T}} - \mathbf{I_T}\|_2^2, \tag{3}$$

where $\hat{\mathbf{I}}_{\mathbf{T}}$ is a function of the parameters Θ (feed-forward step).

2.2   Pre-training

Learning the mapping of two different modalities is a complex task. To assist our network architecture in optimizing the parameters, we initialize the weights with pre-trained ones. For this purpose, we pre-train the weights per-layer relying on the unsupervised learning power of Restricted Boltzmann Machine (RBM) [10], leveraging the tight relationship between Autoencoders and RBM [13]. Specifically, we adopted a *Gaussian-Bernoulli RBM* (GB-RBM) [5] to pre-train the weights and the bias connecting $L1$ and $L2$. Then, the output of this network is provided to a *Bernoulli-Bernoulli RBM* (BB-RBM) [9] that pre-trains the connections between $L2$ and $L3$. The same process is being followed for the layers $L4$ and $L5$, as well as for the layers $L3$ and $L4$, while here there are being used as training images the ones of the target modality instead. Once the parameters in Θ are pre-trained, we perform the fine-tuning and we train the network with back-propagation as discussed previously.

2.3   Inference

At test time, we provide an image from the source modality to the layer $L1$ and we perform a single feed-forward step into the entire network. The activations on the layer $L5$ are the output of the network and represent the actual synthetic image in the target modality domain. This demonstrates the simplicity and elegance of this holistic approach to synthesis.

Retaining this network requires less memory than retaining a patch database. While training the network is computationally demanding this happens offline. Performing a feed-forward step at inference is significantly more efficient than the nearest neighbours being used in most patch-based approaches.

3   Experiments and Results

In this section, we evaluate the proposed deep neural network approach by generating T2 scans from T1 scans and DWI scans from T2. We follow evaluation settings and metrics that there were recently had been used in [29]. Furthermore, we compare with the patch-based method of [29].

Dataset: We used the SISS dataset from the ISLES 2015 workshop [17]. Specifically, we used the training dataset, which includes 28 subjects. For every subject, there are images of four modalities: T1, T2, VFlair, and DWI, of dimension approximately $230 \times 230 \times 150$. We rely on this dataset since it has been already preprocessed and the subjects are co-registered. If we had chosen another popular dataset. It would be necessary to perform various steps of pre-processing. The pre-processing could vary according to the implementation and the tools might had been used, eventually leading to potential bias and inability to compare directly among papers in the same area.

Model of Comparison: Modality Propagation (MP) [29] is a patch-based method for medical image synthesis, which is commonly used for comparisons, even in the most recent papers which use neural networks [23,24]. This method comprises of a database with paired images of different modalities. Assuming fine alignment between the input image and those in the database, the synthesis of the target image is being made through patch matching nearest neighbor search. To reduce the search space within the database, the method uses techniques to reduce both the population and the area searched around a specific point location. Additionally, the method introduces an iterative regularization term that takes advantage of the produced synthetic image. We implemented this method de novo and we used the same parameters as the authors.

Preprocessing: The portion occupied by brain matter is less than the actual size of the image and this does not affect our learning. For a more efficient computation, we crop all the images using the biggest bounding box that encloses

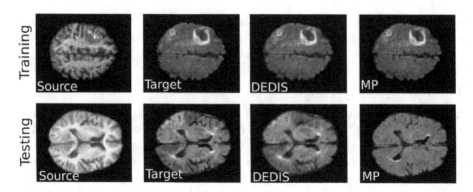

Fig. 2. Example of reconstruction with the proposed DEDIS network and Modality Propagation (MP) [29]. In this picture, we have a training (first row) and testing subject (second row). The first column shows the source modality images T1, the second column shows the ground-truth image in the target modality. Then, the third column shows the output of our DNN. The last column is the result from MP.

the area covered by the brain across all the subjects. Subsequently, plane slices have been rescaled by half. Even though our method is computationally fast, our implementation of Modality Propagation is not. Thus, to keep the comparison fair we used the same image sizes for both methods. After these operations, all the images have dimension 79×100. Then, each image is individually normalized, by removing the mean and dividing by the standard deviation of the intensities within the image. To increase the data to train on and add some bilateral invariance, we augmented the dataset. The augmentation have been made by flipping all training data across the horizontal line, since the brain is almost symmetric for healthy subjects along the interhemispheric fissure, doubling the dataset size.

Experimental Setup: We selected the size of our network as multiples of the input layers, which corresponds to the number of pixels within one slice after preprocessing. The chosen architecture is summarized as follows: [7900, 2250, 1125, 2250, 7900]. Other configurations, e.g. over-complete setup scenarios, that is the layers in between ($L2$ and $L3$) were bigger than the input layer, induced redundant information and were prone to over-fitting. In the other hand, when we reduced the dimensions of the inner layers, we observed that the network had learned better representations.

We adopted 7-fold cross-validation, in which 24 subjects had been used for training, and the remaining 4 had been used for testing. The training, included only the slices containing brain matter. We iterated the pre-training of RBMs with 200 epochs, whereas the fine-tuning had been performed with 300 iterations. We built our network with the *Deep Learning Toolbox*[2] and thus our code had been based mostly in Matlab. We ran our experiments on an Intel Xeon 3.5 GHz CPU with a GeForce GTX Titan X GPU running in Debian.

---

[2] Freely available at https://github.com/rasmusbergpalm/DeepLearnToolbox [18]. We modified the current implementation to enable also GPU (CUDA) processing.

Table 1. Experimental results of our proposed method, when it is trained from modality T1 to VFlair, input and target modality respectively. We compared test results with Modality Propagation [29]. Values are *mean (std)*.

	DEDIS		Modality Propagation [29]	
	Training	Testing	Training	Testing
M.A.E	0.1261 (0.0558)	0.2400 (0.0490)	-	0.1196 (0.0467)
M.S.E	0.0696 (0.0863)	0.2212 (0.1226)	-	0.1501 (0.1151)
Norm. X-Corr	0.9652 (0.0454)	0.8886 (0.0652)	-	0.9292 (0.0559)

Table 2. Similar to Table 1 but synthesizing T2 from DWI.

	DEDIS		Modality Propagation [29]	
	Training	Testing	Training	Testing
M.A.E	0.0544 (0.0123)	0.2697 (0.2898)	-	0.1456 (0.0441)
M.S.E	0.0118 (0.0255)	0.2898 (0.1360)	-	0.2008 (0.1897)
Norm. X-Corr	0.9940 (0.0145)	0.8573 (0.0750)	-	0.9096 (0.0784)

Evaluation Metrics: As commonly done by other works in this area, we adopted three different metrics to quantitatively evaluate our method: (i) mean absolute error (M.A.E.), (ii) mean squared error (M.S.E.), and (iii) normalized cross-correlation (Norm. X-Corr), where for the first two the lower the better and for the third the higher the better.

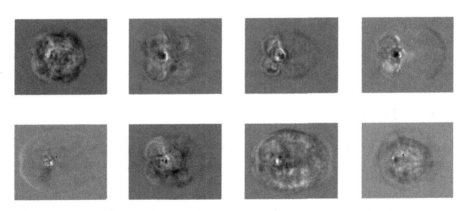

Fig. 3. The first 8 filters from the weight matrix $W^{(1)}$ connecting *L1* and *L2* of DEDIS after 300 iterations of fine-tuning.

Results and Discussion: In Fig. 2 we show a visual example of synthesized images using DEDIS, where images of T1 were used as source modality and as target modality the corresponding VFlair contrast. In this example, we show images from the training and also testing, where both approaches (DEDIS and MP) have not seen the input image. In the last two columns we present estimated instances of DNN and the MP respectively. The first and second row show training and testing examples accordingly. The proposed method is able to preserve anatomical details (e.g., cortical folds), both in training and testing examples. This is particularly evident in the testing case: the MP was unable to reconstruct fully the lateral ventricle, most likely attributed to the large cell size we used. This demonstrates the benefit of using our whole image approach to synthesis. In fact, as Fig. 3 shows, filters learned by DEDIS, preserve both anatomical and contrast related information.

Quantitative results across the study population and the cross-validation are reported in Table 1, for VFlair synthesis with T1 as input, and in Table 2 for T2 synthesis given DWI as input. We show training and testing performance for DEDIS, as well as the testing error of MP [29]. As done in [23] we do not report the training performance of MP as it is not applicable. Whilst training results are above MP, at testing we are slightly lower. Perhaps our network still over-fits and strategies to mitigate that in the future could improve performance.

Critically though, we do gain in computational performance at inference. DEDIS takes 0.004 seconds per slice at test time[3], orders of magnitude less than the 80 seconds required by MP. The implications of the k-NN search required by MP within the image database and the local patch-based search are evident. Note that the search time scales (albeit linearly) with the size of the database (or the window) and as such the more the images in the database the more the computational time is in demand. In contrast, our approach synthesizes the whole image while at the same time, since it is independent of database size for inference.

Similar argument holds for memory size requirements. Our network at these settings occupies 300 MB in memory, whilst MP 800 MB, almost 3-fold more. As database size increases, e.g. the number of training images increases, memory requirements for MP increase, whereas ours remains the same.

4   Conclusion

In this paper, we introduced a Deep Neural Network that can learn to synthesise a modality. Our network is optimized via back-propagation and it needs a set of data belonging to the input and target modality, as it is illustrated in Fig. 1. We pre-trained the network using Restricted Boltzmann Machines, which learned the pair-wise weight matrices that there were fine-tuned at later stage. Example-based methods are expensive both in time and memory resources. Instead our

---

[3] We use only the CPU and not GPU to permit fair comparison with our MP implementation which does not use GPU.

approach, which we termed DEDIS, synthesizes whole images treating the problem as a multi-output regression. Overall, we show that our method gives comparable results with a patch-based method (Modality Propagation) [29] when trained on a preprocessed dataset. But our method is almost 1000 times faster. Being fast is important when for example the synthesis method will be used within a data imputation pipeline of a very large database (e.g., biobank).

Relying on the advantages of the proposed network, the future orientation to explore is the one enabling DEDIS architecture to synthesize a whole volume at once, instead of slice by slice.

Acknowledgement. We thank NVIDIA Inc. for providing us with a Titan X GPU used for our experiments.

References

1. Alexander, D.C., Zikic, D., Zhang, J., Zhang, H., Criminisi, A.: Image quality transfer via random forest regression: applications in diffusion MRI. In: Golland, P., Hata, N., Barillot, C., Hornegger, J., Howe, R. (eds.) MICCAI 2014, Part III. LNCS, vol. 8675, pp. 225–232. Springer, Heidelberg (2014)
2. Artaechevarria, X., Munoz-Barrutia, A., Ortiz-de-Solórzano, C.: Combination strategies in multi-atlas image segmentation: application to brain MR data. IEEE Trans. Med. Imaging **28**(8), 1266–1277 (2009)
3. Burgos, N., Cardoso, M.J., Thielemans, K., Modat, M., Pedemonte, S., Dickson, J., Barnes, A., Ahmed, R., Mahoney, C.J., Schott, J.M., et al.: Attenuation correction synthesis for hybrid PET-MR scanners: application to brain studies. IEEE Trans. Med. Imaging **33**(12), 2332–2341 (2014)
4. Cardoso, M.J., Sudre, C.H., Modat, M., Ourselin, S.: Template-based multimodal joint generative model of brain data. In: Ourselin, S., Alexander, D.C., Westin, C.-F., Cardoso, M.J. (eds.) IPMI 2015. LNCS, vol. 9123, pp. 17–29. Springer, Heidelberg (2015). doi:10.1007/978-3-319-19992-4_2
5. Cho, K.H., Ilin, A., Raiko, T.: Improved learning of Gaussian-Bernoulli restricted Boltzmann machines. In: Honkela, T., Duch, W., Girolami, M., Kaski, S. (eds.) ICANN 2011. LNCS, vol. 6791, pp. 10–17. Springer, Heidelberg (2011). doi:10.1007/978-3-642-21735-7_2
6. Fischl, B., Salat, D.H., van der Kouwe, A.J., Makris, N., Ségonne, F., Quinn, B.T., Dale, A.M.: Sequence-independent segmentation of magnetic resonance images. Neuroimage **23**, S69–S84 (2004)
7. Guimond, A., Roche, A., Ayache, N., Meunier, J.: Three-dimensional multimodal brain warping using the demons algorithm and adaptive intensity corrections. IEEE Trans. Med. Imaging **20**(1), 58–69 (2001)
8. Hertzmann, A., Jacobs, C.E., Oliver, N., Curless, B., Salesin, D.H.: Image analogies. In: Proceedings of the 28th Annual Conference on Computer Graphics and Interactive Techniques, pp. 327–340. ACM (2001)
9. Hinton, G.E.: Training products of experts by minimizing contrastive divergence. Neural Comput. **14**(8), 1771–1800 (2002)
10. Hinton, G.E., Osindero, S., Teh, Y.W.: A fast learning algorithm for deep belief nets. Neural Comput. **18**(7), 1527–1554 (2006)

11. Iglesias, J.E., Konukoglu, E., Zikic, D., Glocker, B., Van Leemput, K., Fischl, B.: Is synthesizing MRI contrast useful for inter-modality analysis? In: Mori, K., Sakuma, I., Sato, Y., Barillot, C., Navab, N. (eds.) MICCAI 2013, Part I. LNCS, vol. 8149, pp. 631–638. Springer, Heidelberg (2013)

12. Jog, A., Roy, S., Carass, A., Prince, J.L.: Magnetic resonance image synthesis through patch regression. In: IEEE 10th ISBI, pp. 350–353. IEEE (2013)

13. Kamyshanska, H., Memisevic, R.: The potential energy of an autoencoder. IEEE Trans. PAMI **37**(6), 1261–1273 (2015)

14. Konukoglu, E., van der Kouwe, A., Sabuncu, M.R., Fischl, B.: Example-based restoration of high-resolution magnetic resonance image acquisitions. In: Mori, K., Sakuma, I., Sato, Y., Barillot, C., Navab, N. (eds.) MICCAI 2013, Part I. LNCS, vol. 8149, pp. 131–138. Springer, Heidelberg (2013)

15. Kroon, D.J., Slump, C.H.: MRI modalitiy transformation in demon registration. In: IEEE International Symposium on Biomedical Imaging: From Nano to Macro, ISBI 2009, pp. 963–966. IEEE (2009)

16. Larochelle, H., Erhan, D., Courville, A., Bergstra, J., Bengio, Y.: An empirical evaluation of deep architectures on problems with many factors of variation. In: Proceedings of the 24th ICML, pp. 473–480 (2007)

17. Maier, O., Wilms, M., von der Gablentz, J., Krämer, U.M., Münte, T.F., Handels, H.: Extra tree forests for sub-acute ischemic stroke lesion segmentation in MR sequences. J. Neurosci. Methods **240**, 89–100 (2015)

18. Palm, R.B.: Prediction as a candidate for learning deep hierarchical models of data. Master's thesis (2012)

19. Rohlfing, T., Russakoff, D.B., Maurer, C.R.: Expectation maximization strategies for multi-atlas multi-label segmentation. In: Taylor, C.J., Noble, J.A. (eds.) IPMI 2003. LNCS, vol. 2732, pp. 210–221. Springer, Heidelberg (2003)

20. Rousseau, F.: Brain hallucination. In: Forsyth, D., Torr, P., Zisserman, A. (eds.) ECCV 2008, Part I. LNCS, vol. 5302, pp. 497–508. Springer, Heidelberg (2008)

21. Roy, S., Carass, A., Prince, J.: A compressed sensing approach for MR tissue contrast synthesis. In: Székely, G., Hahn, H.K. (eds.) IPMI 2011. LNCS, vol. 6801, pp. 371–383. Springer, Heidelberg (2011)

22. Tulder, G., Bruijne, M.: Why does synthesized data improve multi-sequence classification? In: Navab, N., Hornegger, J., Wells, W.M., Frangi, A.F. (eds.) MICCAI 2015. LNCS, vol. 9349, pp. 531–538. Springer, Heidelberg (2015). doi:10.1007/978-3-319-24553-9_65

23. Nguyen, H., Zhou, K., Vemulapalli, R.: Cross-domain synthesis of medical images using efficient location-sensitive deep network. In: Navab, N., Hornegger, J., Wells, W.M., Frangi, A.F. (eds.) MICCAI 2015. LNCS, vol. 9349, pp. 677–684. Springer, Heidelberg (2015). doi:10.1007/978-3-319-24553-9_83

24. Vemulapalli, R., Van Nguyen, H., Zhou, S.K.: Unsupervised cross-modal synthesis of subject-specific scans. In: Proceedings of the IEEE ICCV, pp. 630–638 (2015)

25. Vincent, P., Larochelle, H., Lajoie, I., Bengio, Y., Manzagol, P.A.: Stacked denoising autoencoders: learning useful representations in a deep network with a local denoising criterion. J. Mach. Learn. Res. **11**, 3371–3408 (2010)

26. Wein, W., Brunke, S., Khamene, A., Callstrom, M.R., Navab, N.: Automatic CT-ultrasound registration for diagnostic imaging and image-guided intervention. Med. Image Anal. **12**(5), 577–585 (2008)

27. Williams, D., Hinton, G.: Learning representations by back-propagating errors. Nature **323**, 533–536 (1986)

28. Wolz, R., Chu, C., Misawa, K., Mori, K., Rueckert, D.: Multi-organ abdominal CT segmentation using hierarchically weighted subject-specific atlases. In: Ayache, N., Delingette, H., Golland, P., Mori, K. (eds.) MICCAI 2012, Part I. LNCS, vol. 7510, pp. 10–17. Springer, Heidelberg (2012)
29. Ye, D.H., Zikic, D., Glocker, B., Criminisi, A., Konukoglu, E.: Modality propagation: coherent synthesis of subject-specific scans with data-driven regularization. In: Mori, K., Sakuma, I., Sato, Y., Barillot, C., Navab, N. (eds.) MICCAI 2013, Part I. LNCS, vol. 8149, pp. 606–613. Springer, Heidelberg (2013)

Automated Quality Assessment of Cardiac MR Images Using Convolutional Neural Networks

Le Zhang[1]([✉]), Ali Gooya[1], Bo Dong[1], Rui Hua[1], Steffen E. Petersen[2],
Pau Medrano-Gracia[3], and Alejandro F. Frangi[1]

[1] Centre for Computational Imaging and Simulation Technologies
in Biomedicine (CISTIB), Department of Electronic and Electrical Engineering,
University of Sheffield, Sheffield, UK
le.zhang@sheffield.ac.uk
[2] William Harvey Research Institute, Queen Mary University of London, London, UK
[3] Anatomy with Medical Imaging, University of Auckland, Auckland, New Zealand

Abstract. Image quality assessment (IQA) is crucial in large-scale population imaging so that high-throughput image analysis can extract meaningful imaging biomarkers at scale. Specifically, in this paper, we address a seemingly basic yet unmet need: the automatic detection of missing (apical and basal) slices in Cardiac Magnetic Resonance Imaging (CMRI) scans, which is currently performed by tedious visual assessment. We cast the problem as classification tasks, where the bottom and top slices are tested for the presence of typical basal and apical patterns. Inspired by the success of deep learning methods, we train Convolutional Neural Networks (CNN) to construct a set of discriminative features. We evaluated our approach on a subset of the UK Biobank datasets. Precision and Recall figures for detecting missing apical slice (MAS) (81.61 % and 88.73 %) and missing basal slice (MBS) (74.10 % and 88.75 %) are superior to other state-of-the-art deep learning architectures. Cross-dataset experiments show the generalization ability of our approach.

1 Introduction

Cardiac Magnetic Resonance Imaging (CMRI) can not only reflect anatomic information of the heart but also provide physiological information associated with cardiovascular diseases. Although low image quality can be minimized by careful design of the imaging acquisition protocols, it cannot be fully avoided; particularly in large-scale imaging studies, where data is acquired at different imaging sites, across subjects with a diverse constitution and at a big pace [5].

On the other hand, few objective guidelines exist, clinical or otherwise, that establish what constitutes, in general, a good image and, in particular, a good CMRI study [6]. To ensure that the quality of data collected in such imaging studies is maintained, Image Quality Assessment (IQA) is crucial. Surprisingly, IQA is still usually carried out by visual inspection of the images which can be exhaustive, costly, subjective, error prone, and time consuming [1]. Thus, Automatic IQA (AIQA) methods are required to detect deviations from the desired

© Springer International Publishing AG 2016
S.A. Tsaftaris et al. (Eds.): SASHIMI 2016, LNCS 9968, pp. 138–145, 2016.
DOI: 10.1007/978-3-319-46630-9_14

quality, intervene to correct problems in data collection as soon as possible, and discard low-quality images, whose analysis would otherwise impair any aggregated statistics over the cohort. Additionally, *a priori* and objective knowledge on image quality of a given dataset (and possibly the type of artifact affecting it) could assist in choosing the most appropriate image analysis method to be used. This paves the way to "quality-aware image analysis" [16].

In multimedia, AIQA is a mature research field and usually concerned with detecting specific image distortions [15,17]. Unfortunately, most of these methods cannot be directly translated to medical imaging due to different properties in image statistics and the more complex nature of image artifacts [9]. Thus, AIQA remains as a relatively unexplored research area in medical imaging. It is acknowledged that lack of basal and/or apical slices is probably the most common problem affecting image quality in CMRI and has a major impact on the accuracy of quantitative parameters of cardiac performance [7]. In this paper, we mainly focus on short axis (SA) cine MRI. More specifically, we aim to identify missing apical slice (MAS) or missing basal slice (MBS). To address this problem, we are motivated by the success of deep learning techniques and, in particular, Convolutional Neural Network (CNN) [2,4]. They can achieve effective generalization properties, when applied to complex classification problems such identifying missing SA slices.

To the best of our knowledge, this is the first paper tackling the problem of detecting the missing slices in CMRI. Apart from introducing a new application for the CNN's, and addressing a pressing need, we propose an effective strategy for their training. In practice, the lack of sufficient number of CMR data sets with MBS/MAS deficiencies imposes a severe class imbalance problem. To alleviate this issue, only the bottom and top SA slices are examined to ensure the full coverage of the heart. This allows us to use the middle slices as non BS/AS training samples. We present results for various depth of the networks, and identify the optimal number of the layers. We also compare our framework with an array of other deep learning methods such as Deep Boltzman Machines (DBM) and Stack Auto Encoders (SAE), and show its better performance. In the next section, we briefly introduce the architecture of our networks and provide the specification of our data sets. We then present our classification results and conclude the paper in the final section.

2 Methodology

2.1 Convolutional Neural Network for Feature Learning

As mentioned, we are interested in detecting missing apical and basal slices in CMRI data sets. To this end, for each cardiac subject, the top and bottom SA slices in the scan are classified using two CNNs, each particularly trained for detecting missing slices in basal or apical positions. Each CNN is composed of alternating convolutional and sampling layers, and one fully-connected output layer. Figure 1 shows the configuration of CNNs with total number of 5 layers

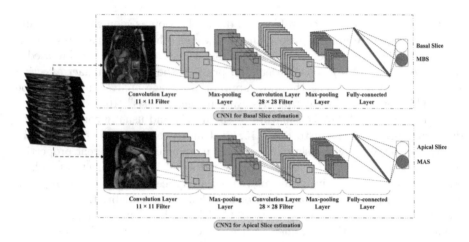

Fig. 1. Overview of our proposed deep learning model for cardiac MRI quality assessment. The CNNs are composed of 5 layers: four multi perceptron convolutional layers plus one fully-connected layer. The bottom and top SA slices are examined individually.

(showing overall the best classification performance). Here, we briefly review the various components in the proposed CNNs with a further detail.

Convolutional Feature Layers: Convolutional layers implement kernels that are used to detect discriminative features from input images [11]. During the training, these kernels are optimized to compute some salient features (such as edges, corners, etc.) that are relevant for discrimination of the observed categorical variables. We define $\mathbf{X}_i^{l-1}$ and $\mathbf{X}_i^l$ as input and output ith feature map of the lth layer. Let $m \times n$ and $k \times k$ be the size of input maps and the convolution kernel for layer l. With this setting of parameters, we can get N output maps with the size $(m - k + 1) \times (n - k + 1)$. The output of a convolutional layer l is given by

$$\mathbf{X}_j^l = f\left(\sum_{i \in M_j} \mathbf{X}_i^{l-1} * \mathbf{k}_{ij}^l + b_j^l \right), \tag{1}$$

where $\mathbf{k}_{ij}^l$ denotes the convolution kernel linking the ith input to the jth output map; b_j^l is the bias vector for the jth output-feature-map of lth layer; f is the activating function $1/(1 + e^{-x})$, and M_j is the input feature map in the former layer.

Sampling Layers: These layers are designed to reduce the number of kernel parameters, minimize the computational complexity, and make the features robust to zoom, shift and rotation. The output of convolution layers are divided into sub-regions having the size of $w \times h$ pixels. Then, each output pixel of a sampling layer is defined as the maximum value in the corresponding input sub-region. These operations can be formulated using the following relationship

$$\mathbf{X}_j^l = f\left(\beta_j^l down\left(\mathbf{X}_j^{l-1}\right) + b_j^l\right),\qquad(2)$$

where $down(\cdot)$ symbolizes the down sampling function; j, l, β and b denote the feature map index, the layer number, the weighting coefficients, and the bias vector, respectively.

Softmax classifiers: To predict the final labels, the CNN detected low-dimensional features are used to train softmax classifiers. Given the feature vector $\mathbf{x}^{(i)}$, we computed the posterior probabilities for $k = 1, 2, ..., K$ classes using

$$p(y^{(i)} = k | \mathbf{x}^{(i)}) = \frac{e^{\boldsymbol{\theta}_j^T \mathbf{x}^{(i)}}}{\sum_{l=1}^{K} e^{\boldsymbol{\theta}_l^T \mathbf{x}^{(i)}}},\qquad(3)$$

where $\boldsymbol{\theta}$ denotes the parameters of the softmax classifier, obtained from the pre-trained CNN network. The neural network was trained over 3 days for 100 epochs with a fixed learning rate 0.01. In the framwork, Rectified Linear Unit (ReLU) [8] was used as a activation function, and back-propagation technique [14] was used for adjusting weights of connections in the network. To test a single image with size 100×100, it only took approximate 0.2 s.

3   Results

3.1   Pre-processing and Data Description

To minimize the influence from the background region, a global mask covering the heart and its vicinity was employed prior to training. We define three classes of qualities in this paper: MAS, MBS, and no missing slices (normal). The last label is obtained by logical combination of the results from the MAS and MBS classifiers. The criterion used to determine a correct basal slice position is to verify if the left ventricular outflow tract (LVOT) is observable at the end-systolic phase [7].

Table 1. The average precision and recall rates of each type of missing slices using different deep learning models.

	Precision rate			Recall rate		
	MAS	MBS	Normal	MAS	MBS	Normal
SAE	79.08 %	68.63 %	78.54 %	88.48 %	88.72 %	88.15 %
DBM	66.67 %	70.09 %	71.47 %	88.38 %	88.71 %	88.32 %
3-CNNs	80.77 %	70.92 %	78.43 %	88.52 %	88.75 %	87.85 %
5-CNNs	81.61 %	74.10 %	79.42 %	88.73 %	88.75 %	88.01 %
7-CNNs	82.19 %	69.43 %	75.06 %	88.62 %	88.76 %	87.01 %

(a)   (b)

Fig. 2. The learned convolution kernels on basal and mid-slices of the first (a), and the second (b) layers of the trained CNN.

We apply our framework to 100 *UK Biobank (UKB)* cardiac MRI pilot data sets. These data sets are obtained by 1.5T MR scanners [12,13] and show overall good quality and no missing slices. Therefore, to generate synthetic deficiencies in the data, we manually removed basal slices from 50 subjects and apical slices from another 50 subjects. For each kind of the considered defect, we randomly selected 80 % of generated data sets as training sets and the left the rest as the testing sets. In order to evaluate our proposed framework's performance, we use the *Precision Rate* $= TP/(TP + FP)$, and the *Recall Rate* $= TP/(TP + FN)$, where TP, FP, and FN denote the number of true positive, false positive, and false negative samples, respectively.

3.2   Evaluation and Comparison to Other Deep Learning Models

We systematically compared our proposed CNNs framework with different types of CNNs architectures and traditional deep learning methods. Table 1 lists the results for different CNNs architectures and other state-of-the-art deep learning methods. As seen, the CNNs with a total number of 5 layers shows the best precision rate and recall rates.

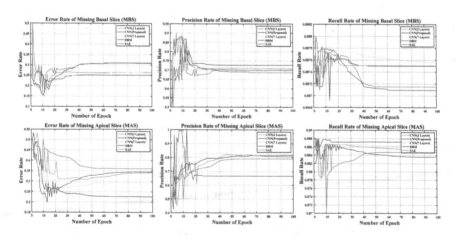

Fig. 3. The distributions of the error, precision, and recall rates over 100 training epochs, showing a superior performance of the CNNs with 5 layers.

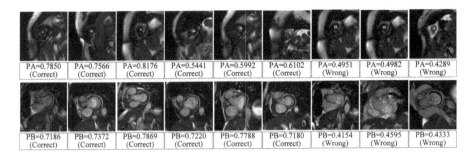

| PA=0.7850 (Correct) | PA=0.7566 (Correct) | PA=0.8176 (Correct) | PA=0.5441 (Correct) | PA=0.5992 (Correct) | PA=0.6102 (Correct) | PA=0.4951 (Wrong) | PA=0.4982 (Wrong) | PA=0.4289 (Wrong) |

| PB=0.7186 (Correct) | PB=0.7372 (Correct) | PB=0.7869 (Correct) | PB=0.7220 (Correct) | PB=0.7788 (Correct) | PB=0.7180 (Correct) | PB=0.4154 (Wrong) | PB=0.4595 (Wrong) | PB=0.4333 (Wrong) |

Fig. 4. Sample test slices and their probability values of being apical (top row) or basal slice (bottom row) are shown. 'PA' means the Probability value of being Apical slice; 'PB' means the Probability value of being Basal slice. The 'correct' and 'wrong' subscripts indicates the classification results.

We also visually examined the learned convolution kernels, and found only a few kernels present structure related appearances. Figure 2 shows the kernels learned for classifying missing basal slices. It is not surprising that some of these kernels show noisy, rather than strong structural and interpretable patterns. This is because our features are trained to be discriminative. In fact, to obtain user interpretable features, generative models such as those outlined in [10] is usually considered.

Furthermore, to demonstrate the convergence behaviour of the compared methods, in Fig. 3 we show the distributions of the error, precision, and recall rates over 100 training epochs. It can be seen the CNNs with 5 layers outperforms other CNN architectures and learning models.

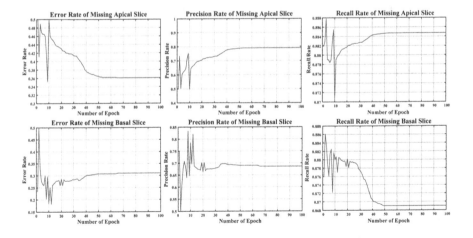

Fig. 5. The error, precision, and recall rates in cross dataset test.

In Fig. 4, a few apical (top row) and basal (bottom row) slices in the test datasets along with their corresponding posterior probability values are shown. We can observe that our framework correctly classifies a few challenging basal slices, but also fails in a few other cases. Furthermore, the basal slices with existing LVOT's indicate higher probability values of being correctly classified. This shows that the training has been successful in capturing the LVOT as a prominent feature in the correctly positioned basal slices.

We also designed a validation experiment with a second collection of CMR data sets to show the generalization ability of our method. To this end, we trained the proposed model using the UK Biobank datasets and tested it using the data sets available from Data Science Bowl Cardiac Challenge data sets [3]. This experiment was repeated for 100 training epochs and the values for error, precision and recall rates are shown in Fig. 5. These results show that our trained convolutional neural network achieves a good generalization efficacy.

4   Conclusion

In this paper, we tackled the problem of identifying the missing apical and basal slices in large imaging databases. We illustrated the concept by applying the method to CMRI studies from the UK Biobank pilot datasets. We designed slice classifiers and learned a set of discriminative features directly by training Convolutional Neural Networks. Casting this problem as a slice classification task, we were able to alleviate the class imbalance issue and effectively train the CNNs using the available data. Different numbers of network layers were examined and compared to other deep learning models (such as Stacked Auto-Encoder and Deep Boltzmann Machines). We showed that a CNN model with 5 layers outperforms the other models. We also validated our model by training the 5-CNNs using UKB pilot datasets and applying them to CMR data sets from Data Science Bowl Cardiac Challenge. The proposed model shows a high consistency with human perception and becomes superior compared to the state-of-the-art methods, showing its high potential. In this paper, the kernel sizes in the convolutional layers of the network were selected somehow arbitrarily. However, in principle these parameters can be optimized by performing exhaustive cross validation experiments. In future, we will further refine the current structure of our model by tuning such parameters.

References

1. Attili, A.K., Schuster, A., Nagel, E., Reiber, J.H., van der Geest, R.J.: Quantification in cardiac MRI: advances in image acquisition and processing. Int. J. Cardiovasc. Imaging **26**(1), 27–40 (2010)
2. Bengio, Y., Courville, A., Vincent, P.: Representation learning: a review and new perspectives. IEEE Trans. Pattern Anal. Mach. Intell. **35**(8), 1798–1828 (2013)
3. Bowl, K.: Data science bowl cardiac challenge data. https://www.kaggle.com/c/second-annual-data-science-bowl/data, Accessed 17 Mar 2016

4. Chen, X., Xu, Y., Yan, S., Wong, D.W.K., Wong, T.Y., Liu, J.: Automatic feature learning for glaucoma detection based on deep learning. In: Navab, N., Hornegger, J., Wells, W.M., Frangi, A.F. (eds.) MICCAI 2015. LNCS, vol. 9351, pp. 669–677. Springer, Heidelberg (2015). doi:10.1007/978-3-319-24574-4_80

5. Ferreira, P.F., Gatehouse, P.D., Mohiaddin, R.H., Firmin, D.N.: Cardiovascular magnetic resonance artefacts. J. Cardiovasc. Magn. Reson. **15**(1), 41 (2013)

6. van der Graaf, A., Bhagirath, P., Ghoerbien, S., Götte, M.: Cardiac magnetic resonance imaging: artefacts for clinicians. Neth. Heart J. **22**(12), 542–549 (2014)

7. Klinke, V., Muzzarelli, S., Lauriers, N., Locca, D., Vincenti, G., Monney, P., Lu, C., Nothnagel, D., Pilz, G., Lombardi, M., et al.: Quality assessment of cardiovascular magnetic resonance in the setting of the european CMR registry: description and validation of standardized criteria. J. Cardiovasc. Magn. Reson. **15**, 55 (2013)

8. Krizhevsky, A., Sutskever, I., Hinton, G.E.: Imagenet classification with deep convolutional neural networks. In: Advances in Neural Information Processing Systems, pp. 1097–1105 (2012)

9. Krupa, K., Bekiesińska-Figatowska, M.: Artifacts in magnetic resonance imaging. Pol. J. Radiol. **80**, 93 (2015)

10. Lee, H., Grosse, R., Ranganath, R., Ng, A.Y.: Convolutional deep belief networks for scalable unsupervised learning of hierarchical representations. In: Proceedings of the 26th Annual International Conference on Machine Learning, pp. 609–616. ACM (2009)

11. Oskoei, M.A., Hu, H.: A Survey on Edge Detection Methods. University of Essex, UK (2010)

12. Petersen, S.E., Matthews, P.M., Bamberg, F., Bluemke, D.A., Francis, J.M., Friedrich, M.G., Leeson, P., Nagel, E., Plein, S., Rademakers, F.E., et al.: Imaging in population science: cardiovascular magnetic resonance in 100,000 participants of uk biobank-rationale, challenges and approaches. J. Cardiovasc. Magn. Reson. **15**(1), 46 (2013)

13. Petersen, S.E., Matthews, P.M., Francis, J.M., Robson, M.D., Zemrak, F., Boubertakh, R., Young, A.A., Hudson, S., Weale, P., Garratt, S., et al.: UK biobanks cardiovascular magnetic resonance protocol. J. Cardiovasc. Magn. Reson. **18**(1), 1 (2016)

14. Rumelhart, D.E., Hinton, G.E., Williams, R.J.: Learning representations by back-propagating errors. Cogn. Model. **5**(3), 1 (1988)

15. Saad, M.A., Bovik, A.C., Charrier, C.: Blind image quality assessment: a natural scene statistics approach in the DCT domain. IEEE Trans. Image Process. **21**(8), 3339–3352 (2012)

16. Wang, Z., Wu, G., Sheikh, H.R., Simoncelli, E.P., Yang, E.H., Bovik, A.C.: Quality-aware images. IEEE Trans. Image Process. **15**(6), 1680–1689 (2006)

17. Xue, W., Mou, X., Zhang, L., Bovik, A.C., Feng, X.: Blind image quality assessment using joint statistics of gradient magnitude and laplacian features. IEEE Trans. Image Process. **23**(11), 4850–4862 (2014)

Patch Based Synthesis of Whole Head MR Images: Application To EPI Distortion Correction

Snehashis Roy[1(✉)], Yi-Yu Chou[1], Amod Jog[2],
John A. Butman[3], and Dzung L. Pham[1]

[1] Center for Neuroscience and Regenerative Medicine,
Henry Jackson Foundation, Bethesda, USA
snehashis.roy@nih.gov
[2] Department of Computer Science,
The Johns Hopkins University, Baltimore, USA
[3] Diagnostic Radiology Department,
National Institute of Health, Bethesda, USA

Abstract. Different magnetic resonance imaging pulse sequences are used to generate image contrasts based on physical properties of tissues, which provide different and often complementary information about them. Therefore multiple image contrasts are useful for multimodal analysis of medical images. Often, medical image processing algorithms are optimized for particular image contrasts. If a desirable contrast is unavailable, contrast synthesis (or modality synthesis) methods try to "synthesize" the unavailable constrasts from the available ones. Most of the recent image synthesis methods generate synthetic brain images, while whole head magnetic resonance (MR) images can also be useful for many applications. We propose an atlas based patch matching algorithm to synthesize T_2-w whole head (including brain, skull, eyes etc.) images from T_1-w images for the purpose of distortion correction of diffusion weighted MR images. The geometric distortion in diffusion MR images due to inhomogeneous B_0 magnetic field are often corrected by non-linearly registering the corresponding $b = 0$ image with zero diffusion gradient to an undistorted T_2-w image. We show that our synthetic T_2-w images can be used as a template in absence of a real T_2-w image. Our patch based method requires multiple atlases with T_1 and T_2 to be registered to a given target T_1. Then for every patch on the target, multiple similar looking matching patches are found on the atlas T_1 images and corresponding patches on the atlas T_2 images are combined to generate a synthetic T_2 of the target. We experimented on image data obtained from 44 patients with traumatic brain injury (TBI), and showed that our synthesized T_2 images produce more accurate distortion correction than a state-of-the-art registration based image synthesis method.

Keywords: Image synthesis · Patches · Distortion correction · EPI

S. Roy—Support for this work included funding from the Department of Defense in the Center for Neuroscience and Regenerative Medicine.

S.A. Tsaftaris et al. (Eds.): SASHIMI 2016, LNCS 9968, pp. 146–156, 2016.
DOI: 10.1007/978-3-319-46630-9_15

1   Introduction

Different contrasts of magnetic resonance (MR) images quantify different information about the underlying tissues. For example, T_1-w and T_2-w images produce signal intensities and contrasts dependent upon the underlying longitudinal (T_1) and transverse (T_2) relaxation times of protons. Therefore the complementary information about tissues observed in multiple MR acquisition sequences can be exploited in multi-contrast image processing algorithms. If one or more image sequences are not available due to limited scan times, artifacts, or poor quality, image synthesis methods have been proposed to generate the missing sequences from the available ones.

Since the MR properties of tissues can be inherently different between two contrasts, it is not possible to exactly replicate a real MR scan (e.g. $PD-$w) from other modalities (e.g. T_1 and T_2-w). Therefore the purpose of current image synthesis methods is to facilitate the existing algorithms by providing a close approximation to a real acquisition. Usually there is a high degree of correlation between T_1 and T_2-w images. Hence one can think of a simple image synthesis as histogram matching, where intensities between two modalities can be transformed by a one-to-one mapping. This does not impart any additional information to the synthesized image beyond what is available in the acquired data. However, most of the current synthesis methods are atlas based. Therefore the synthetic images contain rich information obtained from atlases, which are used to explore the relationship between the available data and the missing contrasts. Synthesis has been shown to improve performance of existing algorithms in the absence of real images [1].

Image synthesis methods are targeted toward various image processing applications. One such application is improving the consistency of acquired images in longitudinal or multi-site studies [2,3]. Synthesizing images for large scale image normalization has been proposed to improve the stability of segmentation algorithms [4,5]. Image synthesis of pathological brains using atlases of normal subjects has also been shown to provide good segmentations of the pathologies, e.g., tumor [6] and lesion segmentation [7,8]. Inter-modality registration has also been improved by enabling more reliable intra-modal registration algorithms via an intermediate synthetic image (e.g., T_1-w to T_2-w [9], CT to ultrasound [10], or MR to CT registration [11]). While registering an MR to a CT image, registration metrics such as mutual information or cross correlation can possess many local minima in the optimization, since the MR and CT intensities are not directly comparable. Therefore first synthesizing a CT from MR, and then registering the synthetic CT to the original CT improves registration accuracy. The idea of having an intermediate synthetic image for single channel registration can be extended to multi-channel registrations [12]. While registering a source T_1 to a target T_2, the accuracy can be improved by synthesizing both source T_2 and target T_1 modalities, and then converting the single channel registration to a multi-channel one using the combination of real and synthetic images. Similar intermediate synthetic T_2-w images can also be used for distortion correction in diffusion imaging [13]. For PET reconstruction from MR-PET scanners, synthetic CT images, generated from the MR, are used for attenuation correction of the PET [14,15]. Other applications of synthesis include super-resolution and artifact correction [16].

In this paper, we propose a patch based synthesis method aimed toward synthesizing whole head images, with the application to distortion correction in diffusion weighted imaging (DWI). Diffusion imaging is based on obtaining T_2-w images using a rapid spatial encoding technique (eco-planar imaging EPI) with and without application of diffusion sensitizing gradients. The strength of the gradient is given by a b-value. Because of the EPI method, these images are sensitive to changes in the B_0 magnetic field which results in spatial distortion. The $b = 0$ image has no diffusion gradient applied, and has contrast comparable to that of a "structural" T_2-w image. The structural image obtained by a spin echo technique compensates for B_0 inhomogeneity and is not distorted. Because the image contrasts of the $b = 0$ and the structural T_2-w are comparable, registration methods can be used to correct for the distortion. Diffusion sensitizing gradients (e.g. $b = 1000$) are applied to generate diffusion weighted images sensitized to diffusion along a particular direction. These images are subject to the distortion due to B_0 inhomogeneity as well as to the distortion resulting from eddy current fields induced by the large diffusion gradients. The geometric distortion from susceptibility in the echoplanar imaging techniques used in DWI are usually corrected by non-linearly registering the $b = 0$ images to a T_2-w structural images. However, in clinical and acute research settings, T_2-w are sometimes not acquired at all to reduce overall scan times. Also, T_2-w images, if available, may not have been generated with geometric parameters suitable for the purposes of distortion correction. For example, thick (5 mm) slices are commonly sufficient in the clinical setting. In the absence of a real high-resolution T_2, synthetic T_2-w images can be used [5,13]. Note that the method in [13] is applicable only for stripped images, while our method can be used to synthesize whole head images as well. Usually first step of distortion correction is a linear registration of $b = 0$ images to a structural image, preferably T_2-w, for a subsequent skull stripping. Therefore synthesis of images with skull are important for optimal registration. Similar to [14], our method also involves registration of multiple atlases, consisting of both T_1 and T_2-w images, to a target T_1. Then we perform patch-matching between the target and the atlases as an additional step. For every patch on the target T_1, we define a neighborhood, and identify multiple similar looking T_1 atlas patches within that neighborhood. Similarity metrics for the matching patches are computed and the corresponding atlas T_2 patches are combined to produce a synthetic T_2 of the subject. Similar ideas of patch matching have been previously used for hippocampus segmentation [17,18], while we extended it to image synthesis problem in this paper. We compared the accuracy of distortion correction with the synthesis method described in [14], called Fusion.

2   Method

Our proposed method uses a combination of atlas registration and patch matching to synthesize T_2-w images from T_1. A patch is defined as a $p \times q \times r$ 3D sub-image around a voxel. We used $3 \times 3 \times 3$ patches in our experiments. An atlas is a pair of images $\{a_1^{(t)}, a_2^{(t)}\}$, where $a_1^{(t)}$s are the T_1 of the tth atlas, and $a_2^{(t)}$s are the atlas T_2-w images, $t = 1, \ldots, T$, T being total number of atlases. All $a_1^{(t)}$ and $a_2^{(t)}$ are assumed to be coregistered. Similarly, a subject is a T_1-w image $\{s_1\}$, while its synthetic T_2-w image is denoted by $\hat{s}_2$. The atlases $a_1^{(t)}$ are first registered to the subject s_1. Although optimal registration of each atlas to the subject would ideally be performed with deformable registration methods, time constraints typically have necessitated the use of affine registrations. However, we used an "approximate" version of the ANTS deformable registration [19] which takes similar time as an affine one. The parameters of the "approximate ANTS" are given in Table 1. Essentially after the affine step, the deformable registration algorithm SyN is applied on a subsampled (by a factor 4) version of the images with a limited number of iterations. This serves three purposes, (1) obvious speed enhancement is observed since the images are subsampled, (2) having TBI subjects in our datasets, limited number of iterations on low resolution images prevent the algorithm from going into local minima in presence of pathologies, (3) having better matching between target and atlases, fewer atlases are required. This version of the deformable registration takes about 2 min between two $1\,mm^3$ images on Intel Xeon 2.80 GHz 20-core processors. On the same images, FLIRT [20] takes about 1.5 min. for an affine registration. We have empirically found that the approximate ANTS provides better matching than affine, while taking similar computation time as other popular affine registration tools. Once the $a_1^{(t)}$s are registered to the s_1, corresponding $a_2^{(t)}$s are also transformed using the same deformations. All images are intensity normalized so that the modes of their white matter intensities are unity. The modes are automatically found by a kernel density estimator [2].

Table 1. Approximate ANTS parameters are shown in this table.

Transform(-t)	Metric(-m)	Iterations(-m)	Smoothing sigma(-s)	Shrink Factor(-f)
Rigid	Mattes	$100 \times 50 \times 25$	$4 \times 2 \times 1$	$3 \times 2 \times 1$
Affine	Mattes	$100 \times 50 \times 25$	$4 \times 2 \times 1$	$3 \times 2 \times 1$
SyN	CC	$100 \times 1 \times 0$	$1 \times 0.5 \times 1$	$4 \times 2 \times 1$

For brevity of notations, we assume that $a_1^{(t)}$ and $a_2^{(t)}$ also denote registered atlases in the subject space. Atlas patches of the T_1 and T_2-w images at the jth voxel are denoted by $\mathbf{a}_1^{(t)}(j)$ and $\mathbf{a}_2^{(t)}(j)$, where $\mathbf{a}_1^{(t)}(j), \mathbf{a}_2^{(t)}(j) \in \mathbb{R}^{d \times 1}$, $d = pqr$. A subject patch at the ith voxel is denoted by $\mathbf{s}_1(i) \in \mathbb{R}^{d \times 1}$. For the ith patch $\mathbf{s}_1(i)$, we define a neighborhood N_i around the ith voxel, and assume that similar looking atlas patches can be found within that neighborhood. Since the atlases and subject are registered, a small $9 \times 9 \times 9$ neighborhood suffices for the purpose [18]. Atlas T_1 and T_2 patches ($\mathbf{a}_1^{(t)}$ and $\mathbf{a}_2^{(t)}$) are collected within the neighborhood N_i from T atlases and combined in two $d \times TL$ matrices $A_1(i)$ and $A_2(i)$, respectively, $L = |N_i|$.

For every $\mathbf{s}_1(i)$, a few similar looking atlas T_1 patches are found from $A_1(i)$ so that their convex combination reconstructs $\mathbf{s}_1(i)$ [2]. This is formulated as,

$$\mathbf{s}_1(i) \approx A_1(i)\mathbf{x}(i), \quad \mathbf{x}(i) \geq \mathbf{0}, \quad \mathbf{x}(i) \in \mathbb{R}^{TL \times 1}, \quad ||\mathbf{x}(i)||_0 \ll TL, \tag{1}$$

where $\mathbf{x}(i)$ is a sparse vector with number of non-zero elements ($||\mathbf{x}(i)||_0$) being much less than its dimension, $\mathbf{0}$ indicates a $TL \times 1$ vector with all elements as 0. Only a few elements of $\mathbf{x}(i)$ are nonzero, indicating a few atlas patches are selected from $A_1(i)$. Eq. 1 is efficiently solved by elastic net regularization [21],

$$\mathbf{x}(i) = \arg \min_{\alpha} ||\mathbf{s}_1(i) - A_1(i)\alpha||_2^2 + \lambda_1 ||\alpha||_1 + \lambda_2 ||\alpha||_2^2, \quad \alpha \geq \mathbf{0}. \tag{2}$$

Both λ_1 and λ_2 are chosen as 0.01. By minimizing both ℓ_1 and ℓ_2 norms of $\mathbf{x}(i)$, the sparsity of $\mathbf{x}(i)$ is maintained as well as all similar looking patches in $A_1(i)$ are given non-zero weights. Once $\mathbf{x}(i)$ is obtained for a subject patch $\mathbf{s}_1(i)$, a corresponding synthetic T_2 patch is generated by $\widehat{\mathbf{s}}_2(i) = A_2(i)\mathbf{x}(i)$. Only the center voxel $\widehat{\mathbf{s}}_2(i)$ is chosen as the ith voxel of the synthetic T_2−w image.

3   Data

We experimented on two datasets with patients having mild to moderate TBI. The first set (called HighRes) contains 32 patients having T_1−w ($1\,\text{mm}^3$, $T_R = 2530\,\text{ms}$, $T_E = 3\,\text{ms}$, $T_I = 1100\,\text{ms}$, flip angle $7°$), high resolution T_2−w ($0.5 \times 0.5 \times 1\,\text{mm}^3$, $T_R = 3200\,\text{ms}$, $T_E = 409\,\text{ms}$, flip angle $120°$), as well as $b = 0$ images ($2 \times 2 \times 2\,\text{mm}^3$). For this set, we assume that a "pseudo" ground truth distortion corrected $b = 0$ is obtained when the distorted one is registered to the original high resolution T_2. The second dataset (called LowRes) also has 32 patients with T_1 ($1\,\text{mm}^3$), lower resolution T_2 ($0.5 \times 0.5 \times 2\,\text{mm}^3$), and blip-up blip-down diffusion weighted images having distorted $b = 0$ images ($2 \times 2 \times 3.5\,\text{mm}^3$), which were corrected by [22]. In this case, we assume the ground truth corrected $b = 0$ to be the one corrected by blip-up blip-down acquisitions [22]. For each of HighRes and LowRes datasets, we arbitrarily chose 10 atlases for Fusion [14], and a subset of $T = 3$ atlases for our synthesis from the same dataset. The similarity metrics, described in the next section, are computed on the remaining 22 subjects from each dataset. Corrected $b = 0$ images using our synthetic T_2 are compared with those using a Fusion [14] synthetic T_2, as well as a baseline $b = 0$ to T_1 registration, when neither T_2 or synthetic T_2 are available.

4   Results

To quantitatively measure the accuracy of synthesis, we use the synthetic images as intermediate steps for distortion correction, where $b = 0$ images are

	T_1-w	T_2-w	FUSION	PROPOSED

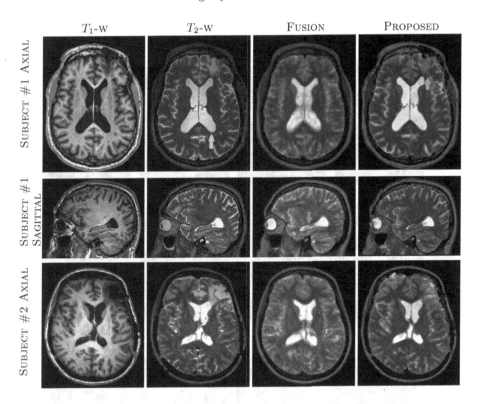

Fig. 1. The top two rows show axial and sagittal views of a patient from `HighRes` dataset, where T_1−w, T_2−w, Fusion [14], and proposed synthesis results are shown. There is a lesion in the frontal lobe (red arrow) which was not synthesized in Fusion. Also ventricles and cortex are fuzzier (yellow arrow) as well as hippocampus (red arrow) has CSF-like intensities in Fusion based T_2. The bottom row shows another subject from the same dataset where the lesion on the left frontal lobe (red arrow) is not well synthesized in either synthetic T_2s. Our method generally produced sharper features in the cortex and anatomically correct intensities near the hippocampus. (Color figure online)

deformably registered by ANTS [19] to the synthetic T_2, which is also in the space of original T_1 images. The corrected $b = 0$ is compared to the ground truth (Sect. 3) $b = 0$ via peak signal to noise ratio (PSNR). Although the synthesis was performed on whole head, PSNR is computed only on the brain so that background noise in the sinuses and air pockets are not used in the computation. Most of the distortion occurs near the brain and skull boundary. Therefore CSF is most affected by the distortion. To compute if the CSF is correctly aligned between T_1 and $b = 0$, we first segmented the T_1−w images [23], and computed median $b = 0$ intensities for only cortical CSF voxels. For this purpose, $b = 0$ images are normalized to have modes of the WM intensities as 1. CSF being hyperintense on $b = 0$, higher median intensities indicate better matching. As

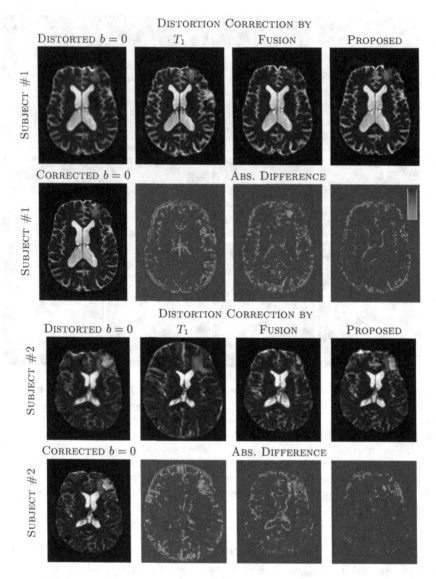

Fig. 2. The top two rows show distorted $b = 0$ and corrected $b = 0$ images via T_1, original T_2, synthetic T_2s from Fusion [14] and the proposed method, along with absolute difference images from the original T_2 corrected $b = 0$. The "Corrected $b = 0$" indicates $b = 0$ image corrected by original high resolution T_2. The same image slices of subject #1 of Fig. 1 are shown. Bottom two rows shows similar slices for the subject #2 from Fig. 1. Yellow arrows indicate the lesions that are better reconstructed with the proposed synthesis. The colormap of the absolute difference images indicate 0 to 30 % of the maximum intensity of the $b = 0$ images. Note that the distortion correction for subject #2 using the T_1−w image yielded gross scaling errors. (Color figure online)

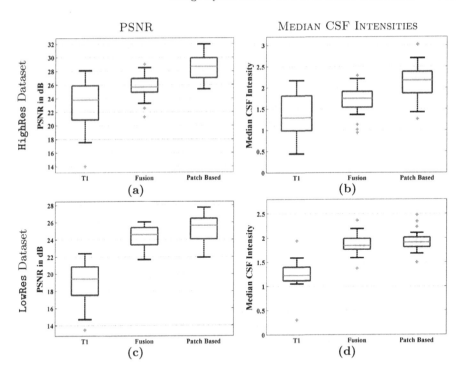

Fig. 3. PSNR between ground truth $b = 0$ (see Sect. 3 for definition) and T_1 or synthetic T_2 corrected $b = 0$ are shown for (**a**) HighRes dataset, (**c**) LowRes dataset. Median CSF intensities from corrected $b = 0$ images are shown for (**b**) HighRes dataset, (**d**) LowRes dataset.

the synthetic images are only used as an intermediate step of the distortion correction, we did not compute any similarity metric between the synthetic T_2 and the original T_2.

Fusion, being a registration based voxel-wise method, usually requires more atlases and more accurate registrations. On the contrary, the proposed method uses patches from a neighborhood, therefore some degree of registration error is permitted. An example is shown in Fig. 1, where original T_1-w, T_2-w, and synthetic T_2-w images are shown for two subjects from HighRes dataset. Fusion produces fuzzier ventricles (e.g., yellow arrow) and cortex due to minor registration mismatch. However, both of them have sharper features in the results from the proposed algorithm. This is evident near the hippocampus (red arrow) as well, which has CSF-like intensities in the Fusion synthesis. Also there is a lesion near the left frontal lobe (red arrows) on both subjects, which was not synthesized well in Fusion, since there were no lesions in the atlases in that region. It is, however, partially synthesized in our method, where CSF patches from nearby voxels contribute to synthesize the lesion. An example of distortion correction is shown in Fig. 2 where distorted and corrected $b = 0$ images of the same subjects as Fig. 1 are shown. The lesions on both subjects are better registered with our synthetic T_2 (yellow arrows). Also the cortex and ventricles are generally better aligned in the proposed method, as seen from the lower values near those regions in the difference images.

Figures 3(a)–(c) shows the PSNR between ground truth $b = 0$ and T_1 or synthetic T_2 based corrected $b = 0$ images. Median PSNRs for the HighRes dataset are 23.79, 25.67, and 28.68 dB for T_1, Fusion, and proposed synthetic T_2 corrected $b = 0$ s. The numbers are 19.02, 24.34, and 25.62 for LowRes dataset. Our synthetic T_2 provides significantly higher PSNR ($p < 0.0001$) than both Fusion and T_1 correction for both datasets. Median CSF intensities on the corrected $b = 0$ images are 1.29, 1.75, and 2.17 for HighRes data, and 1.23, 1.84, and 1.91 for LowRes data. In this case also, our synthetic T_2 is significantly better ($p < 0.001$) on both datasets and for both T_1 and Fusion T_2.

5   Discussion

We have proposed a patch matching method to synthesize whole head T_2-w MR images from T_1-w images and demonstrated on 44 patients with TBI that such synthetic images can substitute for real T_2-w images to perform accurate distortion correction for DWI images. We have compared with a state-of-the-art registration based voxel-wise fusion method [14] and showed that the proposed synthesis produces more accurate results than the fusion method.

To register an atlas and a target, we have employed an "approximate ANTS" registration, which, in comparison to affine registration, is more robust on pathological brains, produces better matching, requires less number of atlases, and takes similar time. Only 3 atlases are used in all experiments. Although the accuracy increases slightly with more atlases, 3 atlases already provided better results than Fusion. Due to the registration, similar patches can be found within a small neighborhood, as done in [18], as opposed to patch search within the whole brain when the atlases are not registered to the subject [2,16]. Also because of the patch matching instead of voxel-wise analysis, some error in registrations between atlases and target can be tolerated.

The LowRes dataset produces slightly worse results than the HighRes dataset, both in terms of PSNR (28.68 vs 25.62 dB) and median CSF intensities (2.17 vs 1.91). The reason is partially due to the fact that the synthesis is performed with the T_2-w atlases having a native 2 mm inferior-to-superior (I-S) resolution compared to 1 mm I-S resolution on HighRes atlases.

As mentioned in Sect. 1, synthetic images can not perfectly replicate the original images. This is especially true in the presence of pathologies, such as Fig. 1, where the lesions are not well synthesized. However, in absence of a real T_2-w, synthetic images can be used as intermediate data for more accurate distortion correction. The combination of registration and patch matching provides greater flexibility than registration alone.

References

1. Tulder, G., Bruijne, M.: Why does synthesized data improve multi-sequence classification? In: Navab, N., Hornegger, J., Wells, W.M., Frangi, A.F. (eds.) MICCAI 2015. LNCS, vol. 9349, pp. 531–538. Springer, Heidelberg (2015). doi:10.1007/978-3-319-24553-9_65
2. Roy, S., Carass, A., Prince, J.L.: Magnetic resonance image example based contrast synthesis. IEEE Trans. Med. Imag. **32**(12), 2348–2363 (2013)
3. Clark, K.A., Woods, R.P., Rottenberg, D.A., Toga, A.W., Mazziotta, J.C.: Impact of acquisition protocols and processing streams on tissue segmentation of T1 weighted MR images. NeuroImage **29**(1), 185–202 (2006)
4. Han, X., Fischl, B.: Atlas renormalization for improved brain MR image segmentation across scanner platforms. IEEE Trans. Med. Imag. **26**(4), 479–486 (2007)
5. Roy, S., Jog, A., Carass, A., Prince, J.L.: Atlas based intensity transformation of brain mr images. In: Shen, L., Liu, T., Yap, P.-T., Huang, H., Shen, D., Westin, C.-F. (eds.) MBIA 2013. LNCS, vol. 8159, pp. 51–62. Springer, Heidelberg (2013). doi:10.1007/978-3-319-02126-3_6
6. Ye, D.H., Zikic, D., Glocker, B., Criminisi, A., Konukoglu, E.: Modality propagation: coherent synthesis of subject-specific scans with data-driven regularization. In: Mori, K., Sakuma, I., Sato, Y., Barillot, C., Navab, N. (eds.) MICCAI 2013. LNCS, vol. 8149, pp. 606–613. Springer, Heidelberg (2013). doi:10.1007/978-3-642-40811-3_76
7. Sudre, C.H., Cardoso, M.J., Bouvy, W., Biessels, G.J., Barnes, J., Ourselin, S.: Bayesian model selection for pathological data. In: Golland, P., Hata, N., Barillot, C., Hornegger, J., Howe, R. (eds.) MICCAI 2014. LNCS, vol. 8673, pp. 323–330. Springer, Heidelberg (2014). doi:10.1007/978-3-319-10404-1_41
8. Roy, S., Carass, A., Prince, J.L.: MR contrast synthesis for lesion segmentation. In: Internationl Symposium on Biomedical Imaging (ISBI), pp. 932–935 (2010)
9. Iglesias, J.E., Konukoglu, E., Zikic, D., Glocker, B., Leemput, K., Fischl, B.: Is synthesizing MRI contrast useful for inter-modality analysis? In: Mori, K., Sakuma, I., Sato, Y., Barillot, C., Navab, N. (eds.) MICCAI 2013. LNCS, vol. 8149, pp. 631–638. Springer, Heidelberg (2013). doi:10.1007/978-3-642-40811-3_79
10. Wein, W., Brunke, S., Khamene, A., Callstrom, M.R., Navab, N.: Automatic CT-ultrasound registration for diagnostic imaging and image-guided intervention. Med. Image Anal. **12**(5), 577–585 (2008)
11. Roy, S., Carass, A., Jog, A., Prince, J.L., Lee, J.: MR to CT registration of brains using image synthesis. In: Proceedings of SPIE, vol. 9034, p. 903419 (2014)
12. Chen, M., Jog, A., Carass, A., Prince, J.L.: Using image synthesis for multi-channel registration of different image modalities. In: Proceedings of SPIE, vol. 9413, p. 94131Q (2015)
13. Bhushan, C., Haldar, J.P., Choi, S., Joshi, A.A., Shattuck, D.W., Leahy, R.M.: Co-registration and distortion correction of diffusion and anatomical images based on inverse contrast normalization. NeuroImage **115**, 269–280 (2015)
14. Burgos, N., Cardoso, M.J., Thielemans, K., Modat, M., Pedemonte, S., Dickson, J., Barnes, A., Ahmed, R., Mahoney, C.J., Schott, J.M., Duncan, J.S., Atkinson, D., Arridge, S.R., Hutton, B.F., Ourselin, S.: Attenuation correction synthesis for hybrid PET-MR scanners: application to brain studies. IEEE Trans. Med. Imag. **33**(12), 2332–2341 (2014)
15. Roy, S., Wang, W.T., Carass, A., Prince, J.L., Butman, J.A., Pham, D.L.: PET attenuation correction using synthetic CT from ultrashort echo-time MR imaging. J. Nucl. Med. **55**(12), 2071–2077 (2014)

16. Jog, A., Carass, A., Roy, S., Pham, D.L., Prince, J.L.: MR image synthesis by contrast learning on neighborhood ensembles. Med. Image Anal. **24**(1), 63–76 (2015)
17. Rousseau, F., Habas, P.A., Studholme, C.: A supervised patch-based approach for human brain labeling. IEEE Trans. Med. Imag. **30**(10), 1852–1862 (2011)
18. Coupe, P., Manjon, J.V., Fonov, V., Pruessner, J., Robles, M., Collins, D.L.: Patch-based segmentation using expert priors: application to hippocampus and ventricle segmentation. NeuroImage **54**(2), 940–954 (2011)
19. Avants, B.B., Epstein, C.L., Grossman, M., Gee, J.C.: Symmetric diffeomorphic image registration with cross-correlation: evaluating automated labeling of elderly and neurodegenerative brain. Med. Image Anal. **12**(1), 26–41 (2008)
20. Jenkinson, M., Smith, S.: A global optimisation method for robust affine registration of brain images. Med. Image Anal. **5**(2), 143–156 (2001)
21. Zou, H., Hastie, T.: Regularization and variable selection via the elastic net. J. Roy. Stat. Soc. Series B **67**(2), 301–320 (2005)
22. Andersson, J.L.R., Skare, S., Ashburner, J.: How to correct susceptibility distortions in spin-echo echo-planar images: application to diffusion tensor imaging. NeuroImage **20**(2), 870–888 (2003)
23. Roy, S., He, Q., Sweeney, E., Carass, A., Reich, D.S., Prince, J.L., Pham, D.L.: Subject specific sparse dictionary learning for atlas based brain MRI segmentation. IEEE J. Biomed. Health Inf. **19**(5), 1598–1609 (2015)

MRI-TRUS Image Synthesis with Application to Image-Guided Prostate Intervention

John A. Onofrey[1]([✉]), Ilkay Oksuz[1,4], Saradwata Sarkar[5],
Rajesh Venkataraman[5], Lawrence H. Staib[1,2,3], and Xenophon Papademetris[1,2]

[1] Departments of Radiology and Biomedical Imaging,
Yale University, New Haven, CT 06520, USA
{john.onofrey,ilkay.oksuz,lawrence.staib,xenophon.papademetris}@yale.edu
[2] Biomedical Engineering, Yale University, New Haven, CT 06520, USA
[3] Electrical Engineering, Yale University, New Haven, CT 06520, USA
[4] IMT Institute for Advanced Studies Lucca, Lucca, Italy
[5] Eigen, Grass Valley, CA 95945, USA
{sarad.sarkar,rajesh.venkataraman}@eigen.com

Abstract. Accurate and robust fusion of pre-procedure magnetic resonance imaging (MRI) to intra-procedure trans-rectal ultrasound (TRUS) imaging is necessary for image-guided prostate cancer biopsy procedures. The current clinical standard for image fusion relies on non-rigid surface-based registration between semi-automatically segmented prostate surfaces in both the MRI and TRUS. This surface-based registration method does not take advantage of internal anatomical prostate structures, which have the potential to provide useful information for image registration. However, non-rigid, multi-modal intensity-based MRI-TRUS registration is challenging due to highly non-linear intensities relationships between MRI and TRUS. In this paper, we present preliminary work using image synthesis to cast this problem into a mono-modal registration task by using a large database of over 100 clinical MRI-TRUS image pairs to learn a joint model of MR-TRUS appearance. Thus, given an MRI, we use this learned joint appearance model to synthesize the patient's corresponding TRUS image appearance with which we could potentially perform mono-modal intensity-based registration. We present preliminary results of this approach.

1   Introduction

Non-rigid registration of multi-modal images is a challenging problem for image-guided interventions. The highly non-linear intensity relationships between such multi-modal images and the high dimensionality of the non-rigid deformation make registration optimization difficult. In contrast to intensity-based registration, image segmentation offers an alternative strategy to register images where corresponding structures in both image are first segmented and then these segmented structures are subsequently registered to each other. However, image segmentation, both automated and manual, is itself a difficult problem that is

© Springer International Publishing AG 2016
S.A. Tsaftaris et al. (Eds.): SASHIMI 2016, LNCS 9968, pp. 157–166, 2016.
DOI: 10.1007/978-3-319-46630-9_16

prone to error and high variability. Furthermore, depending upon the segmentation's granularity, potentially useful information for the registration about the anatomy, *e.g.* fine internal anatomical structures within a volume of interest, could be abstracted away by the segmentation. In this paper, we present preliminary work to convert this multi-modal image registration task into a mono-modal registration task using image synthesis. Using a large set of manually-labeled, multi-modal training data, we learn a model of intensity appearance between two different modality images, and then use this model to synthesize the appearance of a target image given an image of the other modality. We present results applying our approach to synthesize trans-rectal ultrasound (TRUS) imaging from magnetic resonance imaging (MRI) for image-guided prostate biopsy localization.

With over 450,000 men estimated to be diagnosed with prostate cancer in the year 2015 [14], prostate cancer is one of the most commonly occurring forms of cancer and one of the major causes of cancer-related death in the U.S. TRUS image-guided biopsy is the current clinical standard for diagnosing prostate cancer. The biopsy sampling procedure consists of two parts: (*i*) 12 untargeted, systematic tissue cores, in a non-patient-specific plan, from different regions of the prostate; and (*ii*) a small number of TRUS-guided targeted biopsies.

While TRUS itself cannot be reliably used for targeting suspicious lesions because of poor image quality and lack of contrast, multi-parametric MRI (mpMRI) that combines T2-weighted imaging with functional sequences, *e.g.* diffusion-weighted MRI, spectroscopic MRI and dynamic contrast enhanced MRI, shows significantly better localization of suspicious lesions within the prostate [2]. To avoid performing biopsies under MRI guidance, which can be time consuming, expensive and impractical [15], current practice aims to fuse pre-procedure mpMRI with intra-procedure TRUS imaging. In this case, clinicians identify suspicious prostatic tissue using mpMRI and then urologists use TRUS imaging to provide targeted image-guided navigation for biopsy. Rigid registration between the MRI and TRUS is inadequate for accurate biopsy guidance due to prostate gland deformations caused by (*i*) variations in patient orientation, (*ii*) changes in bladder or rectal filling, (*iii*) and presence or absence of an endorectal MR coil, and (*iv*) deformation caused by handheld TRUS probes. Therefore, non-rigid registration is required to accurately compensate for these deformations.

A variety of non-rigid registration methods have been proposed to fuse MR and TRUS images for prostate biopsy. Previously proposed surface registration algorithms to align the segmented prostate surfaces from the MRI and TRUS images [8,9] are highly operator dependent because they rely upon semi-automated segmentation methods, which are both time-consuming and prone to significant variability. As an alternative to surface-based registration, Sparks *et al.* [12] perform image fusion by first performing a probabilistic segmentation of the prostate in TRUS images, and then register this segmentation probability map. Karnik *et al.* [6] suggest that intensity-based registration methods may perform better than surface-based registration methods, and have the additional benefit that they do not require segmentation. Mitra *et al.* [7] propose an intensity-based registration method, but validated it only on mid-gland MRI-TRUS slices. Rather than using raw intensity values, Sun *et al.* [13] propose MRI-TRUS fusion using an intensity-based non-local feature descriptor, but this strategy relies on analogous structures existing in both image volumes, which does not necessarily hold in the poor quality TRUS images. Some other works have used mono-modal TRUS image registration to perform intra-operative updates of the guidance. Xu *et al.* [17] use a combination of image intensity and image intensity gradient information to register 2D TRUS image slices to a 3D TRUS reference volume. Xu *et al.* [16] use mono-modal TRUS registration to perform updates during the biopsy procedure, but their method makes the assumption that the initial pre-operative TRUS acquisition aligns well with the MRI.

Similar to these works, we seek to perform non-rigid mono-modal TRUS image registration to update the image-guided biopsy procedure. In this work, we present a method to synthesize the TRUS image appearance for a given MRI. Rather than adopting a synthesis methodology that models the physics of image acquisition [4,5], in this work we attempt to learn the appearance relationship of one modality from another based on a large set of richly-annotated, clinical MRI-TRUS training data. Our method, described in Sect. 2, builds a subject-specific joint MRI-TRUS appearance model by first warping all MRI-TRUS image pairs into the space of the test MRI. In this paper, we test two different methods to build this model: *(i)* using a principal component analysis (PCA)-based approach; and *(ii)* using a dictionary learning approach. We then use these learned models of appearance to synthesize a novel TRUS image that corresponds to the patients pre-procedure MRI. Our preliminary results, in Sect. 3 demonstrate approaches to synthesize qualitatively realistic TRUS images given an MRI.

2   Methods

Section 2.1 begins by describing the pre-processing steps necessary to create our database of training data. In Sect. 2.2, we detail our methods for jointly modeling MR-TRUS appearance, and how we apply this model to synthesize TRUS images given novel MRIs. Figure 1 illustrates our method's model building and synthesis workflow.

2.1   MRI-TRUS Training Data and Pre-processing

We train our MRI-TRUS model of joint appearance using data from a clinical database of $N = 105$ patients undergoing prostate biopsy at our institution. For each patient, the dataset contains a pre-procedure T2-weighted MRI I_{MR}, an intra-procedure TRUS image I_{TRUS}, as well as segmented prostate surfaces S_{MR} and S_{TRUS} in each image. Both surfaces were generated using a semi-automated, clinical segmentation tool (Eigen, Grass Valley, CA). For each MRI-TRUS image pair, we account for deformations induced by the biopsy procedure by non-rigidly

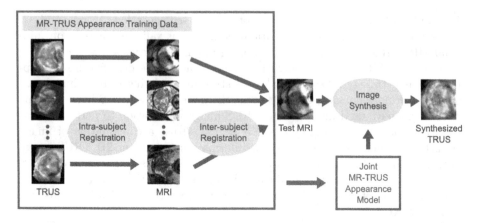

Fig. 1. Our workflow for training a patient-specific joint MRI-TRUS appearance model and synthesizing novel TRUS images. We make use of a large database of richly anno-tated data to learn a model of MRI-TRUS appearance. Given a novel, test MRI, we first warp all the MRI and TRUS images in our database to the test image's space using a series of intra-subject and inter-subject registrations. We then use these transformed image pairs as training data to learn the model of MRI-TRUS appearance. We then use this model to synthesize the corresponding TRUS image for that patient.

registering the TRUS image to the MRI space using a surface-based registration. For each image $i = 1, \ldots, N$, we non-rigidly register $S_{\text{TRUS},i}$ to $S_{\text{MR},i}$ using a robust point matching (RPM) framework [3] with the transformation parame-terized by a free-form deformation (FFD) [10,11] with 10.0 mm isotropic control point spacing; We denote these transformations $T_{\text{TRUS}\rightsquigarrow\text{MR}}$, where $i \rightsquigarrow j$ indi-cates nonrigid transformation from space i to j. We use all this data to create our patient-specific models of joint MRI-TRUS appearance as described in the next section.

2.2 Joint MR-TRUS Appearance Modeling

For a novel MRI I_{MR} not included in the training set, we warp our training data into this image's space. To do this, we perform N inter-subject MRI-MRI registrations. These registrations use a non-rigid RPM registration with 5.0 mm isotropic control point spacing [3,10], and we denote these transforma-tions $T_{\text{MR}\rightsquigarrow\text{MR},i}$ for $i = 1, \ldots, N$. Using these transformations and the intra-subject transformations from Sect. 2.1, we reslice all training images to the MRI reference space using the following:

$$I'_{\text{MR},i} = T_{\text{MR}\rightsquigarrow\text{MR},i} \circ I_{\text{MR},i}$$
$$I'_{\text{TRUS},i} = T_{\text{TRUS}\rightsquigarrow\text{MR},i} \circ T_{\text{MR}\rightsquigarrow\text{MR},i} \circ I_{\text{MR},i}$$

for all $i = 1, \ldots, N$ patients in the training database, where $\circ$ is the transforma-tion operator.

With the N training images resliced to this common space, we construct our joint model of MRI-TRUS appearance. First, we center both the MRI and the TRUS data to have the same median intensity inside the prostate, where the prostate is defined by the segmented surface S_{MR} for the test patient. Rather than modeling the appearance of the entire MRI reference volume $\Omega \subset \mathbb{R}^3$, where anatomical structure is highly variable and prone to large registration errors due to being far away prostate surfaces used to perform the registration, we model the appearance of the prostate volume and the volume immediately outside the gland boundary. Using the whole gland prostate surface segmentation S_{MR}, we use morphological filtering to dilate the binary whole gland mask with a large circular filter to define this region, and we denote voxel locations within this volume $\mathbf{x} \in \Omega_P \subset \Omega$. For each MRI-TRUS image pair, we extract and vectorize the joint MRI-TRUS intensity appearance in this region $\mathbf{j}_i = [\mathbf{m}_i, \mathbf{u}_i]^T$, where $\mathbf{m}_i \in \mathbb{R}^d$ and $\mathbf{u}_i \in \mathbb{R}^d$ are the vectors of d voxel intensities in $I'_{\mathrm{MR},i}(\mathbf{x})$ and $I'_{\mathrm{TRUS},i}(\mathbf{x}), \forall \mathbf{x} \in \Omega_P$, respectively. The N joint appearance vectors are realizations of the distribution of MRI-TRUS joint intensity appearance $\mathcal{J}$ between the pre-procedure MRI and intra-procedure TRUS imaging. In this work, we model the distribution of deformations $\mathcal{J}$ and synthesize TRUS images using two methods: (i) a linear global appearance model using principal component analysis (PCA); and (ii) a non-linear global appearance model using dictionary learning.

Appearance Modeling and Synthesis Using PCA. PCA estimates the eigenvectors of $\mathcal{J}$'s covariance matrix

$$\mathbf{j} = \bar{\mathbf{j}} + \boldsymbol{\Phi}\mathbf{w} \tag{1}$$

where the eigenvectors $\boldsymbol{\Phi} = [\boldsymbol{\phi}_1, \ldots, \boldsymbol{\phi}_N] \in \mathbb{R}^{2d \times N}$ are the N principal modes of MRI-TRUS appearance, $\bar{\mathbf{j}}$ is the mean appearance for the training data, and $\mathbf{w} \in \mathbb{R}^N$ is a vector of eigenvectors weights. Figure 2 illustrates an example set of eigenvectors generated by our model. To synthesize the novel TRUS image, we first get the target MRI intensity vector $\mathbf{m}$, which contains the voxel intensities $I_{\mathrm{MR}}(\mathbf{x}), \forall \mathbf{x} \in \Omega_P$. We then create the joint appearance vector as $\mathbf{j} = [\mathbf{m}, \mathbf{0}]^T$, where $\mathbf{0}$ is a zero vector that reflects the TRUS image that we want to synthesize. We perform the TRUS image synthesis operation by projecting $\mathbf{j}$ onto the appearance eigenvectors and solving for $\mathbf{w}$ in (1)

$$\hat{\mathbf{w}} = \boldsymbol{\Phi}^T(\mathbf{j} - \bar{\mathbf{j}}_m),$$

where we set the TRUS component of the mean appearance vector to zero $\bar{\mathbf{j}}_m = [\bar{\mathbf{m}}, \mathbf{0}]$, and then substitute this result back into (1)

$$\hat{\mathbf{j}} = \bar{\mathbf{j}} + \boldsymbol{\Phi}\hat{\mathbf{w}}. \tag{2}$$

The resulting joint appearance solution $\hat{\mathbf{j}} = [\hat{\mathbf{m}}, \hat{\mathbf{u}}]^T$ provides both the MRI reconstruction of minimum error $\hat{\mathbf{m}}$ with respect to the PCA model and the novel synthesized TRUS image in $\hat{\mathbf{u}}$.

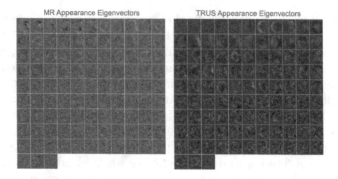

MR Appearance Eigenvectors   TRUS Appearance Eigenvectors

Fig. 2. Sample eigenvectors showing joint MRI-TRUS intensity appearance found using PCA. The joint eigenvector is the concatenation of the MRI eigenvector and the TRUS eigenvector at the same positions in the two corresponding matrices. The first principal component with the largest eigenvalue is shown in the top left corner and the remaining principal components are sorted in decreasing order of their eigenvalues from left to right and top to bottom.

Appearance Modeling and Synthesis Using Dictionary Learning. Dictionary learning, in comparison to PCA, provides a non-linear model of the distribution joint appearance $\mathcal{J}$. We use K-SVD to generate an overcomplete dictionary $\mathbf{D} = [\mathbf{d}_1, \ldots, \mathbf{d}_k] \in \mathbb{R}^{2d \times k}$ of K sparse joint appearance atoms [1]. While the atoms were created using the joint appearance vectors, each atom $k = 1, \ldots, K$ may be partitioned into separate MRI and TRUS components $\mathbf{d}_k = [\mathbf{d}_{\mathrm{MR},k}, \mathbf{d}_{\mathrm{TRUS},k},]^T$. Figure 3 shows atoms from a sample dictionary of joint MRI-TRUS appearance. To reconstruct an MRI-TRUS appearance sample $\mathbf{j} = [\mathbf{m}, \mathbf{0}]^T$, where $\mathbf{0}$ is a zero vector that reflects the TRUS image that we want to synthesize, we solve the sparse coding problem

$$\hat{\gamma} = \min_{\gamma} \|\mathbf{j} - \mathbf{D}_m \gamma\|_2^2 \quad \text{s.t.} \quad \|\gamma\|_0 \leq \Gamma_0 \tag{3}$$

where $\mathbf{D}_m$ is the dictionary $\mathbf{D}$ with all K atoms having their TRUS appearance vectors set to zero $\mathbf{d}_{\mathrm{TRUS},k} = \mathbf{0}$, γ is the sparse dictionary weighting coefficients, and Γ_0 is the dictionary's target sparsity constraint. We use orthogonal matching pursuit (OMP) to solve for (3). From (3), we have $\hat{\mathbf{j}} = \mathbf{D}\hat{\gamma}$, where $\hat{\mathbf{j}} = [\hat{\mathbf{m}}, \hat{\mathbf{u}}]^T$ provides both the MRI reconstruction of minimum reconstruction error $\hat{\mathbf{m}}$ with respect to the dictionary model and the novel synthesized TRUS image in $\hat{\mathbf{u}}$.

3   Results and Discussion

From our database of $N = 105$ prostate biopsy patients, we perform leave-one-out testing. In each leave-one-out test, we selected the i-th patient's MRI as the reference image, and created a unique joint appearance model using the remaining $N - 1$ images as described in Sect. 2.2. For PCA-based modeling, we

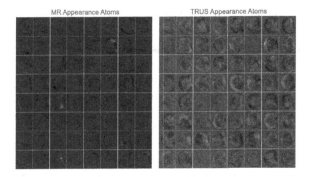

Fig. 3. Sample dictionary atoms showing joint MRI-TRUS intensity appearance found using K-SVD. The joint eigenvector is the concatenation of the MRI eigenvector and the TRUS eigenvector at the same positions in the two corresponding matrices.

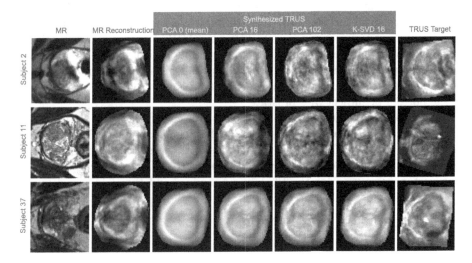

Fig. 4. Example MRI-TRUS image synthesis results from three subjects. From left to right, we show each patient's prostate MRI, the reconstructed MRI from the joint appearance model (using PCA 102), synthesized TRUS images found using both the PCA and dictionary learning (K-SVD) methods, and the patient's target TRUS image. Here, PCA X indicates that X eigenvectors were used for the synthesis, with PCA 0 indicating that the mean TRUS image. K-SVD 16 indicates a sparsity constraint of 16 atoms for the synthesis.

limited the model to use the first 3, 16, 46, and 102 eigenvectors, which corresponded to 50, 75, 90, and 100 % of the model's cumulative variance, respectively. We also used the mean of the training TRUS images, which corresponded to using 0 eigenvectors in the PCA model, to synthesize the TRUS. For the dictionary learning-based model, we set our dictionary to have $K = 64$ atoms and a sparsity constraint $\Gamma_0 = 16$. All MR images were resampled to have 1.0 mm isotropic voxel spacing.

We evaluated TRUS image synthesis both qualitatively and quantitatively by comparing how similar the synthesized image was to patient i's corresponding target TRUS image. Figure 4 shows example synthesized TRUS images and compares them to their respective target TRUS. These results show the synthesized TRUS images appearing more realistic as more eigenvalues are used in the PCA models. The synthesized TRUS appearance changes from the smooth mean TRUS appearance using 0 eigenvectors to gradually include more appearance details as more eigenvectors are used. The dictionary learning-based model synthesized TRUS images nearly identical in appearance to the PCA model using 102 eigenvectors, but did so using only 16 atoms, an 84% reduction in appearance dimensionality. Ideally, the synthesized TRUS and target TRUS images should exhibit similar structural appearance at corresponding locations, however we note that registration errors might still exists between the MRI and TRUS images since surface-based registration was used to align the datasets in Sect. 2.1. Figure 4 also shows the reconstructed MRIs (created using the PCA-based model with 102 eigenvectors) for the example patients. These MRI reconstructions appear to capture the overall appearance of the original MRI, but omit some of the subtle anatomical features, for example the low intensity lesion at the bottom of subject 37's prostate.

Quantitatively, we calculated the correlation coefficient (CC) between the synthesized TRUS image and the target TRUS image, using only the voxels close to the prostate gland in Ω_P. Figure 5 shows the distributions of CC values for the various appearance models. The mean CC values decreased as more eigenvectors were used for the PCA-based models, and the PCA-based model

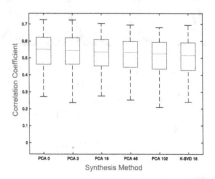

Fig. 5. Boxplots show the distribution of correlation coefficient similarity measures between synthesized TRUS images and their corresponding target TRUS image using different appearance model methods. Here, PCA X indicates that X eigenvectors were used for the synthesis, with PCA 0 indicating that the mean TRUS image. K-SVD 16 indicates a sparsity constraint of 16 atoms for the synthesis. Only PCA 102 and K-SVD 16 had no significant differences (two-tailed, paired t-test, $p = 0.32$), while all other method comparisons showed significant differences (two-tailed, paired t-test, $p \leq 0.05$).

using 102 eigenvectors and dictionary learning model showed no significant differences (two-tailed, paired t-test, $p = 0.32$). All other combinations of methods compared gave significantly different similarity values (two-tailed, paired t-test, $p \leq 0.05$). These results appear to indicate that while the synthesized TRUS images in Fig. 4 appear more realistic, the structures synthesized do not actually correlate well with those in target TRUS. Interestingly, the smoothest synthetic TRUS images, those created using the mean intensity of the TRUS data (PCA 0) had the highest mean CC.

4   Conclusion

The method proposed in this paper can be used to create models of multi-modal image appearance, which in turn can be used to generate synthetic images of one modality from the other. Our results show that using a data-driven approach to image appearance modeling can both produce realistic MRI reconstructions and synthesize realistic TRUS images. We tested two different approaches to modeling MRI-TRUS appearance, using PCA and dictionary learning-based methods. Interestingly, the dictionary learning approach appears to provide similar qualitative and quantitative synthesis results compared to PCA, but does so with an 84 % reduction in appearance dimensionality. For this preliminary study, we utilized a global approach to appearance synthesis. However, the results show that such a global model of image appearance may not sufficiently capture the unique anatomical features present in the test images. Patch-based learning and synthesis methods may be better suited for learning such non-global appearances. In future work, we aim to explore using local, patch-based joint appearance modeling, and we envision that our global model of appearance presented in this work could serve as an initial pre-processing step prior to local appearance modeling and synthesis. Future work will also incorporate these synthetic TRUS images into the image registration process, and then quantifying target registration error of expertly identified matching landmarks identified in both the pre-procedure MRI and intra-procedure TRUS imaging to see how it compares with the current clinical standard that uses surface-based registration.

Acknowledgments. This work was supported in part by the NIH under grant R41/42-CA186414.

Disclosure: Dr. Papademetris is a consultant for Electrical Geodesics, Inc.

References

1. Aharon, M., Elad, M., Bruckstein, A.: K -SVD: an algorithm for designing overcomplete dictionaries for sparse representation. IEEE Trans. Sig. Process. **54**(11), 4311–4322 (2006)
2. Barentsz, J.O., Richenberg, J., Clements, R., Choyke, P., Verma, S., Villeirs, G., Rouviere, O., Logager, V., Fütterer, J.J.: ESUR prostate MR guidelines 2012. Eur. Radiol. **22**(4), 746–757 (2012)

3. Chui, H., Rangarajan, A.: A new point matching algorithm for non-rigid registration. Comput. Vis. Image Underst. **89**(2–3), 114–141 (2003)
4. Jog, A., Carass, A., Roy, S., Pham, D.L., Prince, J.L.: MR image synthesis by contrast learning on neighborhood ensembles. Med. Image Anal. **24**(1), 63–76 (2015)
5. Jog, A., Roy, S., Carass, A., Prince, J.L.: Magnetic resonance image synthesis through patch regression. In: IEEE 10th International Symposium on Biomedical Imaging (ISBI) 2013, pp. 350–353 (2013)
6. Karnik, V.V., Fenster, A., Bax, J., Cool, D.W., Gardi, L., Gyacskov, I., Romagnoli, C., Ward, A.D.: Assessment of image registration accuracy in three-dimensional transrectal ultrasound guided prostate biopsy. Med. Phys. **37**(2), 802–813 (2010)
7. Mitra, J., Mart, R., Oliver, A., Llad, X., Ghose, S., Vilanova, J., Meriaudeau, F.: Prostate multimodality image registration based on B-splines and quadrature local energy. Int. J. Comput. Assist. Radiol. Surg. **7**(3), 445–454 (2012)
8. Moradi, M., Janoos, F., Fedorov, A., Risholm, P., Kapur, T., Wolfsberger, L., Nguyen, P., Tempany, C., Wells, W.: Two solutions for registration of ultrasound to MRI for image-guided prostate interventions. In: IEEE EMBC, pp. 1129–1132 (2012)
9. Narayanan, R., Kurhanewicz, J., Shinohara, K., Crawford, E.D., Simoneau, A., Suri, J.: MRI-ultrasound registration for targeted prostate biopsy. In: IEEE ISBI, pp. 991–994 (2009)
10. Papademetris, X., Jackowski, A.P., Schultz, R.T., Staib, L.H., Duncan, J.S.: Computing 3D non-rigid brain registration using extended robust point matching for composite multisubject fMRI analysis. In: Ellis, R.E., Peters, T.M. (eds.) MICCAI 2003. LNCS, vol. 2879, pp. 788–795. Springer, Heidelberg (2003)
11. Rueckert, D., Sonoda, L., Hayes, C., Hill, D., Leach, M., Hawkes, D.: Nonrigid registration using free-form deformations: application to breast MR images. IEEE TMI **18**(8), 712–721 (1999)
12. Sparks, R., Nicolas Bloch, B., Feleppa, E., Barratt, D., Moses, D., Ponsky, L., Madabhush, A.: Multiattribute probabilistic prostate elastic registration (MAPPER): application to fusion of ultrasound and magnetic resonance imaging. Med. Phys. **42**(3), 1153–1163 (2015)
13. Sun, Y., Yuan, J., Rajchl, M., Qiu, W., Romagnoli, C., Fenster, A.: Efficient convex optimization approach to 3D non-rigid MR-TRUS registration. In: Mori, K., Sakuma, I., Sato, Y., Barillot, C., Navab, N. (eds.) MICCAI 2013, Part I. LNCS, vol. 8149, pp. 195–202. Springer, Heidelberg (2013)
14. Tempany, C., Straus, S., Hata, N., Haker, S.: MR-guided prostate interventions. J. Magn. Reson. Imaging **27**(2), 356–367 (2008)
15. Ukimura, O., Faber, K., Gill, I.S.: Intraprostatic targeting. Curr. Opin. Urol. **22**(2), 97–103 (2012)
16. Xu, S., Kruecker, J., Guion, P., Glossop, N., Neeman, Z., Choyke, P.L., Singh, A.K., Wood, B.J.: Closed-loop control in fused MR-TRUS image-guided prostate biopsy. In: Ayache, N., Ourselin, S., Maeder, A. (eds.) MICCAI 2007, Part I. LNCS, vol. 4791, pp. 128–135. Springer, Heidelberg (2007)
17. Xu, S., Kruecker, J., Turkbey, B., Glossop, N., Singh, A.K., Choyke, P., Pinto, P., Wood, B.J.: Real-time MRI-TRUS fusion for guidance of targeted prostate biopsies. Comput. Aided Surg. **13**(5), 255–264 (2008)

Automatic Generation of Synthetic Retinal Fundus Images: Vascular Network

Elisa Menti[1,3], Lorenza Bonaldi[1,3], Lucia Ballerini[2(✉)],
Alfredo Ruggeri[3], and Emanuele Trucco[1]

[1] VAMPIRE Project, Computing, School of Science and Engineering,
University of Dundee, Dundee, UK
[2] VAMPIRE Project, Department of Neuroimaging Sciences,
University of Edinburgh, Edinburgh, UK
lucia.ballerini@ed.ac.uk
[3] Department of Information Engineering, University of Padova, Padova, Italy
http://vampire.computing.dundee.ac.uk

Abstract. This work is part of an ongoing project aimed to generate synthetic retinal fundus images. This paper concentrates on the generation of synthetic vascular networks with realistic shape and texture characteristics. An example-based method, the Active Shape Model, is used to synthesize reliable vessels' shapes. An approach based on Kalman Filtering combined with an extension of a Multiresolution Hermite vascular cross-section model has been developed for the simulation of vessels' textures. The proposed method is able to generate realistic synthetic vascular networks with morphological properties that guarantee the correct flow of the blood and the oxygenation of the retinal surface as observed with fundus cameras. The validity of our synthetic retinal images is demonstrated by qualitative assessment and quantitative analysis.

Keywords: Synthetic retinal images · Shape · Texture · Validation

1 Introduction

Retinal Image Analysis (RIA) aims to develop computational and mathematical techniques for helping clinicians with the diagnosis of diseases such as diabetes, glaucoma and cardiovascular conditions, that may cause changes in retinal blood vessel patterns like tortuosity, bifurcations, variation of vessel width and colour [1,18]. RIA algorithms have to be validated to avoid obtaining misleading results. Validation can be defined as the process of showing that an algorithm performs correctly by comparing its output with a reference standard [16]. A common practice for validation of medical image algorithms is to use Ground Truth (GT) provided by medical experts. Obtaining manually GT images annotated by clinicians is an expensive and laborious task which motivates the creation of synthetic datasets providing GT of adequate quality for algorithm validation. Medical phantoms are used extensively in medical imaging [3,9]. However,

© Springer International Publishing AG 2016
S.A. Tsaftaris et al. (Eds.): SASHIMI 2016, LNCS 9968, pp. 167–176, 2016.
DOI: 10.1007/978-3-319-46630-9_17

to our best knowledge, there are no publicly available databases of synthetic retinal fundus images, and providing annotations for large image repositories remains impractical (e.g. UK Biobank alone stores fundus images for 68,000 patients). Synthesized high-resolution fundus images, along with GT free from inter-/intra-observer variability, would allow an efficient validation of algorithms for segmentation and analysis of retinal anatomical structures: by tuning morphological and textural characteristics of these images, we can represent the hallmarks of several diseases or different populations. This work focuses on the generation of retinal vessels and their integration with non-vessel regions, i.e. retinal background, fovea and Optic Disc (OD), previously reported by Fiorini et al. [5], to yield complete fundus camera images. The resulting synthetic retinal fundus images include explicit GT for vessels binary maps, bifurcation point locations, vessel widths and artery/vein classification.

This paper is organized as follows. In Sect. 2 we describe the proposed method for the generation of the morphological properties (Subsect. 2.2) and the textural features (Subsect. 2.3) of the vasculature. In Sect. 3 we report results and summarize and discuss our experiments to evaluate them. Finally in Sect. 4 we give concluding remarks and hints for future work.

2 Method

2.1 Overview

The proposed approach consists of a learning phase and a generation phase. In the former phase, data describing vascular morphology and texture are collected from annotations of real images. Models are specified and their parameters learned from the training data. In the latter phase, the models obtained are used to create synthetic vascular networks. Arteries (A) and Veins (V) are created separately with the same protocol, and then combined together. This work is based on the publicly available High-Resolution Fundus[1] (HRF) images database [13], and on a subset of retinal images of the GoDARTS bioresource[2].

2.2 Vascular Morphology

The generation of synthetic vessel morphology has been achieved using the well-known Active Shape Model (ASM) [4]. This model provides a statistical representation of shape represented by a set of points, called *landmark points*. By analysing the variations in shape over the training set, a PCA model is built. The training samples (vessel centerlines in our case) are aligned into a common coordinate frame and the deviations from the mean shape are analysed. Each training shape is represented as a fixed number n of landmark points placed along a vessel and equally spaced. These landmarks form a $2n$ vector $\mathbf{x}$, the

---

[1] The HRF database can be free downloaded at http://www5.cs.fau.de/research/data/fundus-images/.
[2] The GoDARTS resource is described at http://medicine.dundee.ac.uk/godarts.

dimensionality of which is reduced using PCA, assuming that the most interesting feature is the one with the largest variance. Hence, each shape can be approximated as:

$$\mathbf{x_i} \approx \mathbf{\bar{x}} + \mathbf{Pb_i} \tag{1}$$

where $\mathbf{\bar{x}}$ is the mean shape of the aligned data, $\mathbf{P}$ contains the first t eigenvectors corresponding to the largest t eigenvalues of the covariance matrix of the training shapes, and $\mathbf{b_i}$ is a t dimensional vector of parameters of a deformable shape model. We choose t, so that the model represents 98 % of the total variance of our training data. By varying the element in $\mathbf{b_i}$, randomly choosing them from a multivatiate normal distribution learned across the training set shapes, we generate a new synthetic vessel using Eq. (1).

The data describing the shape of the vessels of each type (A and V) for the main arcades, nasal and temporal ($n = 81$ landmarks), and their branches ($n = 31$ landmarks) up to three levels of branching have been previously collected from 50 GoDARTS retinal fundus images. We used polar coordinates centred in the OD and with the main axis in the direction of the OD-Fovea axis (i.e. the line connecting the OD centre and the fovea), adopted by the VAMPIRE software suite [15]. Vessel shapes are represented into this system using a transformation that includes a rigid translation and rotation. Similarly the shapes of the branches have been aligned using a rigid transformation that shifts their starting point to the origin of the same coordinate system. Fig. 1 shows the aligned set of shapes and the mean shape for the temporal arcade (a) and a vessel branch (b).

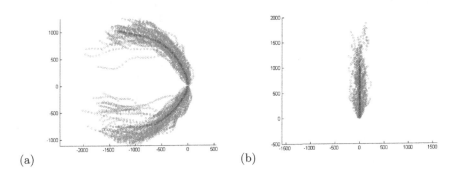

(a)   (b)

Fig. 1. Vessels aligned shapes (green) and their mean shape (red) for the temporal arcades (a) a vessel branch (b). (Color figure online)

Individually generated synthetic vessels are then connected to create the vascular network skeleton. The location of vessel bifurcations is estimated from real images as follows. First we calculate the spatial density distribution map (Fig. 2(a)) of all bifurcation points annotated on real images. Then we map our synthetic vessel onto it, obtaining a probability score for each point of the vessel to become a bifurcation point (Fig. 2(b)). We select one of the points having maximum score as the first bifurcation point of the main arcades. We select the following bifurcation point as one of the points having maximum score located at a distance $d \in [l/2n, l/n]$ from the previous one, where l is the length of the vessel and n is the desired number of bifurcations. These bounds are required to obtain a biologically plausible structure. We continue to select points until the desired number of bifurcation points is achieved. This number is chosen empirically, based on accurate analysis of the number of bifurcations in real images.

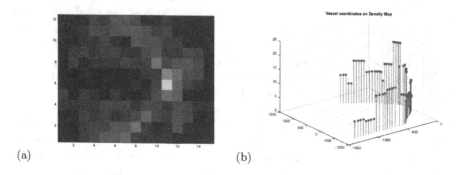

(a)   (b)

Fig. 2. (a) Density Map distribution of artery bifurcation points in the image plane. (b) A synthetic vessel with the probability score of each point to be a bifurcation point.

We compute orientation and calibre for each branch vessel originating at a bifurcation point using Murray's bifurcation model [12], linking branching angles with vessel calibres. Newly generated synthetic branches need to fit with the context of the vascular tree already generated: all vessels should be inside the Field of View (FOV), but outside the foveal region, avoiding intersections between vessels of the same type, and converging toward the fovea.

The binary map of the vascular tree (see example in Fig. 3) is obtained by adding calibre information using mathematical morphological dilation of the skeleton. The initial calibre of the main arcades is sampled from the estimate distribution of the largest vessel calibre of real images. The initial calibre of the branches is obtained from the parent vessel calibre following Murray's Law.

2.3   Vascular Texture

To generate synthetic vessel textures we collected examples of intensity values along vessels and of textural features of the surrounding area (background). We then created a model combining both information, capturing the transition of intensities between vessels and background.

Data Collection. Cross-sections of the vessel of interest were defined, spaced by 5 pixels along the vessel centerline. We extracted the intensity RGB profile on lines perpendicular to the direction of the vessel as depicted in Fig. 4(a).

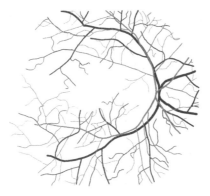

Fig. 3. Example of synthetic vascular tree (arteries in red and veins in blue for display purpose). (Color figure online)

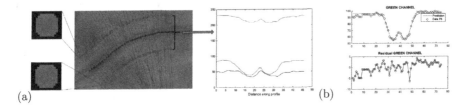

(a)   (b)

Fig. 4. (a) Cross-sections perpendicular to vessel direction, background regions and RGB intensity profile along one of the cross-sections. (b) Green channel fitting profile using the Extended Multiresolution Hermite Model. (Color figure online)

The green channel intensities are fitted (Fig. 4(b)) with a weighted NonLinear Least Squares model using a 6-parameters Extended Multiresolution Hermite Model [11] (EMHM) to fit the cross-sectional intensity profiles. The EMHM accounts for non-symmetric and symmetric profiles, with or without central reflex, expressed by the formula:

$$H(a, m, \delta, \sigma, p, q, x) = -p\{1 + a[(x - m - \delta)^2 - 1]\}e^{-\frac{(x-m)^2}{2\sigma^2}} + q \qquad (2)$$

where $a \in [-1, 1]$ models the depth of the central reflection; $m \in [1, length(profile)]$ is the mean of the Gaussian and allows shifts along the x-axis and $length(profile)$ is the length of the vessel region around the target location; $\delta \in [-2, 2]$ accounts for asymmetry; $\sigma \in [1, 15]$ is the standard deviation of the Gaussian; $q \in [0, 255]$ shifts the function along y-axis, avoiding negative pixels values; $p \in [0, 150]$ guarantees that vessels are darker than the background; x is a vector of the same length of the cross-section of the vessel. The initial conditions are $a = 0$, $m = length(profile)/2$, $\delta = 0.2$, $\sigma = length(profile)/std(profile)$, $q = max(profile)$, $p = max(profile) - min(profile)$.

At the endpoints of each cross-section (green circles in Fig. 4(a)) we computed five statistical texture descriptors [7,14] (Mean, Std, Skewness, Kurtosis and Entropy) on two near-circular windows of 6 pixel radii.

The ensemble of these data, 6 EMHM parameters $(\mathbf{X}_{n\times 6})$ and 5×2 background texture descriptors $(\mathbf{Y}_{n\times 10})$ for each profile, for a total of 975 artery and 1593 vein profiles, collected from the 15 healthy subjects of HRF dataset, constitute the measurements for the procedure proposed below.

Generation of Vessel Textures. The procedure for creating reliable synthetic vessel texture takes into account both the continuity of intensity profiles along the vessel and their consistence with background intensities. We apply a Kalman Filter [8], casting our problem as a state space system:

$$\begin{cases} \mathbf{x}_k = \mathbf{F}\mathbf{x}_{k-1} + \mathbf{w}_{k-1} & \text{System model} \\ \mathbf{y}_k = \mathbf{H}\mathbf{x}_k + \mathbf{v}_k & \text{Measurement model} \end{cases} \tag{3}$$

where $\mathbf{x}_k$ is the state vector containing the 6 parameters describing the intensity profile, $\mathbf{F}$ is the state transition matrix (set to identity matrix), $\mathbf{y}_k$ is the vector of measurements given by 10 textural descriptors of the synthetic background and the two vectors $\mathbf{w}_{k-1}$ and $\mathbf{v}_k$ are unrelated realizations of white zero-mean Gaussian noise. The measurement matrix $\mathbf{H}$ has been obtained, using Multivariate Multiple Linear Regression, solving the system:

$$\begin{bmatrix} y_{1,1} & \cdots & y_{1,10} \\ \vdots & \ddots & \vdots \\ y_{n,1} & \cdots & y_{n,10} \end{bmatrix} = \begin{bmatrix} x_{1,1} & \cdots & x_{1,6} \\ \vdots & \ddots & \vdots \\ x_{n,1} & \cdots & x_{n,6} \end{bmatrix} \begin{bmatrix} h_{1,1} & \cdots & h_{1,10} \\ \vdots & \ddots & \vdots \\ h_{6,1} & \cdots & h_{6,10} \end{bmatrix} + \begin{bmatrix} \epsilon_{1,1} & \cdots & \epsilon_{1,10} \\ \vdots & \ddots & \vdots \\ \epsilon_{n,1} & \cdots & \epsilon_{n,10} \end{bmatrix} \tag{4}$$

where the matrices $\mathbf{X}_{n\times 6}$ and $\mathbf{Y}_{n\times 10}$ are the measurements calculated as described in Sect. 2.3 and ϵ represents the system error.

Equation (3) recursively estimate, through a predictor-corrector method, the state $\mathbf{x}_k$ and its covariance $\mathbf{P}_k$. The initial estimate of the state $\hat{\mathbf{x}}_0$ (first profile) is assumed to be known and its covariance matrix $\mathbf{P}_0$ is initialized to zero. The first profile for the major arcades is the profile having background descriptors more similar to the current synthetic ones. The first profile for the branches is the profile of the parent vessel at the bifurcation point from which they originate.

Iterating this procedure, each new intensity profile of the green channel is generated taking into account the previous one and the surrounding background. A similar procedure was applied to the red and blue channels. However, based on experimental results, we later decided to simply use the average intensity profile of the training ones for the latter two channels. The red component is weighted with underlying background red intensity level, in order to take into account the spatial colour distribution of the whole image. Finally, the RGB intensity profile is cut with the full-width-at-half-maximum algorithm [10] to keep the mere component of the vessel, and re-sampled using the Bresenham line-drawing algorithm [2]. Experiments showed that the quality of the synthetic images generated would not improve using the full Kalman estimator in the red and blue channels.

The two vascular trees obtained (arteries and veins) are combined and superimposed on synthetic backgrounds, reported elsewhere [5], to create complete synthetic fundus camera images. Gaussian filtering is finally applied to smooth vessel edges and in general unrealistically sharp intensity changes.

The image size of the final synthetic is 3,125 × 2,336 pixels with FOV diameter of 2,662 pixels, in line with the resolution of state-of-the-art fundus cameras. The whole method and an user-friendly GUI of the simulation tool have been implemented in Matlab®2014b. An extended dataset of synthetic images and the simulation tool will be publicly available after publication.

3   Results

In Fig. 5 we visually compare real images (a, b) with synthetic images (c, d). We notice that the synthetic vessels are characterized by a realistic morphology, including typical tortuosity. The temporal segments of the arcades go toward and around the macula, and the nasal segments radiate radially from the nerve head. The vessels colouring is always darker than the background, following real images: vessels appear brighter around the OD and darker towards the fovea and the extremities of the FOV. The arteries appear, as in real images, brighter and narrower than veins. Because of the changes in intensity profile along the tree, the central reflex (a central, thin, bright reflection appearing sometimes along the centerline of large vessels, especially arteries) is automatically provided.

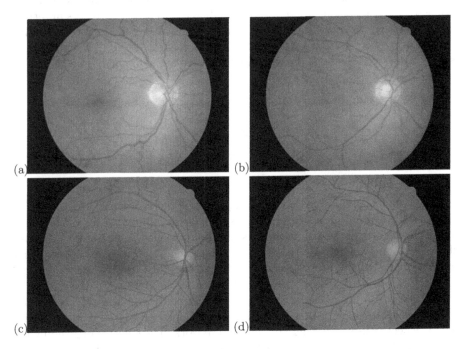

Fig. 5. Comparison between real fundus images from the GoDARTS dataset (a, b) and two complete synthetic retinal fundus images generated by our method (c, d).

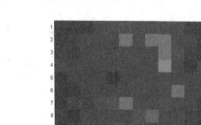
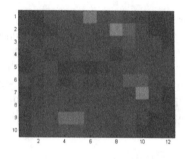

(a)   (b)

Fig. 6. Density Map distribution of bifurcation points in synthetic images for artery (a) and vein (b).

As can be seen in Fig. 6, the bifurcation probability maps of our synthetic images are plausible and similar to the one of the real images.

Our method is fully capable of modelling any biological plausible patterns and outliers given examples of such patterns in the training images. Moreover, the proposed method is potentially capable of dealing with pathologies without increasing its complexity. Indeed, our models can learn their parameters from training set of pathological images.

In absence of quantitative quality criteria, we performed a simple qualitative assessment by asking 7 experts (ophthalmologists and researchers in retinal image analysis) to score the degree of realism of 12 synthetic retinal fundus images, using a scale from 1 to 4, where $1 =$ not realistic at all, $2 =$ slightly realistic, $3 =$ nearly realistic, $4 =$ very realistic. Scores are summarized in Table 1.

Table 1. Qualitative assessment: scores given by the experts for each image

Image	#1	#2	#3	#4	#5	#6	#7	#8	#9	#10	#11	#12
mean	2.14	1.36	2.00	2.43	2.14	1.71	2.79	2.50	2.29	2.36	2.00	1.86
±std	±0.64	±0.44	±0.93	±1.05	±0.99	±0.70	±1.06	±0.89	±1.03	±0.87	±0.53	±0.64

The best image obtained a score of 2.79, while the average score over all the images is 2.13. We did not ask the experts to make any allowance for the fact that many characteristics of fundus images are not modelled (e.g. small capillaries, the vascular network inside the OD). Considering this, the scores suggest that our synthetic images are plausible, as far as the only features generated go. The experts also suggested some improvements: the density of the vessels in some zone is too high, the largest vessels occasionally end abruptly, some first level branches appear too straight and the direction of growth sometimes recoils. These aspects will be considered in our future work. The comments given by the experts will be analysed systematically and properly addressed. A qualitative evaluation on a larger dataset will be used for this scope.

The main purpose of this project was to generate a synthetic dataset providing GT for validation of retinal image analysis algorithms, e.g. vasculature

Table 2. Performance comparison of VAMPIRE segmentation algorithm on real (HRF) and synthetic images: True Positive Rate (TPR), False Positive Rate (FPR), Specificity (Sp), Accuracy (Acc) (mean ± standard deviation).

	TPR	FPR	Sp	Acc
Real images	0.9874 ± 0.0015	0.0058 ± 0.0070	0.9942 ± 0.0070	0.9936 ± 0.0063
Synthetic images	0.9703 ± 0.0185	0.0151 ± 0.0125	0.9849 ± 0.0125	0.9835 ± 0.0122

and landmark detection. To demonstrate the suitability of our dataset for this purpose, we compared the performance of a retinal vessel segmentation software, VAMPIRE [17], when run on our synthetic images and on real images. We used 10 images of healthy eyes with manual GT from the HRF dataset, and 10 of our synthetic images including their synthetic binary maps. Segmentation results are evaluated in term of the standard statistical criteria [16]. The comparison of these 2 experiments, summarized in Table 2, shows that our synthetic images behave comparably with real ones in term of vasculature segmentation and certainly in line with the performance of algorithms reported recently in the literature [6]. We note generally small differences between all values.

4   Conclusions

This paper has presented a novel technique to generate a reliable synthetic retinal vasculature, as part of an ongoing project aimed to generate full, realistic, synthetic fundus camera images. The results are promising for both the morphology and the texture of the vessel networks. To our best knowledge no similar method has been reported in literature. The encouraging quality of our initial results is supported, so far, by small-scale visual inspection and quantitative experiments. Further improvements to this preliminary work will take into account further properties of real fundus images, including the geometric interaction between arteries and veins, the way vessels radiate from the OD, the vascular network inside the OD, and the appearance of further structures like small capillaries and the retinal nerve fibre layer. Another future direction will be the simulation of lesions.

Acknowledgements. The authors would like to thank the experts who performed the qualitative evaluation. They are also grateful to the anonymous reviewers for their valuable comments and suggestions, which contributed to improve this paper.

References

1. Annunziata, R., Garzelli, A., Ballerini, L., Mecocci, A., Trucco, E.: Leveraging multiscale hessian-based enhancement with a novel exudate inpainting technique for retinal vessel segmentation. IEEE J. Biomed. Health Inform. **20**(4), 1129–1138 (2016)

2. Bresenham, J.E.: Algorithm for computer control of a digital plotter. IBM Syst. J. **4**(1), 25–30 (1965)
3. Collins, D.L., Zijdenbos, A.P., Kollokian, V., Sled, J.G., Kabani, N.J., Holmes, C.J., Evans, A.C.: Design and construction of a realistic digital brain phantom. IEEE Trans. Med. Imaging **17**(3), 463–468 (1998)
4. Cootes, T.F., Taylor, C.J., Cooper, D.H., Graham, J.: Active shape models-their training and application. Comput. Vis. Image Underst. **61**(1), 38–59 (1995)
5. Fiorini, S., Ballerini, L., Trucco, E., Ruggeri, A.: Automatic generation of synthetic retinal fundus images. In: Medical Image Understanding and Analysis (MIUA), pp. 7–12 (2014)
6. Fraz, M., Remagnino, P., Hoppe, A., Uyyanonvara, B., Rudnicka, A., Owen, C., Barman, S.: Blood vessel segmentation methodologies in retinal images: a survey. Comput. Methods Program. Biomed. **108**(1), 407–433 (2012)
7. Haralick, R.M.: Statistical and structural approaches to texture. Proc. IEEE **67**(5), 786–804 (1979)
8. Kalman, R.E.: A new approach to linear filtering and prediction problems. Trans. ASME J. Basic Eng. **82**(Series D), 35–45 (1960)
9. Lehmussola, A., Ruusuvuori, P., Selinummi, J., Huttunen, H., Yli-Harja, O.: Computational framework for simulating fluorescence microscope images with cell populations. IEEE Trans. Med. Imaging **26**(7), 1010–1016 (2007)
10. Lowell, J., Hunter, A., Steel, D., Basu, A., Ryder, R., Kennedy, R.: Measurement of retinal vessel widths from fundus images based on 2-D modeling. IEEE Trans. Med. Imaging **23**(10), 1196–1204 (2004)
11. Lupascu, C.A., Tegolo, D., Trucco, E.: Accurate estimation of retinal vessel width using bagged decision trees and an extended multiresolution Hermite model. Med. Image Anal. **17**(8), 1164–1180 (2013)
12. Murray, C.D.: The physiological principle of minimum work applied to the angle of branching of arteries. J. Gen. Physiol. **9**(6), 835–841 (1926)
13. Odstrcilik, J., Kolar, R., Budai, A., et al.: Retinal vessel segmentation by improved matched filtering: evaluation on a new high-resolution fundus image database. IET Image Process. **7**(4), 373–383 (2013)
14. Poletti, E., Veronese, E., Calabrese, M., Bertoldo, A., Grisan, E.: Supervised classification of brain tissues through local multi-scale texture analysis by coupling DIR and FLAIR MR sequences. In: Proceedings of the SPIE, vol. 8314, p. 83142T–83142T-7 (2012)
15. Trucco, E., Ballerini, L., Relan, D., et al.: Novel VAMPIRE algorithms for quantitative analysis of the retinal vasculature. In: Proceedings of the IEEE ISSNIP/BRC, pp. 1–4 (2013)
16. Trucco, E., Ruggeri, A., Karnowski, T., et al.: Validating retinal fundus image analysis algorithms: issues and a proposal. Invest. Ophthalmol. Vis. Sci. **54**(5), 3546–3559 (2013)
17. Trucco, E., Giachetti, A., Ballerini, L., Relan, D., Cavinato, A., MacGillivray, T.: Morphometric measurements of the retinal vasculature in fundus images with VAMPIRE. In: Lim, J.H., Ong, S.H., Xiong, W. (eds.) Biomedical Image Understanding, Methods and Applications, pp. 91–111. Wiley, New York (2015)
18. Yin, Y., Adel, M., Bourennane, S.: Retinal vessel segmentation using a probabilistic tracking method. Pattern Recogn. **45**(4), 1235–1244 (2012)

Author Index

Printed in the United States
By Bookmasters